GHOSTS
WASHINGTON REVISITED

The Ghostlore of the Nation's Capital

John Alexander

Schiffer Publishing Ltd®

4880 Lower Valley Road, Atglen, PA 19310 USA

Dedication

This book became a reality because of the encouragement of my wife Sheila. When I was doing my original research our two daughters, Robin and Angela, were small and my hours were long. When I was writing those first drafts Sheila always had time to proof them and to offer her constructive criticism. She has also been at my side during this update, some twenty years later. I am indebted.

Published by Schiffer Publishing Ltd.
4880 Lower Valley Road
Atglen, PA 19310
Phone: (610) 593-1777; Fax: (610) 593-2002
E-mail: Info@schifferbooks.com
Please visit our web site catalog at
www.schifferbooks.com

This book may be purchased from the publisher.
Include $3.95 for shipping. Please try your bookstore first.
We are always looking for people to write books on new and related subjects. If you have an idea for a book please contact us at the above address.
You may write for a free catalog.

In Europe, Schiffer books are distributed by
Bushwood Books
6 Marksbury Avenue
Kew Gardens
Surrey TW9 4JF England
Phone: 44 (0) 20-8392-8585; Fax: 44 (0) 20-8392-9876
E-mail: info@bushwoodbooks.co.uk
Free postage in the UK. Europe: air mail at cost.

Contents

Acknowledgments

There are quite a few people to whom I owe a hearty thanks. I'll begin with WMAL Radio, Washington, D.C., where I created and produced the Halloween special *"Washington Revisited."* A few years later, after I had decided to dig deeper, collect more stories, and write a book, Larry Adler—then of the *Washingtonian Magazine*—recognized the possibilities. There were a half-dozen or so curators and contacts whose jovial assistance made up for the few dour sources who not only didn't want to talk about old ghost stories, but were afraid the book I was working on would "soil the image" of their institution(s). I thank John Kirkwood, then of the U.S. Capitol Historical Society; James Ketchum, then Curator, Arts & Antiquities, U.S. Senate; John Pearce, then Curator, Decatur House; and Sara Jameson, then Curator, Octagon House. A special thanks goes to Lee Shephard who brought along his camera for a personal tour of the haunts I wanted photographed. I thank those who purchased the book or read a library copy, and especially to those of you who wrote to me. I'm sorry, I just couldn't respond to every letter.

When Ashleigh Nichole Holt was old enough to be aware that her grandfather had written a book of ghost stories, she began pleading with him to read them to her. Well, about the only one I could "revise" to suite a four year old was "The Demon Cat." It has become her favorite. My favorite (and only) granddaughter is part of the inspiration I needed to dig back into this subject. I have revised and expanded the book so that it will remain fresh to future generations of ghostlore lovers. And I thank *you* for buying this book. If you really like old ghost stories you won't be disappointed!

Introduction

Some of my fondest childhood memories are of sitting under a tree at night with other neighborhood kids and swapping ghost stories. A vivid imagination was a necessity. This book grew out of those experiences and from a desire to preserve some marvelous stories that date back to a time when conversation was valued and story telling was an art form. Storytellers seldom let facts get in the way of perpetuating a legend; although a few facts add seasoning and make the legend more believable. One doesn't set out to intentionally alter the truth, just enhance it and make it more memorable. A tale spinner's goal is entertainment.

When I was a correspondent at WMAL Radio in Washington, I had an opportunity to cross that line from reporting to tale-spinning. I created an hour-long radio special for Halloween of 1970. It was patterned somewhat after the old radio melodramas of the 1940s and 1950s. I remember listening to them as a child on my secret headset long after the lights were out and I was supposed to have been asleep.

Washington Revisited was a supernatural tour of the Federal City. It was complete with spooky music, terrifying screams, and sound effects to help one visualize things that go bump in the night. The response was not only gratifying, it was overwhelming. Ohio State University's Institute for Radio and Television honored the program with a prestigious award for *excellence in radio documentary production.* Listeners to WMAL began calling the station the following September requesting another Halloween replay. *Washington Revisited* became a Washington radio Halloween tradition for almost a decade.

When I began my research for an old ghost story to spin that Halloween I had no idea that I would find so many. I uncovered a rich treasure of ghostly lore that was in danger of disappearing. I found quite a few leads in old newspapers that were yellow and crumbled when touched. Most of these sto-ries had not been told for years. When I went into the neighborhoods, tracking down leads, I found that it was the older residents who were most helpful. Some provided other versions of the stories and a few pointed me to other houses they recalled from their youth that were said to be haunted.

Quite a few of the houses in Washington said to have ghosts have been haunted for so long that the spirits who return to them have practically become members of the family. Indeed, who is to say they weren't at one time? Sometimes, however, it is impossible to pinpoint the exact location of a haunted house. In the retelling of tales the location of a house can become distorted, even lost. In some cases wary inhabitants are reluctant to discuss their nocturnal visitors at all. If they do talk to reporters, they sometimes ask for anonymity.

Down through the years people have been pretty much the same. We've always been fascinated with the rich and powerful, so most stories revolve around politicians, preachers, generals, and scandals. The only difference is that way-back-when people tended to try to keep some of the more prominent people alive—or with them—longer than reality dictated. Today the tabloids regularly chronicle sightings of Hitler, JFK, and Elvis among others. John Wayne has been resurrected for beer commercials. Come to think of it, nothing much has changed.

April 18, 1891 *The Washington Star* proclaimed "Washington Is the Greatest Town for Ghosts in this Country."

The *Washington Star* proclaimed in 1891 **"Washington is the greatest town for ghosts in this country!"** Why Washington? Could it be the power, stress, and unfinished business? Almost a hundred years later Charles Paul Freund, writing in the *Washington Post,* August 13, 1989, said "Washington is the nation's Gothic capital, the shining city on a haunted hill."

Of course ghost stories have always been a part of every community, but in the 1850s spiritualism had begun to sweep the nation, and attempts to communicate with the dead became a popular pastime. Newspaper reporters often chronicled the exploits of mediums, exposing more than a few as frauds. Newspapers featured stories about people who lived in haunted houses or believed they had encountered ghosts. In reviewing these old papers, it is quite obvious that great numbers of the American people had developed a fascination for ghosts that lasted for more than a half-century.

However, by the 1930s most newspaper articles, it seemed, were simply retelling the older stories, but with less zest and flair than had earlier writers. When the big push into science came in the 1950s it shoved the ghost story to the back page, if it made the paper at all.

I expressed surprise in the introduction of my first book on Washington ghosts that I had found no tales of Abraham Lincoln or John Wilkes Booth at Ford's Theater; and that although Blair House, the Frederick Douglass House, and the Smithsonian Castle seemed to be ideally suited for ghostlore, my search showed they were void of ghosts.

Within a few years, however, I was pleased to learn that both President Lincoln and John Wilkes Booth had put in appearances at Ford's Theater. People were coming forth with more stories. Ghostly tales involving several of those old places surfaced. Rekindled imaginations, or were restive ghosts frequenting new locations?

Although I have a background as a journalist, and brought those investigative skills into my research, I consider myself a storyteller. It is not necessarily the explanation of how a tale may have originated that I am concerned with, but rather its preservation. Ghostlore is a fascinating way to remember people—to weave legends in which heroes and villains can be larger, and last longer, than life itself. I don't know what it is that we call a ghost. I do know that the more science investigates, the more questions scientists seem to ask. Do we really want to know everything? The unknown is enticing. It can be scary. It can also be entertaining.

Are all of these stories actually encounters with ghosts? It is highly unlikely. Some of them are beyond our ability to understand or explain. Others may be more obvious: a person who had too much to drink or someone with a fertile imagination. Some of the stories may have originated or been used as devices of non-violent social control. Many tales of phantom coaches or headless ghosts roaming the roads or haunting bridges were deliberately spread by grave robbers. They sought to deflect suspicion off their own real coaches as they traveled through the black of night from graveyards to no-questions-asked medical schools. Of course the tale may be exactly what it appears to be: a ghostly encounter.

Regardless of origin, the stories in this book are deeply embedded in the folklore and history of our Nation's Capital. In the Washington you are about to enter the past and the present are sometimes intertwined. You will wander in and out of two centuries of history along with the ghosts of Washington who, if we are to believe these tales, revisit their beloved city from time to time.

(signed) John Alexander

Georgetown Ghosts

The Curse of the Three Sisters

As you leave the Capital Beltway and drive along the scenic George Washington Parkway on the Virginia side of the Potomac, you are on land that was once part of the mighty Powhatan Confederacy. Between the Chain Bridge and Francis Scott Key Bridge, three large granite rocks rise out of the river. They are part of a legendary Indian curse that persists to this day: No one will cross the river at this point.

Scores of people who have tried to cross the river here have died in the attempt. Almost four hundred years ago Captain John Smith, referring to the curse, wrote in his diary about the sounds of moaning and sobbing coming from the vicinity of the Three Sisters Rocks. Some say it is the curse of the three sisters that has thwarted the efforts of those who wanted to erect a massive bridge across the Potomac high above the three small rock islands. The bridge was begun in the early 1970s and steel pilings appeared briefly near the District of Columbia shore. It has yet to be built.

To understand why the Three Sisters Rocks, and the curse that surrounds them, command such respect from many Washingtonians it is necessary to go back to almost a full century before the Europeans settled Jamestown in 1607.

Indian enclaves and confederacies dotted the fertile region west of the Chesapeake Bay and on either side of the Potomac River. Tribal medicine men were important leaders because of the powerful magic they received directly from the Great Spirit. Our story involves three daughters of one such spiritual leader.

From settlements along the river Indians launched their hunting trips and their war parties. The region was rich in resources. In addition to the seasonal fish runs, game, wild berries, nuts, and seeds were plentiful in the woodlands. The Indians also grew their own maize, beans, and squash.

Those small islands in the Potomac are mute reminders of the curse that has plagued this section of the river for four hundred years. *Martin Luther King, Jr. Public Library, District of Columbia*

There was quite a bit of animosity between the groups that lived in what is now Maryland and those that settled along the Potomac in what is now Virginia. Northern Indians of Iroquoian stock, and the Susquehannocks, often made raids across the river into the area of the Powhatan Confederacy (composed of several Algonquian tribes). The warfare was frequent and ruthless. Control of the entire region's abundant resources was the prize for the victor. Battle captives were almost always tortured, sometimes enslaved, and infrequently adopted.

One day, after what had been a particularly long siege, the chief of a Virginia village decided that the situation had stabilized enough so that he could take his men out in search of venison and other game. Food supplies in the palisaded village were depleted. The warriors had fought many days to break the siege and drive the Susquehannock raiders back across the river. Hunger had weakened them, and their survival hinged on that one last desperate effort to end the siege. Starvation had already claimed a few old men and women who had sacrificed their rations so that the warriors and the young might live. When the chief decided he and his men could undertake the hunt, he refused to give three of his young sons permission to come along. He thought they weren't old enough to defend themselves if the hunters encountered their enemy outside the village.

The sons were greatly disappointed. Eager to prove their bravery, and to impress their father, they devised a plan. They would launch a clandestine expedition and bring back enough fresh fish to feed the women, children, and old men until the hunting party returned.

The greatest abundance of fish was near the northern shore, and although the young men knew how dangerous it would be to venture there, that did not affect their determination to prove their manhood to their father. During the siege all but one of the village canoes had been ripped to shreds by the Susquehannocks. The chief's sons had hidden it, and as dawn drew near, they slipped the canoe from its hiding place and quietly paddled across the river before the sun could burn away the early morning fog.

Unfortunately, the Susquehannocks had left behind a scouting party. The three brothers were fishing only a short while when they were attacked. In full view of those who had remained in the village across the river, the chief's sons were tortured and murdered.

Among the villagers who watched helplessly were the Shaman's three beautiful daughters, who were deeply in love with the unfortunate braves. Although numb with shock and disbelief, the maidens called upon all their inner strength to seek revenge. They decided to cross the river and persuade the rival chief to give them to the warriors who had slain their lovers. The maidens envisioned a slow, torturous death for these hated enemies once they had them in the power of their beauty and their father's medicine.

Tears streamed down their faces as they lashed together several logs to improvise a makeshift raft. Wading into the water, they climbed onto the logs and shoved off from the shore. None of the other villagers noticed that they were gone until it was too late.

The river proved too swift. The winds were too strong. Currents began carrying the raft downstream toward the open sea. Stricken by the tragedy they had just witnessed and frustrated by their inability to navigate the Potomac, the maidens' sad faces glistened with their tears. They seemed to draw supernatural strength from each other. They clasped their arms around each other and shouted a curse. If they—the privileged daughters of the Shaman of the most powerful confederacy on earth—could not cross the river, then no one would cross at that point again. *Ever.*

The three sisters sealed the curse by jumping into the swiftly flowing waters, and, through death, rejoined their young braves.

The sky darkened as the young women sank from sight. Distant rumblings of thunder moved closer and closer. Lightning danced overhead. Occasionally bolts darted down to earth and touched the waters where the maidens had perished. The storm continued through the night, swelling the waters and whipping them into a white-capped frenzy.

At sunrise the waters subsided. A calm spread over the surface. As the clouds rolled away, the sun reflected brilliantly off the sparkling water, and off three granite boulders that had not been there the day before.

To this day the three rocks continue to take their toll of those who dare to defy the maidens' curse. Metropolitan Harbor Police add names to the list of victims each year. Among these are swimmers, fishermen, and canoeists who try to cross the river at this point. Old rivermen say that a mournful cry heard drifting over the Potomac during a storm means there will soon be another drowning—another unsuspecting victim of the ancient curse of the three sisters.

The beginning of bridge construction to the right of the Three Sisters Rocks was swept away during the storm of the century in the late 1970s. That was the last attempt made to confront the ancient curse. *Courtesy Lee Shephard*

As the controversy between bridge builders and environmentalists reached its peak in 1972—those who knew the legend saw a strange parallel in a storm that descended at a critical juncture, just as it had when the three Indian maidens invoked their curse. The skies over Washington darkened, distant rumblings of thunder moved closer, winds churned the mighty Potomac into a white frenzy. Lightning flashed overhead, and it is said that bolts darted down to earth and touched the waters. Flood waters from the most devastating storm in the city's history swept away the construction framework at the proposed site for the Three Sisters Bridge. More than one bridge worker considered this mute testimony to the power of the ancient curse.

All hope of building the bridge seems to have been abandoned. Even plans to name the span for the three sisters failed to break the spell they cast over that section of the river.

The white men will never be alone.
These shores will swarm with the invisible dead.
The dead are not powerless.
Dead, did I say?
There is no death, only a change of worlds.
—Words of a Long-Departed Indian Chief

The sound of British General Edward Braddock and his troops marching off to meet their death during the French and Indian War is still heard in the streets of Georgetown. *Library of Congress*

Braddock's Death March

As you cross the Potomac from Virginia into Washington over Francis Scott Key Bridge, you see the pre-Revolutionary War port of Georgetown on the high ground directly ahead. The port is built on the ruins of what was once the Indian village of Tohoga. When the hour is late, and only on a certain date, the hillside rising out of the waters is said to echo with the sounds of soldiers on the march—soldiers from another time, killed at another place, yet inextricably involved in the old port's history.

The Europeans were determined to settle the region after the glowing reports sent back by Captain John Smith, who had sailed his ship up the Potomac. Henry Fleet, another Englishman, couldn't get Smith's description out of his mind. Within a few years after he read the Captain's diary, Fleet made plans to see the region for himself. What could a land be like that had "waters so clear the bottom could be seen to a depth of several fathoms," as Smith described the Potomac? Fleet found out. He anchored his ship in the channel near Tohoga and spent some twelve years with the Indians.

Other Europeans followed to see for themselves this land that was so rich and fertile. The Indians were pushed farther back into the wilderness. As they became disgruntled, they found what they mistakenly thought was an ally in the French.

It was during the French and Indian War that Georgetown's most famous legend was born. British General Edward Braddock had been brought to the Colonies in 1755 to fight the French after sensational victories in Holland. He would never return home. The optimistic Braddock landed his fourteen hundred troops in Alexandria, where they linked up with seven hundred Colonial militiamen and marched to the Georgetown Ferry. From there he sent half the men along the Potomac on the Virginia side, and personally led about one thousand troops across the river and up the hill through Georgetown. He planned to join the forces again in Cumberland, Maryland, where they would cross the Allegheny Mountains and attack the French at Fort Duquesne. He would make short work of these enemies of the Crown, Braddock thought.

However, Braddock and his men were ambushed at the forks of the Ohio River by a much smaller French and Indian force. In the ensuing blood bath, Braddock and more than seven hundred of his men met their death.

On the bluffs above the Potomac where Braddock began his death march more than one Georgetowner has reported hearing harshly barked orders, the rattling of sabers, and the clatter of horses' hooves and men's boots on the old cobblestones. Those sounds of the distant past shattered the stillness of Georgetown for more than a century—always on the anniversary of the start of Braddock's march. Today Georgetown is a crowded, noisy, business district with lots of traffic and late-night diners and shoppers. However, there are those who still insist if you know the right night and listen carefully at the right time you can still separate the sounds of the phantom army on the march from the din of the night life.

One of the best accounts of an encounter with Braddock's invisible infantry occurred during the War Between The States.

During the Civil War a small Union patrol mistook the ghostly sounds of General Edward Braddock's troops for an advancing Confederate army. *Courtesy Library of Congress*

A Civil War era journalist wrote about a Union patrol's encounter with what might have been General Edward Braddock's doomed troops from the French and Indian War a hundred years earlier.

Long Bridge was always well guarded, as were all other bridges crossing the Potomac into the Confederacy. The writer says Union sentries of a force encamped along the District banks of the river heard the distant sounds of troops and equipment moving across Long Bridge. It was too dark to see anything, but troops quietly moved into battle position. When his men were set, the officer in charge sent a small patrol to scout the Rebel's position and strength.

The patrol came back wet to the skin and totally mystified. When they heard what they thought was the advancing Confederate force they jumped over the side of Long Bridge to keep the enemy from spotting them. After the sounds faded away, the patrol moved cautiously back toward their encampment fully expecting to have been cut off behind their own lines.

The reporter said it was as if the Southern troops had vanished in the middle of the bridge. He speculated that it could have been the spirits of soldiers of another war, doomed to march that road toward death throughout eternity, that the Union patrol heard.

Colonel George Washington served as an aid to General Braddock on that fateful march. He is shown here reading over the burial of Braddock. Washington wasn't wounded although he had two horses shot from under him. *Courtesy Library of Congress*

Mysterious Happenings at Halcyon House

The spirit of Benjamin Stoddert, first Secretary of the Navy, has been seen over the years in his Georgetown house. *The Author's Collection*

Among the survivors of the Braddock massacre was a young lieutenant colonel of the Virginia militia, George Washington. He learned well from early defeats, and when the time came for him to assume a leadership role, he did not fail.

After the Revolution the new nation was in need of a Federal City, but the controversy over where to build it lasted longer than had the fight for freedom. From its temporary home in Philadelphia, Congress ended the seven-year issue by selecting a one-hundred-square-mile tract of land on the banks of the Potomac. The location was chosen because it was halfway between New Hampshire, then the northernmost state, and Georgia, then the southernmost state.

Early attempts to make a city out of the District of Columbia, as the federal project had been named, met with something less than success. Most of the area was largely meadows and mosquito-infested marshland. It seemed foolish to live anywhere but in the established port towns of Georgetown and Alexandria. Both were located within the new District borders, originally. In 1848 the port of Alexandria was given back to the state of Virginia.

The man President George Washington commissioned to purchase tracts of land for the District had a home in Georgetown. Benjamin Stoddert, a former Revolutionary War cavalry officer, also conducted his shipping business from there—except for one period of a few years when he served as the first Secretary of the United States Navy.

Stoddert's home still stands on a Georgetown Bluff. Located on what is now Prospect Avenue, NW, Halcyon House, as Stoddert named it, bears little resemblance to the beautiful and smaller home he had erected on that site. Perhaps that partly explains all of the mysterious occurrences that have been reported inside the turbulent old house: rapping and tapping sounds, an "unfamiliar figure" that sometimes appears, and other supernatural happenings.

Halcyon House—named for the mythical bird whose presence is said to calm the seas—has been anything but calm since the death of Stoddert. He had been a wealthy man and

a friend to many of the nation's great leaders, including President Washington.

As a man who made his living from the sea it seemed natural that Stoddert would want his home as near to it as possible. The land he chose sloped gently down to the Potomac. He commissioned the noted French planner Pierre Charles L'Enfant to design a magnificently terraced garden that enhanced the Potomac view. It also gave Stoddert a vantage point from which he could watch the merchant ships and frigates come and go with the winds. He must have felt mixed emotions as he gazed on such a placid scene. Most of the time that he served as Secretary of the Navy his frigates were involved in an entanglement with the French that was anything but placid. In spite of this undeclared and minor sea war, Stoddert managed to get quite a bit accomplished in his government post. Tributes to his tireless energies were the expansion of the fleet and acquisition of land along the banks of the Anacostia River to construct navy yards for building more ships. It was also Stoddert who was responsible for organizing the Marine Corps on its present basis.

Stoddert was not quite so successful, however, at maintaining his personal affairs. When he stepped down as Navy Secretary at the end of John Adams's administration, Stoddert's shipping business was in such bad shape he simply couldn't salvage it. Within twelve years Benjamin Stoddert died, a frustrated and destitute man.

This is the rear of Halcyon House as it looked before eccentric Albert Clemons went to work on it. Benjamin Stoddert had his home built so that the front overlooked his gardens and the Potomac River. *Courtesy Martin Luther King, Jr. Public Library, District of Columbia.*

Several families passed through Halcyon House over the next few years. During the years preceding the Civil War, and possibly during the war too, it may have served as a crucial link in the Underground Railroad. An old Georgetown carpenter told me stories he had heard as a boy about runaway slaves,

The rear of **Halcyon House** became the front when Clemons erected this **facade** as part of his never-ending building project, which he thought would give him everlasting life. His ghost is said to haunt the house, often manifesting its presence by turning off the electric lights that he would have no part of in life. *The Author's Collection*

Albert Clemons used to shield statues of angels that adorned Halcyon House by placing pie tins on their heads to protect them from the weather. *Courtesy Library of Congress*

heading northward to freedom. He didn't know how many died trying to swim the Potomac. For some who made it across, and found the tunnel at river's edge leading to Halcyon House, freedom was short lived. The weaker ones, in poor health, died in the dampness of its cellar.

"I have heard their cries, heard them plain as day," he said as his voice grew softer and his eyes took on a distant, glassy stare. The carpenter told me that when he was a young man, in the early 1900s, he had been requested to wall up a tunnel in the cellar of Halcyon House. The family was having trouble with rats and was afraid they would find a way to the upstairs. The carpenter related how he took his lumber, nails, mortar, and several lanterns into the cellar one day to begin his task.

He had not heard the stories of the Underground Railroad passing through the house or of escaped slaves dying. All he knew was that there were rats down there and he was scared. It was not the rats, however, that drove him from the cellar before he had completed plastering the wooden barricade that would forever seal the old tunnel. At first, he said, he thought it was the wind that he heard blowing through the tunnel. But the original low moan became a sob, another moan joined it, and then there was more sobbing.

He worked quickly, trying to concentrate on what he was doing and to convince himself it was only the wind—or maybe someone sick upstairs.

But just as he plastered up most of the new wall there was a blood-chilling scream, followed by the kind of sobbing only heard beside a deathbed. A gust of wind, which he swore could not have come from the walled up tunnel, blew out his lanterns. The carpenter fled the cellar, never returning to pick up his tools. He could not get the sounds out of his mind, so he began asking questions about the history of the old house. That is when he learned more than enough to convince him that those few hours he had spent in that cold, dank cellar were a visit into an unearthly world.

"Sometimes," he told me, "I wake up screaming in the middle of the night; my sweat's cold. It's been fifty to sixty years since I heard them sounds, and I'm still haunted by 'em. Haunted by my own mind trying to put faces to them poor people." He shook his head as though trying to clear his mind of the unpleasantness. "Guess I'll carry those ghostly cries to my grave." He did. A few months after I talked with him, the old Georgetown carpenter died.

By walling up the old tunnel he may have stopped the rats, but when the night is quiet and the hour is late, the moans, sobs, and cries of despair of which he spoke have continued to haunt some residents and visitors.

As I searched the old and yellowed newspapers I found a particular Georgetown house where recurring supernatural events were reported. The house was described variously as a "house overlooking the river from the bluffs of Georgetown" or "overhanging M Street" or an "old sea captain's home." Most accounts, however, contained enough information to lead me to the conclusion that all of these writers were talking about Halcyon House. It was in the 1800s that these unexplainable happenings began to attract the attention of reporters, and still no one has provided satisfactory answers to what causes them.

In the beginning decade of the twentieth century the wife of a retired Marine Corps major who lived in Halcyon House had a startling experience. The newspaper account I read said she encountered a "woman dressed in a costume of a forgotten period" while walking through a darkened hall one evening. The article also mentioned a history of "murmurs from servants" who "complained of weird noises during the night, and seeing strange shapes in rooms." The writer said the couple moved. There was no speculation as to who the wispy woman may have been.

In the early 1930s a widow who owned the house kept quiet as long as she could and then finally told her story to a reporter just before she died. She described frequent tapping and rapping on the wall like that made by a heavy branch brushing it; yet, the reporter said, there were no trees that close to the house. The story also included accounts of servants who had met with a "strange person on the stairway who immediately disappeared." The widow told the reporter that for years she had pretended not to hear "muffled footsteps or the sounds of slippered feet," and would never discuss it. The widow suspected that Stoddert, who had died despondent, sick, and a virtual pauper, still walked through his home. The reporter recalled how "he just sat and waited for the day death would call him away from his invalid existence…He used to sit by the window of his upstairs bedroom, with old-fashioned spy glass in hand, watching the harbor, watching the wharf…and watching the people."

After the widow died, the house remained vacant for a year or so before an eccentric named Albert Adsit Clemons acquired the property. He was not satisfied with the appearance of Stoddert's brick home, and set about to change it. Some think he just needed more room for his collection of religious paraphernalia, others think he began to collect it only after an encounter with Stoddert's ghost put the fear of God into him.

One person who has done considerable research into Clemon's life told me the old man was fascinated by all forms of religion, and was particularly in awe of some Eastern philosophies. He is said to have embraced a belief that as long as he continued to build onto his earthly home he would not die. Perhaps that is why Clemons pursued his construction with missionary zeal. He wrapped the north side of the house in a facade, four stories tall. Then he set about building apartments between the facade and Stoddert's original house.

The fear of death was deeply rooted in Clemons. He is said to have taken time out from building to ceremoniously bury two mummies in the garden. One represented his lost figure; the other, his lost youth. In the old coach house he constructed an apartment that contained a crypt in the middle of the floor. There is a rumor that he sometimes slept in it, but no one seems to know for whom he intended it, since he did not plan to die. Others think that it may have been used as some sort of altar. Clemons liked stained glass and he filled Halcyon House with it. Some shattered multicolored evidence was still on the floor in the highest of three attics when I toured the old house. Like the stained glass on the floor, the beams in that third level attic came from St. Matthew's Church on Rhode Island Avenue.

A researcher at the University of Maryland said he understood that Clemons obtained a cast-off pulpit when the old sanctuary at St. Matthew's was razed. There is a platform in that third level loft and a high ceiling that could have accommodated the pulpit. The researcher said that some former tenants told him that Clemons also had a giant crucifix carved from a tree up there.

It was outside this attic, on the ledge overlooking Prospect Avenue, that Clemons had placed several statues of angels. He is said to have placed pie tins on the angels' heads to protect them when it rained. Another person with whom I spoke said that Clemons, while vacationing in Italy, supposedly had purchased an old church and had its contents shipped back to Halcyon House.

The eccentric's obsession that continuing construction meant continuing life drove him to persuade a carpenter to move in with him. Diligently they set to work. It is charged by some old Georgetowner's that Clemons and his helper built with used lumber, often salvaged from homes being demolished, and that their workmanship was shoddy. Seldom did Clemons or the carpenter paint anything, let alone take time to draw up plans before reaching for the nails and hammer.

The fever that infested Clemons compelled him to build without rhyme or reason. The inside of the house soon looked like a crazy quilt: some rooms were built without walls; there were doors that opened into blank walls; a stairway that led nowhere—covered over to become a closet.

When Stoddert owned the home, the main staircase rose from the garden side of the house, but Clemons reversed it to the Prospect Avenue side. Clemons also joined the old coach house to the main building. It was said that the only criticism the carpenter ever had of his boss was that Clemons seldom knew what he wanted done. The carpenter often would spend a whole day tearing down much of the previous day's work because Clemons had changed his mind.

These were some of the apartments Albert Clemons constructed on the 34th Street side of Halcyon House. *The Author's Collection*

One of Clemons's pet projects was the ten apartments he helped to build inside the facade that extended out from the main part of Halcyon House by twenty feet. To help finance his work he rented them. He posted a sign on a lamppost out on the sidewalk that read:
Apartments for rent.
No Children.
No Dogs.
No Leases.
No Electricity Permitted.

It was that last restriction that was the real grabber. The lack of electricity in the 1930s kept quite a few people away. The old man feared it and never permitted the house to be wired while he lived.

One of the stories that circulates around Georgetown is that Clemons used to make the renters change apartments ever year so that he could equalize the strain on the foundations. Apparently he was afraid that such an unequal strain might affect his own physical health.

On March 17, 1938, Alfred Clemons proved the fallacy of his belief in eternal life by dying. The existence of a crypt and the fact that Clemons had drawn up a will were strong indications that he really didn't believe continued construction on his home would prolong his earthly life.

In addition to his hoard of religious paraphernalia, the old man had been a prodigious collector of all kinds of things. For instance, one of the doors of Halcyon House was supposed to have come from the old Francis Scott Key home that had once stood nearby. Some of the other items listed in the inventory of the house when Clemons died were:
Eleven sandstone griffins
Samurai armor
Pictures of nude women
A row of seats from Ford's Theater
A carriage once used by President Abraham Lincoln.

Clemons's eccentricity was also underscored in his last will and testament:
"I Albert Adsit Clemons, being of sound and disposing mind and memory and not acting under duress or fraud or acting under undue influence of any person whatever, do make, publish, and declare this my last will and testament. First, I direct that upon my death having been definitely determined, the attending physician shall thereafter pierce or puncture my heart sufficiently for the purpose of absolute certainty of death."

A few occultists have pointed to Clemons's crypt and said that if he did sleep in it, then the first directive of his will must have been an attempt to clue the doctor to give a vampire eternal rest by plunging a silver instrument through his heart. They suspect that Clemons had fallen victim to a vampire that is said to have once stalked through Washington. They theorize that his obsession with religious trappings was an attempt to cure himself of the dreaded curse. Although I found accounts of the vampire's visits (and chronicle them elsewhere in this book), I found nothing to connect Clemons to it.

Clemons's death certificate made no mention of his heart having been punctured, so it is doubtful that his wish—his last wish—was honored.

Clemons's death had a positive effect on those who rented the apartments in Halcyon House. For one thing, they were no longer required to shift apartments. The new owners wasted no time in converting the house to electricity, either. Another major undertaking was the removal of as much of the grotesque construction work as possible. Ever since Clemons's passing there has been an effort to restore as much of Halcyon House to its former state as possible. But Stoddert's house is old, and its turbulent history and the multitude of renters have left some marks that cannot be erased.

Most former residents have been reluctant to talk of their experiences, but enough have expressed their fears, or amazement, over the years to provide a fairly detailed chronicle of the goings-on in the house. Housekeepers, workers, and other staff have been quoted, owners have been quoted, and renters have been quoted. Some have told of a figure on the stairway that vanishes whenever someone gets too close, of weird sounds echoing in the night, of unearthly shapes in rooms shrouded in darkness. There have also been reports of "an unintelligible whisper" sometimes heard floating through the once beautiful garden "on certain starry nights." It is said to come from the area where a sunken tub, or pool, with a large French mirror had once been located.

A few years after Clemons's death, a woman who rented one of the apartments in Halcyon House related an uncanny experience. She told of returning home from downtown to find a large engraving that hung over the mantel lying on the floor. The spike from which it had hung remained in the wall. The house had been locked up tight during her absence and she was certain no one could have entered.

Several months later there was a similar incident. The woman returned home after a brief absence to find the engraving on the floor, but this time there was a big, bold black X scrawled across the face of it. She was so frightened that she fled the house and moved elsewhere.

I found a newspaper account from the 1960s in which another former resident of Halcyon House told a reporter how he was awakened by footsteps and found himself floating above his bed. The window that he had closed before retiring was wide open. The curtains fluttered in the breeze. As he debated whether to scream, try to move, or faint, he was gently lowered back onto the bed by unseen hands.

The federal government once considered taking on the restoration of Halcyon House. In the mid-1960s they sent architects and housing experts to examine the old home and determine whether it was fit to become the home for the Vice President—at that time Hubert Humphrey. The experts found the architectural atrocities of Clemons, the weather, and time had taken too high a toll to make restoration feasible. Was that the real reason? Or did Humphrey, serving under President Johnson, decide that there was just too much political turbulence in his life to risk living in the most actively haunted house in Washington?

A few years later, at the time I was researching the first edition of this book, I became acquainted with the couple who lived in the house. None of the encounters, and there had been many during the thirteen years they had lived there, had driven them from the house they obviously love very much. Although they graciously accepted me into their home, they requested that I not use their names. The husband was retired from the foreign service. They had raised their family in the large old house, and were planning to move, in a few years, to an apartment following the celebration of their fortieth wedding anniversary. Respecting their right to privacy, as journalists before me did with previous owners of the house, I agreed.

There is a special aura about Halcyon House, whatever its infirmities. The moment you enter the house you sense the inner conflict. Looking closely there is evidence of the beautiful home Benjamin Stoddert had built, but the garish decoration wrought by Clemons—which, unfortunately, cannot be hidden—predominates. You also see the attempts at restoration made by owners who followed Clemons.

The couple impressed me as being responsible witnesses to the uncanny events they recounted. They carefully chose their words as though they didn't expect others to believe their stories. There was no tension, no nervousness. They seemed comfortable co-existing with the supernatural.

I talked with them, individually and together, about the house several times in the years following that initial meeting. Sometimes I would be told of new incidents. About all the husband ever admitted about the incidents was "there's something a little off center here." The wife was more to the point. "Someone's here. I often see him sitting here in the captain's chair."

The small-framed woman in her early seventies pointed to the chair in the south drawing room, on the first floor, where she said quite a few of the incidents occurred. Her shoulders were draped in a crocheted shawl. There was always a light draft in the house, even in summer. She went on to describe a "balding, fat, short, older person wearing a tan suit." She said she had seen him several times in the last dozen years as she came down the stairs. Once, on a fall evening in 1974, she looked up from her evening prayer to see him sitting in that drawing room captain's chair with his legs crossed. She was troubled that his features were never discernible and that he never spoke

She confided that on fewer occasions she has seen another, more sinister looking fellow. "A shadowy figure dressed in black and moving very slowly," she recalled with little additional insight. Stoddert? Clemons? If someone else, who? I wondered. She couldn't say. There were no pictures of Clemons in Halcyon House, but there was a cameo portrait of Stoddert hanging in the entrance hall. His hair line had receded and his round face was a indication of an aging portly body.

A few years before I made my first visit to Halcyon House the married daughter and the daughter-in-law of the owners saw the face of an old woman in a colonial dress in an upstairs window. The image stopped the two women in their tracks as they walked toward the patio from the garden. Their description of the apparition, unknown to them, matched that of the woman whom "the Major's wife" saw in her encounter some sixty years earlier.

A few months later, during another visit by the couple's children, a six-year old grandchild began to cry out in the middle of the night. It happened more than once. When someone would come to his bedroom to comfort him his story was always the same. A scary old woman who woke him up rearranging his bedcovers frightened him.

A few days later, at breakfast, the child seemed to be in a particularly good mood. "Guess what?" He asked those seated at the table and then beamed as he proclaimed that he didn't have to worry about being scared by the old woman anymore. When she visited him the night before, he said, she whispered

Benjamin Stoddert's ghost has often been seen sitting in this captain's chair in the first floor Drawing Room of Halcyon House. *Courtesy Lee Shephard*

From this second-floor bedroom come tales of levitation and of footsteps that can be heard in the attic above. *The Author's Collection*

"Don't worry, I won't return." With that she kissed him and disappeared out the second story window of his bedroom. His grandmother told me no one has reported seeing the wispy old lady since. Who she was, and why she had haunted Halcyon House for a hundred years or more, probably will never be answered.

The grandchild's story marked a third generation within that family who had encountered ghostly turbulence in Halcyon House. Over the years, and with no one having ever been injured, a certain level of tolerance had been reached.

As a young man, their son described his life in a haunted house for *Parade Magazine*. One incident that he related involved a light that he had seen burning in the basement. He went down the steps to investigate. "Who's there?" He called out, but no one answered. However, the light went out leaving him standing in total blackness. He said he had never been filled with such "a blood-chilling dread." He yelled for his father to get the police as he made his way to the door. When they arrived a search was made of the cellar, but there was no one there, and no clues. The light switch worked perfectly. The young man said no one could have escaped because they would have to have gotten past him to get to the door.

Many of the other occurrences he described in that April 21, 1963, article still go on as they have for more than a hundred years. "Lights go out, but we just turn them on again," the lady of the house said to me matter-of-factly more than a decade later.

There is a bedroom in Halcyon House in which people sometimes defy gravity. Several inexplicable levitations are documented. A young woman, who was a guest many decades ago, was assigned this room. It was the middle of the night when she was awakened by a feeling of weightlessness and realized she was actually suspended in midair above the bed. Too frightened to move or scream, she felt invisible, clammy hands slowly turn and lower her. When she rested on the bed again her feet were on the pillow.

The woman of the house smiled as she recalled her family's first experience with levitation. Knowing nothing of the bedroom's reputation when they moved in, she and her husband chose it as the Master Bedroom because of its size. They slept there several years without incident. When they decided to go away for the weekend, relatives who volunteered to house-sit were given this room in which to sleep. Their first day in the old house was uneventful, but when the man and his wife awoke the next morning they discovered their heads were resting at the foot of the bed. The owners say neither of them has experienced the phenomenon in all their years at Halcyon House.

In early 1975 I received a call from Halcyon House. The woman told me that she and her husband were going to be moving soon, but that she had another—and very recent—incident to tell me about. She then proceeded to tell me about a college student whom they had known for some time, and whom they hired to house-sit for a few days. She insisted that the only reason they suggested he sleep in the Master Bedroom was that it was the most comfortable on summer nights because it had a window air-conditioner. Besides, she said, there was a phone right by the bed.

The very first evening the owners were away the student asked a few friends to drop by. When they left, he showered, and went to sleep. At 2:00 A.M. he phoned his family in nearby McLean, Virginia, to tell them he was headed home. The next day he phoned the owners and told them that he would be checking the house three times a day—during daylight hours—but that he would no longer come near the house at night. She said they had not been able to get him to tell them what had frightened him so much.

The Master Bedroom is believed to have also been the bedroom of Benjamin Stoddert. Above it is one of the attics from which ghostly noises have been reported by scores of people over the years. The man of the house confirmed that he and his wife often heard what sounds like "a person walking or running up there." He told me the ceiling had been lowered since the days of Stoddert, but that he had never been up in that attic. "I'm not going to get up and see. I don't care." That apathy demonstrated the attitude that had seen him through more than a dozen years at Halcyon House.

In spite of what he and his family have experienced, and the events that caused relatives and guests to cut short visits, the man prefers to classify most of these events as eccentricities of an aging and decaying house. "We've enjoyed living here and our extrasensory companions, if any, certainly haven't upset me any," he said the last time I saw him.

Halcyon House has been restored. Neither the age nor the condition of the old house stood in the way of these professionals. The interior was completely gutted and most of Albert Clemons' hodgepodge construction removed. Sculptor John Dreyfuss spearheaded this labor of love and, at great expense, tried to restore the house to its Georgian architectural roots, to make the home more closely resemble the one in which Benjamin Stoddert lived. Dreyfuss told Diana McLellan in the November 1991 issue of *Washingtonian Magazine* "this house definitely has its own energy, and part of it, I feel, comes from the 150 year old spirit of Benjamin Stoddert."

As Dreyfuss's project neared completion in 1993, Bruce Lenthall, writing for the *Northwest Current*, quoted Dreyfuss: "I hope it (Halcyon House) will be a historical resource for the community. Making the wrong decisions about our cultural resources is the greatest sin of all."

It's too early yet to comment on whether this endeavor has settled the turbulence inside Halcyon House. It will be interesting to watch and listen. Has a calm finally come to the corner of Prospect Street and 34 Street Northwest?

The Francis Scott Key House

This is a painting of the home of Francis Scott Key as it looked just after Key moved in. The young lawyer and poet maintained his office there, too, so he could remain close to his family. *The Author's Collection*

The northeast exit ramp of the Francis Scott Key Bridge was built on the spot where the home of the man who wrote *The Star Spangled Banner* used to stand. Some say the planners named the bridge after Key in order to quell his angry spirit.

Key, who was a practicing attorney in Maryland and the District of Columbia, lived in the Georgetown house for some thirty years. It had been built in 1802. He raised his family there, wrote his poetry there, and maintained his law office in the home, too. The rear of the house overlooked the majestic Potomac. Later in his life, as Key looked upon the tranquil waters of the peaceful river, there were probably times when his mind flashed back to a more turbulent time. Key, 34, had been a prisoner on board a British ship in Baltimore Harbor during the bombardment of Fort McHenry during the War of 1812. When he saw the American flag still flying over the fort at daybreak he was inspired to write *The Star Spangled Banner*. That poem, set to music, became our National Anthem in 1931.

Poetry and the law weren't Key's only interests. Twenty years after he wrote *The Star Spangled Banner* he authored *The Power of Literature and Its Connection with Religion*. Life seemed good to Key. As a respected attorney, his oldest son Philip had followed him into the practice of law, and his youngest son had been accepted into the U.S. Naval Academy at Annapolis, Maryland. Two years later, while still a midshipman, young Daniel was killed in a duel. Some say the spark in his life left the senior Key at that time. Francis Scott Key died at the age of 64 in 1843.

Opposite page: Virginians had this view of Georgetown in the mid-1800s. Halcyon House is visible on the ridge line slightly left of center. It is the house with two chimneys. Benjamin Stoddert once owned all of the land sloping to the Potomac River, but it was sold off to meet estate expenses. Just to the right of the Aqueduct Bridge is the home where *Star-Spangled Banner* author Francis Scott Key lived and raised his family. Key's lot sloped gently to the river, so it appears the home has four stories. Until the Civil War the Aqueduct Bridge was actually a trough filled with water so that boats on the C & O Canal could carry their loads across the Potomac to Virginia. During the war dirt replaced the water so it could become a roadway for troop movement. *Courtesy Library of Congress*

It is unfortunate that those who took over the Key house did not share his concern for the property. The new owners were more interested in exploiting the Key name to attract renters than with maintaining the property. Attracting them was no problem, keeping them was.

Newspapers reported those who tried to live in the Key house were driven away by "sinister sounds" that were said to have begun soon after Key's death. It wasn't long before the house had a reputation of being haunted. A newspaper account from the late 1800s, and another from the early 1900s, said floors creaked when no one could be seen walking on them. Rafters seemed to moan. Doors squeaked open and slammed shut.

In the early 1920s a family moved into the decaying Key house vowing that they would not be driven from the home "in spite of the occurrences." According to one newspaper account the fact that the house had previously been vacant for prolonged periods did not worry this family—at first. However, after several sleepless nights the new occupants launched a widespread search throughout the old house in an effort to learn what caused the noises that were keeping them awake. The reporter said they discovered a section of the attic that appeared to have been closed off for years. There, splattered on the ceiling, they saw dried bloodstains. There was little else but cobwebs. Not without apprehension the father replaced the boards that had covered the opening and returned to the living quarters. That night moans unlike any they had ever heard reverberated from that portion of the attic, forcing them to change their minds. They decided that moving was not such a bad idea. Just how blood stains got on the attic ceiling remains a mystery.

Over the next few years more renters came and went. The periods of vacancy, however, grew longer. The decay of the Key house quickened. Some say the sounds and omens increased as the deterioration of the house spread. A few people wanted to tear it down and rid Georgetown of an eyesore—a haunted eyesore at that. However, the owners were finally persuaded to make a serious attempt to restore the house to the condition it had been in when Key lived there. The sinister sounds ceased when restoration was completed. At least that's the story the owners told as they now attempted to attract tourists, rather than renters.

These photographs of the Key home show it after restoration, but give little hint of what was going on inside the old house on M Street. *Courtesy Martin Luther King, Jr. Public Library, District of Columbia (closeup on next page)*

See previous page bottom right.

Is it possible that the erratic noises came from the restive spirit of Key, upset that the home he so loved had been allowed to deteriorate? Perhaps, but if the house was no longer a residence who was there late at night to hear any sinister sounds if they were continuing; and what about those bloodstains on the attic ceiling? One Georgetown old-timer told me that even when the restoration was completed—and that included painting all attic ceilings—that the bloodstains continued to show through the paint. What harrowing act caused them? When? Had Key been involved?

Some say it was the spirit of Francis Scott Key that haunted his Georgetown house in the hopes of scaring the owners into restoring the property to its former condition. *Courtesy Library of Congress*

The house that spawned those questions is no more. Although there was much debate the long-time home of Francis Scott Key was torn down in the name of progress for the Whitehurst Freeway and a span across the Potomac. Virginia commuters got another bridge (named for Key, of course), and Georgetown and the nation lost an historic, albeit haunted, landmark.

The Little Falls Drummer

To the west and south of Washington, one can still witness the full force of the powerful Potomac River as it cascades over Great Falls. Once the river makes its way over that magnificent drop, it must still wind through an area of treacherous rocks known as Little Falls before it widens and its flow appears much more placid. It is from this area, near where the Chain Bridge now stands, that a tale is told of a young hero.

As the British advanced on Washington in March of 1814 and began to torch the Federal City, the contingent of American soldiers began to fall back. As darkness approached, the commander of one group looked with favor on the fast-gathering clouds. With clouds covering the moon there would be even less of a chance that a British patrol might spot his troops as they crossed the river into Virginia. Crossing so far upstream, even in daylight, was risky. The current was fast and the rocks slippery. However, there was a little drummer boy with the outfit who knew this part of the river. He volunteered to stand on the large moss-covered boulder in mid-channel that marked the most treacherous spot. From there he would beat his drum to let the soldiers know they were to pass well to their right.

Reluctantly, the commander agreed and made ready his troops for the crossing. A red glow now lighted the sky to their rear. It looked as though all of Washington was ablaze. Just then there was a clap of thunder and a few sprinkles were followed by a steady down pouring of rain. It would help extinguish the flames in Washington, but the storm would make it harder for the soldiers to see and hear the drummer boy.

Heroically, the young lad stood his ground. He continually beat his drum as the men slowly and carefully picked their way across the rocks to the Virginia side. There, they would re-form, and when reinforcements arrived they would counterattack. As the last soldier reached safety, the little drummer boy lost his balance as he turned to climb from his dangerous perch. He slipped and fell into the fast, swirling currents. Before anyone could extend a hand his body was being beaten against the rocks as it, and his drum, were swept downstream. It happened so quickly that he never had a chance to cry out.

Death has not stilled his drum, they say. Old rivermen were the first to hear what they described as "a muffled, distant drum, beating a warning." Down through the years others too suspected the drummer boy of maintaining his vigil. They claimed that on dark and stormy nights they sometimes heard that hauntingly mournful drum beating out its slow and muffled cadence. However, the stories began to diminish with the construction of Chain Bridge. Now, there is a safe way to cross at Little Falls and perhaps the little hero is resting in peace.

Are these the windows from which neighbors witnessed a ten o'clock ritual performed by a long departed housekeeper? *The Author's Collection*

Henry Foxall's Columbian Ordinance Works can be seen on the banks of the Potomac, at the extreme left. It was in this foundry that most of the cannons for the War of 1812 were made. At the far right is Georgetown University, founded in 1789. *Courtesy Library of Congress*

Foxall stands in stately splendor just about a block off Wisconsin Avenue, Georgetown's busiest shopping street. The limbs of massive and ancient trees both obscure and protect the homes of Dumbarton Avenue. Among these stately homes stands a sturdily constructed relic known as Foxall—once so frequently revisited by a ghost that her appearance became known as "the ten o'clock ritual."

This handsome mansion was the pride of Henry Foxall. He had moved to Washington at the insistence of his dear friend, Thomas Jefferson. The two had met what seemed like a lifetime ago, when both were young men in Philadelphia, and the colonies were still subject to British rule. Foxall was building a business and young Jefferson was drafting a declaration on which a new nation could be built. When the two reunited in Washington, Jefferson was one of the leader's of that new nation and Foxall's growing Columbian Ordinance Foundry supplied the armaments to keep it secure.

Both men were violinists. It was this musical bond that cemented their lasting friendship. They often enjoyed evenings of relaxation, at the Foxall mansion, with their music. On warm summer evening's neighbors along Dumbarton sometimes stopped what they were doing to listen to the melodies wafting through the air from the Foxall drawing room. The prospering industrialist was no stranger at the President's House, either. He was received both socially and for business. His foundry supplied many of the cannons for the American Navy when it went after the Barbary Pirates in the Mediterranean, and for all American forces when the second war with Britain erupted in 1812.

A few years after the War of 1812, when his only surviving child married Samuel McKinney, Foxall gave her the Dumbarton Avenue home. It was quite a few years after that when the so-called "ten-o'clock ritual" began. I found a newspaper account from late in the nineteenth century, in the gas light era, of a "house in Georgetown that was cursed with darkness every evening at ten." The article wasn't specific about how long the blackout had been taking place, but implied that it had been tolerated for many years. Various other articles in newspapers and books down through the years have also mentioned the phenomenon, which defied electricity when it replaced gas lights.

Several references to encounters with "a diaphanous aged woman" have been reported. Most who had encountered her said that she floated through the third floor hallway, and vanished if they approached. All of her recorded appearances were "just before ten o'clock at night." Her description has stimulated speculation among some old Georgetowners who say that she resembles a daguerreotype of a housekeeper who had served Foxall families for a number of years. The most often repeated legend is that all the families she had served during her life at Foxall had used the third floor as the children's floor. They say that as housekeeper she enforced the rule of "lights out at ten" and that even after death, sometime in the last third of the nineteenth century, she returned to perform her "nightly ritual."

No one with whom I talked when I was doing my original research for this book seemed to know just when the last incident had been reported. Newspaper references to the legend since the early 1950s seem to be retelling previous accounts. Only long-time neighbors could even recall the legend, and none with whom I talked admitted ever having witnessed the ten o'clock blackout. I also spoke with Foxall's owner at that time. He had lived with his family in the house since 1955. Although he was cordial I was not invited inside. He said that his children, when hearing of the legend, had tried "on several occasions" to get the little old lady back. "They even reverted to candle power, but nothing. Absolutely nothing." He added with a smile, "We've never had any indication the place was haunted."

Almost twenty years later, in 1992, as I was preparing to tell some of the stories from this book to an audience at The National Geographic Society's Grosvenor Auditorium I had a hand-delivered letter brought to me back stage. I wish I could tell you that it was a dark and stormy night, but it was actually a clear, crisp, and beautiful evening—without a full moon.

"Dear Mr. Alexander—

Re: The Foxall House in Georgetown.

There are **two** ghosts despite what my father apparently told you…If you want more specifics, feel free to phone…"

I accepted the woman's invitation and called her. I got the "real" version of what had gone on inside Foxall since the mid-1950s when her family moved into the newly refurbished home that had been vacant several years—or so they thought.

The woman was a teenager back then. Her brother was a few years older. She freely talked about her experiences in a house she believed was haunted, although there was "no *nightly* ritual while we lived there."

Soon after they moved in her brother was talking on the telephone by a desk in the study. The study was just off the foyer and to the right of the large, heavy wooden front door. That door, she said, had a stubborn and noisy lock. He was home alone. No one was in the foyer. No one had come up the walk because he could see out of the window from where he was talking on the phone. Suddenly, he heard the front door open and close. Then he heard footfalls. For a moment he froze. Putting down the phone, the anxious teenager crept back from the desk, and looked into the hall. There were no other sounds. There was no one in the hall.

Over the years there were other strange phenomena. The woman and her brother sometimes heard someone walking up and down the stairs when no one was visible. Once, when the family was gathered for an evening of television, an incident happened that unnerved everyone. She told me the TV set was typical of that period. It was in the days before remote controls. There was a small knob that you pulled out to turn the set on and pushed in to turn the set off. "At ten o'clock the set went dark. It was as though someone had turned it off," she told me. When her father got up to check the TV he found that the knob had been "pushed in by an unseen hand." The woman said her father was always rationalizing the disturbances and was most reluctant to admit they lived in a haunted house, even though he had heard the stories about the "ten o'clock ritual."

"I guess he was trying to protect us," she told me. "He certainly didn't want publicity disturbing our lives."

One morning when the family came down to breakfast the large family portrait that hung on a wall at the foot of the stairs was resting on the table beneath the hanging space. The woman suspected it was another prank of the little old housekeeper.

"Mother saw her, a wisp of a person once, and sensed her presence on another occasion." She added, "Mother could be unkind so the ghost kept a distance from her."

Several years later, when the family decided to get away for a week, they invited a friend who was a teacher to house sit for them. They received a phone call within a few days. The teacher startled the family by calmly inquiring "What's the name of your ghost? I'm sure it's a ghost who came out upstairs and walked around the hall." The teacher continued to house sit for another week or so, but apparently she had no luck in contacting the ghost.

My source had what she describes as the strangest experience of her life late one evening, but she doesn't believe it had anything to do with the nocturnal nanny. She thinks there is another spirit, less frequent in appearance, that also haunts Foxall.

The incident happened during a summer when she was home from college and working days. This particular night she had a girl friend over. Her parents were traveling so the girls were playing the radio rather loudly. She told me she and her friend were getting ready for bed when she heard a noise downstairs.

"There were no rugs on the floors and it sounded as though furniture was being moved." She described the noise as "loud enough for us to hear it above the rock 'n roll music on the radio," which she asked her friend to turn down. They listened more intently—moving to the top of the second floor stairs. The sounds came from the Dining Room.

"It sounded like someone was rearranging the chairs, just moving them back and forth and around," the woman recalled. She said she finally mustered up enough courage to sneak down the stairs. The noise, which lasted for what seemed to her about ten minutes, stopped when she got half-way down the stairs. When she looked around the corner into the Dining Room everything was in its place.

That incident stimulated her curiosity about the old house. During the next few weeks she took time to learn more about the history of Foxall. Among the stories that intrigued her was one of a previous owner, many years before, who hid love letters beneath floor boards in the Dining Room. Apparently the cache had been discovered by workmen years later during one of the many renovations Foxall underwent.

The woman told me that an elderly neighbor who lived down the street added another element to the story: the man's ghost still tries, on occasion, to retrieve those old letters.

Who was that lone room arranger and what could possibly have been in those love letters to cause his spirit to remain so restless? I guess we will never know. My new Foxall source could shed no additional light on the mystery she had uncovered. However, she did bring closure to her experiences with the nocturnal nanny.

The incident happened a few years after she and her brother had been away at college. A housekeeper, who had been employed by the family for years, routinely saw house guests and friends come and go. It was she who may have been the last to see her ghostly counterpart depart. According to my source the housekeeper came upon an elderly lady in the front hall early one evening. Startled, but gaining her composure, the housekeeper asked "Can I help you?"

"I'm just going upstairs to get my things. I'm leaving now," said the unannounced visitor to the somewhat perplexed housekeeper. She knew there were no house guests, so as the uninvited started for the stairs, the housekeeper went for help. The unannounced visitor was never found, but the housekeepers' description closely matched the one others had provided of the ghostly old lady. That encounter, said my source, took place in the late 1970s. She said it was the last encounter her family had involving the shadowy sitter. It came at a time when Foxall no longer had children, or teenagers, living there. As she recalled these incidents to me there was a hint of nostalgia in her voice, "I miss her. I was sorry she left the house. She was nice. I'm sorry my kids didn't get to be in the house with her."

The Ghost of the Murdered Madam

There is one old house, perhaps gone now, that was constructed somewhere on 29th Street in Georgetown just after the Revolution. Residents and some visitors report being haunted by "swishing sounds," going up the stairs; similar to those made by the starched petticoats worn by women of the 1800s. Old newspaper accounts quote witnesses as saying that after following the sounds upstairs they glimpsed a "shadowy substance slipping into a room at the top of the stairs." There is no record of the phenomenon ever preceding anyone *down* those stairs.

I was told, but not surprisingly was unable to confirm, that the old house was once one of Georgetown's finer brothels. The madam prided herself on maintaining a small, but select, group of women who were not only lovely to look at, but excellent conversationalists; should a customer desire that as well. Legend relates that the madam came to Georgetown as a runaway from an old Atlanta plantation. She had been the daughter of a rich, but dictatorial, southern planter. He had caught her with a handsome field hand in the hayloft of one of the barns. Before the young man could reach for his pants the father shot him dead. He severely beat the girl, and carried her back to the mansion, where he locked her inside her room. In the darkness of the night, the young woman put a few things together and climbed out her window. She was never again seen in that area.

The story of what had happened spread throughout the county. Field hand told field hand; house servants told their masters. The girl had brought disgrace to her father; but worse, in the mind of the young man to whom she was betrothed, she had dishonored *him*. The young man was ridiculed everywhere. His friends wouldn't let him forget that his girl had taken up with a slave. He awoke one morning to find a bale of hay at his front door. He blamed his former fiancee for destroying his life. As hatred for the girl he once loved grew, he resolved to get revenge; and set off to find her.

The young woman had tried to hide her trail. She had gone south to Macon before boarding a stage north. Also traveling by the same stage, according to the legend, was a member of Georgia's delegation to the United States Congress. The two became very close on that grueling stage ride, and the congressman found the girl not only attractive but intelligent.

She confessed to her middle-aged companion that she was running away from home but concealed the hayloft adventure. The congressman was more than sympathetic. When they arrived in the Nation's Capital he suggested an inexpensive yet respectable ladies' boarding house for the young girl. He promised to call on her again soon and, if possible, to help her obtain some form of employment.

During the long stage ride the young woman had developed a few ideas of her own; based on what the congressman had told her about his work, his colleagues, and Washington society. She became more than a friend to her stagecoach companion. Before too many weeks passed she talked the

gentleman out of a large sum of money in order to purchase her own home in Georgetown. As the months went by, she kept her ears and eyes open. Her great charm made her an instant success at several of the functions to which the congressman from Georgia escorted her.

One evening after a most satisfying dinner and a carriage ride down by Rock Creek the young woman unveiled her plan to her ally. She would open a discreet brothel, employing only cultured women that would be capable of satisfying a man's mind as well as his body. She personally vowed to be faithful only to her congressman.

At first the Georgia politician was reluctant, but his mistress had a way of making him change his mind. They spent several months organizing the business and then quietly letting it be known that a new and most unusual "gentleman's club" was about to open. From the beginning the lavishly decorated brothel was a success. Months passed but the initial success did not fade. Perhaps it was because neither the congressman nor his consort was greedy. They were content to keep their "gentleman's club" small, employing only four girls and concentrating on quality: in companionship and in clientele.

Time passed quickly. It was late one spring evening, a few years later, when a routine knock on the door was answered by the madam. She screamed. Standing in the doorway cursing and spitting out vile language at the top of his voice was the man her father had chosen for her to marry so long ago in Atlanta.

His face was weather-beaten and unshaven; his broad shoulders rounded from the hours he had spent outdoors in the saddle. He grabbed her wrist. The hatred he had suppressed through the years propelled his slap across her face. The force of the slap broke his hold on her arm. The woman spun loose and raced back into the house. He chased her.

Two employees and a man in the parlor were startled by the commotion. They stood speechless, watching as the crazed intruder chased the screaming woman up the stairs shouting profanities about her last days on her father's plantation.

He cornered her in a room just off the top of the stairs. Another scream erupted, but died as though choked off. That's when the others were jarred into action and rushed up the stairs. They were too late. Lying on the floor was the crumpled body of the young madam. Her throat still bore finger marks. Tears still glistened on her cheeks. The window on the far side of the room was open. The curtains fluttered in the night breeze. There was no one else in the room. Legend has it that the murderer got away. The member of Congress moved behind the scenes to sell the house, hoping that it would help him to forget his lost love, and what had happened to her there.

Down through the years, though, it seemed that the ghost of the disgraced young woman couldn't forget that last climb up the stairs; and so climbed them again, and again, disappearing into the room at the top, hoping each time that the outcome would be different.

The *Evening Star,* in an August 13, 1934 story, described the ghost of a wispy young woman in blue crinoline who supposedly frequented the stairs and hallway of a home on 29th Street Northwest. The article's source was a woman who apparently had recently moved into the house. Whether she encountered the murdered madam can't be said for certain because the legend doesn't reveal just where in Georgetown the southern belle lived. However, the woman's description certainly does make one wonder. She told the *Star* reporter, "I wouldn't really say I'd seen a ghost, because I'm not sure what a ghost should look like…I only know I was terribly startled by the realness of the girl in the blue crinoline." The woman described the ghost as "a tall, misty white thing." The encounter scared her so much she stopped using the front stairs at night.

This is Georgetown's busiest street, Wisconsin Avenue, as it appeared in the 1890s. Several of these old buildings have haunted histories, but only a few of the current owners are willing to discuss the old stories or to admit to any ghostly encounters. It is said that almost one hundred fifty years ago many of the buildings in the 1200 block served as quarters for slaves who were laborers on the C & O Canal or in nearby warehouses. Legend has it they lived in what is now the cellars, and would use some of the upper floors as places to entertain each other during what little leisure time they had. It is said the laughter, joviality, and the music from the plays and dances sometimes mingles in the late night air with the cries and sobs. Some swear to having heard the crack of a bullwhip an instant before a blood curdling scream. Others have heard a tinkling piano and the shuffling feet of people dancing, only to find deserted warehouse space when they investigated. Most of the reports have come from a building that was once a pub known as "Mr. Henry's." In a 1974 article in the *Georgetown Voice* Charles Kahwaty wrote, "There was a morbid quality to the establishment; in the past there had been five suicides in the house." *Courtesy Columbia Historical Society*

International Incidents

It seems the ghosts of Georgetown don't care whom they haunt. I came across a couple of articles in old newspapers where supernatural incidents were reported by members of the diplomatic corps. Diplomatic immunity didn't shield them from ghostly visits. Although these accounts provoked no international incidents they did nothing to foster better foreign relations.

A "former Portuguese Minister" once occupied an old home that was haunted by the spirit of a "long dead British soldier." Whether the soldier died from wounds suffered in the American Revolution or during the War of 1812 isn't known. This rather vague article, dated from the 1930s, only located the house "in Georgetown." The article is actually an explanation of why the minister had chosen to move from the house.

The account relates how the diplomat's wife encountered the ghost early one morning in a hallway. She told the reporter that she first thought it was a servant who had also risen early; but when it drew closer, her blood ran cold as she realized that the thing coming toward her was not of this world. The soldier, whom she described as having a rather pale and haggard look, continued to approach. The frightened woman became fixed to the spot. The scream she tried to muster caught in her throat. She flattened her body against the wall. She told the reporter she began to feel faint.

As unconsciousness was overtaking her; the wistful eyes of that ghostly pale face stared into hers. She remembered that as she crumpled to the floor, she felt the cold, clammy touch of the soldier's hand as he apparently reached out for her elbow in an attempt to prevent her from falling. It took her several days under a doctor's care to recover from the experience. When she had recovered, they moved. To my knowledge no other article was written about that house and its ghost, and I have not heard the story anywhere else.

The second international incident I came across occurred in the 1920s and involved a Russian diplomat. Some rather

Several bridges like these once spanned Rock Creek to make travel between the District of Columbia and Georgetown easier. There was a time when Rock Creek was navigable all the way up to P Street Northwest. There was also a time when several of these old bridges were places you didn't want to be on a dark and stormy night. *Courtesy Lee Shephard*

loud tapping sounds coming from the ground level window in his study frequently interrupted his paperwork during late evening hours. His bedroom was also on that first floor wing, so even when he did get to bed early there were nights when the tapping sounds would awaken him. He was frustrated at not being able to find the source of the tapping. The reporter who chronicled this story said the minister, who had survived several purges by the Czar just before the Russian Revolution, wasn't easily frightened. I got the idea from the article that he had already personally investigated the disturbances and ruled out mischievous neighborhood children, wind blown branches, loose shutters, and similar causes. He told the reporter he suspected the noises might have been an attempt at communication from the afterworld and was interested in studying the phenomenon.

One rainy night he put a lantern by his desk and waited. Almost with the first tapping sound the minister grabbed up the lantern and bolted from the house to the window from which the sound came. He found no footprints, yet wherever he stepped he left a deep print in the soft ground of the flower bed beside the house. This confirmed his personal suspicion: the tapper was a ghostly visitor. The Russian minister fancied himself a student of American history. He speculated to the reporter that since a neighbor's house had been a stop on the Underground Railroad; he wouldn't be surprised if the ghost was that of an escaped slave killed while tapping on the window of a house he had wrongly suspected of offering sanctuary.

Other Haunted Bridges

Georgetown is bordered on the east by Rock Creek and on the south by the Potomac River. Several bridges provide access to the port from the District of Columbia and from Virginia. Long Bridge, which spanned the Potomac, wasn't the only bridge on which strange things happened. Other bridges have spawned some interesting stories over the years. One of the bridges that used to span Rock Creek was a long wooden affair. It no longer stands, but for years Georgetowners shuddered at some of the tales spun around two accidents. One of the stories dates to the days just after the Revolution. It involved yet another drummer boy. The youth was from nearby Falls Church, Virginia, according to most accounts. One windy day, as he crossed the bridge, a great gust of wind blew him off balance, and he tumbled over the side with his drum and drowned. His body was never found. There were reports of muffled drumbeats being carried on the air currents for several years thereafter. An article in one Georgetown publication said, "There are residents who insist that when the nights are quiet and Rock Creek is but a babble, one may hear the muffled roll of a drum trembling in the air." The sound supposedly begins faintly, from far away, but grows ever louder as it reaches the area of the bridge where the youth fell over the side. Then— there is silence.

The other incident involving that same Rock Creek bridge occurred many years later. The wooden span had become rather rickety with age but was still used. One night, during a fierce storm, the old relic collapsed just as a stagecoach went thundering across. The driver and the horses met their death in the swollen, muddy waters below.

For years after that incident, whispers drifted around the Georgetown wharf, through the pubs, and among people on the streets that the drama continued to be re-enacted on certain moonless nights. Fear could be detected in the voices of those living near where the old bridge used to be as they would recall in somber tones what they had glimpsed on more than one stormy night.

They told of a ghostly coach, with a driver who whipped his horses in panic, as he tried to cross a bridge that was no longer there. The "aphonic" apparition always vanished in a clap of thunder and a flash of lightning in what would have been the middle of the bridge.

These stories began to die out within a few decades after the collapse of the rickety old span. Apparently, without the bridge as a reminder, Georgetowners didn't think about the incidents so often. Besides, another nearby bridge was vying for attention, and its ghost was much more frightening.

Travelers of almost two centuries ago, going from Georgetown to the business and government offices in the District of Columbia, most often used the old K Street Bridge that crossed Rock Creek. It too had a legend that persisted over the years it stood, although the number of reports diminished after electricity brightened the nearby streets, and stores and shops replaced its forested approaches. Nevertheless, there were those who feared street crime much less than an encounter with the horrible "headless man of the K Street bridge."

The stories of this macabre apparition first sprang up in the last century. Seldom did anyone who encountered the disembodied spirit ever return to travel the bridge again. At its very mention, fear would be reflected in their eyes.

It has been difficult to determine just how this phantom came to haunt the bridge, or for that matter, how he lost his head. I have read a couple of theories. One that was put forth in an old newspaper account surmised that the phantom had lost his head "in noble battle during the War Between the States." Seldom was he ever referred to elsewhere in such sympathetic tones. It was obvious that the writer had never come in contact with the specter, nor had he ever met anyone else who had.

More often the accounts expressed a belief that the silent spirit of the K Street Bridge was the victim of punishment for some heinous crime. One report conjectured that the beheading had been carried out by vigilantes. Actually, those citizens who had the misfortune to meet the headless ghost of the K Street Bridge seldom took time to wonder how he had lost his head. They were only anxious that he not take theirs before they could escape.

Lafayette Square

The square across from the White House has not always carried the name of the Frenchman who fought bravely for American independence. For many years after construction of the President's House (as the White House was first known), the square across the street was known as "The President's Square." As you read these tales involving many of the residents of the square, you may find yourself in agreement with Washingtonians who refer to it as "Tragedy Square."

The Guardians of St. John's Church

The sight of wagons and families moving in or out on Jackson Place, Lafayette Square, was not an uncommon one. If old tales are to be believed, ghostly turbulence in this area caused many families to seek more peaceful surroundings. *The Author's Collection*

No other section of Washington has had so much intrigue, mystery, murder, and macabre happenings as has the area on the north side of 1600 Pennsylvania Avenue. Few of the original homes of the square remain, and that may partially explain the turbulence of the ghosts who revisit their old neighborhood.

Whenever the one-thousand pound bell, housed in the steeple of St. John's Church, tolls the passing of famous Washingtonians, we are told strange things happen inside the Sanctuary. *Courtesy Lee Shephard*

The first structure erected on Lafayette Square (besides the White House) was St. John's Church. It was designed by Benjamin Latrobe, who topped the steeple with a one-thousand-pound bell. Completed in 1821, the church has counted many American Presidents among those who have attended services there.

The sanctuary is almost always open, and those who enter sense that they are not only in a house of worship, but in a house shrouded in history. The pews, of a deep, rich hardwood, are the same ones parishioners have sat on for more than 150 years.

Legend has it that when the large old bell tolls the death of a famous man, the white-robed spirits of "six great Washingtonians," whose names have been obscured by time, appear at midnight. They sit in the pew of the Presidents with arms folded and heads facing forward, pay their respects, and vanish as silently as they appeared.

The spirits of some of the statesmen who worshipped at St. John's Church materialize whenever one of America's leaders dies. The ghosts of great Americans make their way to the Pew of the Presidents, pay their respects, and vanish. *Courtesy Lee Shephard*

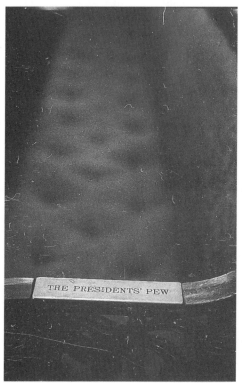

This brass plaque marks the pew where the ghostly statesmen appear briefly to honor the life of service given. *Courtesy Lee Shephard*

The Peripatetic Ghost of Dolley Madison

There was a time when anyone who was anyone, or had ambitions to achieve greatness, lived or was entertained in one or more of the houses on the President's Square. Cabinet members, congressional leaders, representatives of the diplomatic corps, newspaper publishers and editors, admirals, generals, presidential aspirants, men of the judiciary, beautiful women of society, and men-about-town gathered here.

Among the early residents of the square was the noted philanthropist and art collector William Corcoran. Another was Dolley Madison, who spent her declining years in the house that still stands on the corner of what is now Madison and H Streets, Northwest. Late at night, men leaving the popular Washington Club, when it was a few doors down the street, used to tip their hats to the ghost of Mrs. Madison. Many swore to having seen her on her porch; shawl around her shoulders, gently rocking in her favorite chair in shadows highlighted by the glow of the moon. Dolley's spirit is one of the most active in Washington. It has also been seen in the White House Rose Garden and at the Octagon, but then Dolley's life was quite active, too.

The Dolley Madison house is by no means the only one on Lafayette Square where encounters with the spirit world have been reported.

When the hour is late and the moon is bright enough, some say you can see Dolley Madison rocking on the porch of this house on Lafayette Square. It's where she spent her last days. *Courtesy Lee Shephard*

The Disastrous Duel of Stephen Decatur or Pride over Passion

Stephen Decatur, America's favorite hero of the early 1800s was in his mid-thirties when he and his wife, Susan, moved to Washington. His reputation as a leader had been made during the Barbary Wars. When this handsome, rich, and idolized naval hero decided to build a home on Lafayette Square, only the President's House, and St. John's Church were there.

Decatur loved his new home. It was designed by the much-sought-after architect Benjamin Latrobe. There were so many happy hours there with his wife, and so much regret over his final decision that it is said that Decatur frequently revisits his elegant brick home. Perhaps he is still searching for an answer to how he could have lost his life when he had so much to live for.

Stephen Decatur's exploits in the Barbary Wars were detailed and enhanced by the press. Here an artist shows Decatur's life being saved by a wounded seaman. *Courtesy Library of Congress*

This portrait of Stephen Decatur, whose brilliant career was cut short by a duel, hangs inside his home on Jackson Place. *National Trust for Historic Preservation-photographed by Lee Shephard*

Decatur was from a family of seafarers out of Sinepuxent, Maryland. He served in the Caribbean as a lieutenant during the undeclared naval hostilities with France when the new United States Navy under Secretary Benjamin Stoddert was flexing its muscles. He also proved himself in the Mediterranean, and in 1803 was given command of his first ship. By the next year the swashbuckling Marylander had destroyed the captured American frigate *Philadelphia* in Tripoli Harbor. That earned him a captaincy and kept tales of his exploits circulating through the remainder of the war. At age 25, Decatur was the youngest captain ever in the American Navy. Word of his brilliance and courage in combat reached port ahead of his returning ship. Hampton Roads was buzzing about Stephen Decatur. He was lionized by Norfolk society, and it was there that he met Susan Wheeler, daughter of the mayor. Five months later they were married.

A year or so after their marriage, an incident occurred on the high seas—not directly involving Decatur—that eventually led to his premature death.

It had been a quarter of a century since the United States had fought Britain for independence, yet British ships sometimes still tried unsuccessfully to intimidate American vessels on the high seas. The balance changed in 1807, however, when the British frigate *Leopard* encountered the American frigate *Chesapeake*. The *Leopard's* commander fired one shot across the bow of the *Chesapeake*. That was all it took for the *Chesapeake's* Commodore, James Barron, to allow a boarding party to remove four sailors that the British charged were deserters from His Majesty's Royal Navy. Word of the incident spread rapidly. Americans were outraged that one of their naval commanders could be bullied by the British.

When Barron sailed his frigate back into Norfolk he was greeted with an order for a court-martial. The nine-member board, which included Captain Stephen Decatur, suspended Barron from the Navy for five years on charges that he had failed to clear his ship for action. The *Chesapeake-Leopard* incident proved to be the slow-burning fuse that ignited the War of 1812 five years later.

Commodore Barron never quite forgave Decatur for his role in that court-martial. No doubt the fact that the Navy named Decatur commander of the *Chesapeake* explains, at least in part, why Barron singled him out from the others on that board as a target for his resentment. Decatur sailed off toward more heroic exploits in the War of 1812, and the embittered Barron, exiled from the Navy, plotted his adversary's death.

At the war's end, the laurels of a grateful public awaited the courageous naval strategist, and there is no doubt that Decatur could have realized any political ambitions he might have had. He and his wife, Susan, moved to the young nation's capital. The exploits of the dashing Decatur kept conversation going at many social gatherings. There were few men in Washington, or elsewhere, who could rival the Commodore. His charm and poise, added to his reputation for heroism, were more than enough to captivate the ladies of the Federal City. Husbands were just as enamored of the beautiful and soft-spoken Susan as their wives were of Decatur.

Susan Decatur was overjoyed to have her husband home; but being at home was a new and different life-style for the seagoing Commodore. For his part, it was a major readjustment. Marie T. Beall writes in her book *Decatur House and Its Inhabitants* that it was difficult for the Commodore to cope with such peaceful surroundings. The restive Decatur once complained in a letter to a friend that there were no signs of war, and revealed how ashamed he would be "to die in my bed."

Had Commodore James Barron known of Decatur's boredom he might have moved more quickly. Barron's hostility toward Decatur increased each time he was thwarted in his attempt at getting command of another ship. He had been reinstated in the Navy at half pay after his suspension expired, but he was always passed over for the posts he sought. Barron was convinced that Decatur was the source of the opposition with which he was meeting, and he mounted a campaign to provoke Decatur into a duel.

It wasn't easy. Although Decatur had fought several duels earlier in his life, there are indications that he was not eager to return to the field of honor. The vengeful Barron was persistent, however, and Decatur's pride would no longer let him ignore Barron's personal attacks. Reluctantly, Decatur wrote to his nemesis: "…if we fight, it must be on your own seeking." The letter was touted by Barron as Decatur's acceptance to do battle.

The Panic of 1819 was gradually losing its grip on the American economy. Congress was debating the Missouri Compromise as a way of resolving the bickering between slave states and free states over new states. However, all of Washington—including Susan Decatur—was caught up in the social event of the year. President James Monroe and his wife Elizabeth had announced that daughter Maria was to be married. The competition was underway to see who, among the scores of requests, would be chosen to host the parties. We don't know when the Commodore told his wife of his impending duel with Barron, but we do know that the Monroe's awarded the Decatur's the honor of hosting the first of the parties for Maria. Legend has it that the party was hosted at the Decatur home on President's Square on the eve of the Commodore's duel with Barron.

The Commodore, although cordial to his guests, seemed detached from the festivities. Oppressed by a feeling of approaching doom, he walked into his bedroom and over to a window facing north. Ever so often a late night carriage would roll by on H Street, but Decatur seemed oblivious to his surroundings. His sad face was reflected against the glass by the candlelight. His marriage was entering its fifteenth year, but the past fourteen months had held special significance. He and Susan had spent them peacefully in their new home. He was learning to live without war. The smell of gunpowder had never seemed so remote. He had discovered a new passion for life, but he felt he must preserve his pride.

Killing Barron would not improve Decatur's reputation, nor did he believe that Barron could profit by his death. Stephen Decatur had survived a naval career spanning four wars. He had fought hand to hand while boarding vessels on the high seas. He had seen his brother fall dead at his side. His best friend had chosen to be blown to bits in a shipboard explosion rather than be captured. Decatur had faced death many times before. He faced it again now.

There are those who tell of seeing the ghost of Commodore Stephen Decatur slip through this door at the back of his house in the pre-dawn hours on the anniversary of his fatal duel. *Courtesy Lee Shephard*

Before the sun could break through the darkness on the morning of March 14, 1820, Decatur slipped from his wife's warm side to meet his destiny. His friend William Bainbridge met him in the square. They rode in somber silence out the Baltimore Road; crossed the District of Columbia boundary line, and stopped in a field adjacent to the small Bladensburg tavern. The predawn sound of the crickets was drowned out by the birds that had begun to sing. A few yards away a brook called Blood Run trickled by the edge of the notorious dueling field.

The morning serenity was pierced by the occasional clicking of metal on metal as the two men checked their weapons. The duel was at eight paces, murderously close. Presumably, this was a concession to the nearsighted Barron.

As first light tinted the sky, Bainbridge recited the instructions: The men could not fire before the count of one, nor after the count of three. Witnesses reported that two shots sounded as one when Bainbridge reached the count of two. Barron fell immediately with a bullet in his hip. Many argue that Decatur was not off target and that he never intended to kill Barron.

Decatur stood there, pistol smoking, staring down at the fallen Barron, who lay in agony almost at his feet. Decatur was not smiling. The naval hero winced in pain, put his hand to his right side, and fell.

The mortally wounded Decatur was brought back to his home on the President's Square. One account of the tragedy said that his wife Susan was so paralyzed by his condition that she could not bring herself to see him. Decatur knew he was dying, and his last words were, "If it were in the cause of my country, it would be nothing."

Susan Wheeler Decatur could not bring herself to look at her mortally wounded husband when he was brought home. After his death she could not bear to stay in the house they had shared. General John Bomford, a longtime friend of the Decatur's allowed her to use the Kalorama tomb for her husband. He also invited her to be a guest at his estate for a while. Later, Susan had her husband's body moved to Philadelphia for burial beside his parents. She took up residence at 2812 N Street NW. One writer said, "Mrs. Decatur's grief was viewed as somewhat exaggerated even in her own day." She became a recluse, never venturing out into the society she had once so charmed. Although she did receive some visitors into her home, they stayed but a short time. Most were uncomfortable with the sadness and grief. Legend has it Susan grew old wringing her hands and weeping for her lost husband, and that her ghost still resides in that old N Street house. Many who have been in it since say they soon left to avoid being overcome with emotions of sorrow and despair that permeated the air. *Courtesy National Trust for Historic Preservation, Photographed by Lee Shephard*

It was in this bed that American hero Stephen Decatur died from a wound suffered in a duel. "If it were in the cause of my country, it would be nothing," are reported to have been his last words. *Courtesy Lee Shephard*

The nation lost one of its greatest heroes that night. Flags flew at half-mast. When Decatur's funeral cortege passed through the streets of Washington, thousands stood in mourning. He was buried with full military honors. Later, towns in Georgia, Illinois, and Alabama would be named for him.

A year after the Commodore's death some of the household staff were returning home late one night and saw Decatur's ghost as it made its first appearance at that same H Street window where he had stood on the evening before his death.

Stephen Decatur's house, designed by Benjamin Latrobe, still stands on Lafayette Square. Although the first, first-floor window on H Street appears to just be shuttered, it is actually walled up—supposedly in an unsuccessful attempt to prevent the Commodore's apparition from returning to stare out the window in the bedroom where he died. *Courtesy Lee Shephard*

The writing desk and chest belonged to Commodore Stephen Decatur. The chest stands where a corner window, scene of Decatur's ghost on several occasions, was walled up. *Courtesy Lee Shephard*

The window was ordered walled up. But that did not prevent Decatur from revisiting his home. His transparent form has been reported on numerous occasions since. Passers-by on H Street who have claimed to have spotted it at the walled-up window describe his expression as melancholy. Some household staff members early in the twentieth century attested to having seen a transparent figure silently slipping out the back door just before dawn, with a black box under its arm—just as Stephen Decatur did that March morning in 1820 when he left to meet Commodore James Barron on the field of honor at Bladensburg.

Midnight Callers

Some claim that Postmaster General Aaron Brown's career was wrecked and his health ruined because of the supernatural goings-on in his house, which was the former home of Attorney General William Wirt. *Courtesy U.S. Post Office*

Somewhere just to the north and west of Lafayette Square there once stood another of the Federal District houses that attracted those in the higher echelons of government. As a matter of fact, a former Attorney General and the Supreme Court Chief Justice before whom he had argued a great many historic cases were said to be among those who continued to frequent the home for many years after their death.

Tales were being whispered about the house even before Aaron V. Brown moved in, in the 1850s. The former Tennessee governor had served three terms in Congress and was no stranger to Washington. Now, Brown was to be Postmaster General under President James Buchanan. He and his wife, Cynthia, felt proud to have found such an historic house, apparently placing no stock in the whispered stories. One article I read said that Brown used to boast to friends about it having belonged to Attorney General William Wirt, who had served Presidents James Madison and John Quincy Adams. Brown used to tell his guests about the famous people who had visited his home—South Carolina's John C. Calhoun, who once served as Vice President; Speaker of the House of Representatives Henry Clay; famous orator Daniel Webster; and fellow Tennessean President Andrew Jackson.

After he had lived in the house a short time, however, Brown's personality began to change. Those close to him noticed that he had become rather edgy, often grumpy, and that he complained with increasing frequency of noises keeping him awake at night. One reporter said that he bickered with his household staff about their late hours, but they pleaded innocence.

None of the servants had seen a soul stirring in the midnight hours, but several said that they had heard strange voices drifting through the halls on more than one moonless night, and that they too had trouble sleeping at night. There are indications that they began to return to their own homes to sleep. Brown wrongfully assumed that he would get more sleep with the servants gone. Dark circles began to appear under his eyes. One story dwelt on how short his temper was with staff members. He seldom smiled anymore.

U.S. Supreme Court Justice John Marshall's ghost is said to have been among the nocturnal visitors to the old William Wirt house. *Courtesy Library of Congress*

Attorney General William Wirt once owned a house just north and west of Lafayette Square. His ghost is said to have entertained several other ghosts of famous Washingtonians of years gone by who gathered in his home to debate State's Rights. *Courtesy Library of Congress*

One newspaper account I read said that the Postmaster General was convinced that former owner Attorney General Wirt was returning to his home on certain nights to discuss and argue law with former Chief Justice John Marshall and other long-dead political figures. It was while Marshall was Chief Justice that one of the Supreme Court's most momentous precedents was set: allowing the court to declare an act of Congress unconstitutional. This expanded the powers of the still-new federal government while restricting those of the states. According to legend, it was this action that summoned the spirits of the country's most fervent States' Rightists to the Wirt home. Among those voices alleged to have been raised in ethereal debate, witnesses claimed to have heard South Carolina's firebrand John C. Calhoun's oratorical tones and Virginia's "eccentric and rhetorical Congressman John Randolph's shrill—almost soprano—voice."

The way Brown was running the Post Office Department was becoming an increasingly open scandal. "The morals that characterized his administration of the Post Office were deplorable," says Gerald Cullinan in his book *The Post Office Department*, adding "Politics was everything." Among the outrages: a swindling New York postmaster was permitted to "escape" to Mexico with $155,000.00 in postal funds because,

Cullinan says, he was a "sterling Democratic politician." By 1858 Brown had run up record budget deficits for the postal service. Was his work affecting his home life, or was his home life affecting his work?

It is certain that the strange voices he heard drifting through the blackness of his house greatly disturbed the Postmaster General until his sudden death. *The Evening Star* of March 8, 1859, says Brown "suffered from a painful illness of some ten day's duration." The Postmaster General had died that morning. All public business was suspended and Brown lay in state in the East Room of the White House. Speculation at the time that Brown went crazy and then began hearing voices seems unfounded. Articles describing other encounters in the old Wirt house continued after his death. Apparently, until it was torn down, there was no letup in the supernatural sessions. The disturbing noises were said to have driven one owner to suicide, but since he left no note, no one knows the real reason he ended his life. I guess we will never know whether demolition of the old home forced Wirt and Marshall to argue elsewhere with their cronies, or whether these adversaries of the past settled their dispute.

A Haunting Affair

Theresa Sickles and Philip Barton Key had a love affair and that led to Key's death, in 1859, at the hands of her husband, a flamboyant former New York Congressman. Some say Key's restless spirit still haunts Lafayette Square. *Courtesy Library of Congress*

In 1859 Washington's social foundations were rocked by a shocking scandal involving the flamboyant former Congressman Daniel Sickles and Philip Barton Key, a son of the composer of the *Star Spangled Banner*. How they became two of Washington's most noticeable ghosts is a story worth retelling.

Sickles was a good-looking former congressman from New York. He had been married for a little over five years to the beautiful daughter of an Italian music teacher. Theresa Sickles was described in *Harper's Weekly* as "very pretty and girlish and extremely attractive in manner; well educated, and charming in every way."

After his marriage, Sickles was "without office" for a few years. He latched onto a job in the Foreign Service and spent some time in London. When he and his wife returned to Washington, he immediately channeled his energies into James Buchanan's bid for President—and in winning back the seat he had once held in Congress. They moved into a home on Lafayette Square and threw themselves into the city's social whirl. Twice weekly Sickles and his wife wined and dined the influential of Washington. Lafayette Square was the hub of the city's social and political circles, yet few houses on the square could boast as much carriage traffic as that of the Sickles' house.

Although Theresa Sickles was only seventeen when she married, Daniel knew that she would be an asset to his career. A *Harper's* reporter said, "She was soul and charm of these affairs. There was something inexpressibly fascinating about her fresh girlish face, and her sweet amiable manner."

Yet, after Buchanan's election, in which he won back his seat in Congress, Sickles seemed to showcase his lovely wife less and spend more time away from her and home. He spent considerable time with constituents in his New York district, and when in Washington, quite a bit of time appreciating the belles of the District of Columbia. At soirees, Daniel Sickles was often in the company of other women or listening to some politician or lobbyist. For a while Theresa was content to remain home alone. However, as time passed she began to spend more of her time with the handsome widower Philip Barton Key, a noted attorney who was carrying on his fathers' practice. Before he married, Key had been described as "a renowned lady's man," and *Harper's* said, "as a widower his ancient prestige returned to him."

From almost the first meeting the couple seemed inseparable. "At balls, at parties, in the street, at receptions, at theaters, everywhere, Mrs. Sickles invariably is accompanied by Philip Barton Key, District Attorney," said one newspaper of the day. Key seemed to add sparkle to Theresa's life. She smiled more often and her eyes twinkled as they had not in years.

The *Harper's* writer suggested that neither Mr. Key nor Mrs. Sickles acted with "ordinary prudence." That may have been an understatement. Key had an apartment on 15th Street NW, just a block or so away, and they had a handkerchief-waving signal that had not escaped the notice of Washington gossips.

Theresa Sickles's happiness was short-lived. Someone slipped her husband an anonymous note telling him about "a guilty intrigue" between his wife and Key. It even named the rendezvous site. When Sickles confronted his wife with a charge of adultery, *Harper's* quotes her as saying "Oh, I see I am discovered," and says she "implored her husband to spare her." Sickles did spare her, after she signed a confession in front of two witnesses. (It would be good evidence for a temporary insanity plea later.) By the next Sunday, Sickles was described as "totally distraught" in more than one account of the events of that day. "I am a dishonored and ruined man," he told a friend who visited him. When Key walked past the

Sickles house that morning, en route to the Washington Club, he allegedly signaled Theresa Sickles; it was the last straw. "I've seen the scoundrel making his signals," Sickles said to his friend, shaking his head and shouting, "My God! This is horrible."

Later that day, when he saw Key leave the Washington Club, Sickles rushed out into the square. As Key walked toward 16th Street NW, Sickles headed him off. "Key, you scoundrel, you have dishonored my house—you must die!" Witnesses reported he shouted. Sickles fired one of his pistols. Almost at the same instant Key grabbed at his vest and lunged at Sickles, trying to prevent him from reloading. But Sickles stepped back into the middle of the street and produced another pistol. Key saw it and began backing up toward the Washington Club. Sickles stalked him. When he was ten feet away he fired, and as Key leaned against a tree pleading, "Don't shoot me," he fired once more.

In this scene from a drawing in Frank Leslie's illustrated newspaper, irate husband Daniel Sickles is shown killing Philip Barton Key as the attorney was on his way to a rendezvous with Sickles's wife. *Courtesy Library of Congress*

As Key fell his eyes moved once again toward that window across the square. It was the one he often used to watch for Theresa's signal through opera glasses from the Washington Club, according to *Harper's* Washington correspondent. Although he may have been looking for Theresa, it's likely that the last image his eyes registered was the smoking pistols of her vengeful husband. Within minutes there was an explosion of screams and sobs from the Sickles house. Theresa had learned what happened.

The lifeless body of Key was removed and buried with proper respect. However, it is said that the ghost of the debonair lawyer has never left Lafayette Square. Stories of encounters with his persistent phantom have been handed down through the years. For more than one hundred years people have said they have seen Key. A few times newspapers have printed descriptions of Key's ghost as related to them by scores of eyewitnesses. Some have seen it walking out of the old Washington Club. Others claim to have encountered it on the sidewalk near where Key was slain. A shadowy silhouette is also reported to have ventured into the square on occasion. According to the legend, it is the ghost of a single-minded Key intent upon keeping a rendezvous with his mistress.

The attitude that Daniel Sickles assumed toward his twenty-two year old wife "has gained him a great deal of sympathy," according to an article in *Harper's Weekly* shortly after the shooting. "He does not conceal his continued love for

her; and while firmly insisting upon a divorce, he bestows upon her all the pity she needs." The trial was a spectacular one. Sickles hired the best lawyers money could buy. He was acquitted on grounds of "temporary aberration of mind." It was the first time that what has become known as "temporary insanity" had been used in a legal case. Some observers of the trial claimed that the congressman's relationship with President Buchanan was well known to the jurors and intimated that the jury would not convict a man of such position and influence.

Although Sickles and his wife separated, his career did not falter. Theresa's life had ended with Key's death and within a few years she too died. Sickles, however, continued his duties and attended to his social obligations as though nothing had ever happened. When the Civil War erupted, he raised his own contingent of men in New York. They rode off into battle. His patriotism endeared him to President and Mrs. Abraham Lincoln, and assured him of a post after the war.

"He certainly is a very kind-hearted man," Mrs. Lincoln said of General Sickles who sometimes dined at the White House. The loss of a leg in the battle at Gettysburg did not diminish the General's appeal to the opposite sex, nor did it slow him down in his career. Sickles is said to have worn his disability as a badge of courage. He thought so much of his severed leg that he personally bequeathed it to the Army's National Medical Museum. Within a few years he successfully manipulated himself into a position to be named minister to Spain by President Ulysses S. Grant.

Daniel Sickles is flanked by two colleagues as they revisit the Gettysburg battlefield where he lost a leg. It has been said that he wore that disability as a badge of courage. He saved the amputated leg and donated it to the Army Medical Museum. He would often drop by the Washington museum, bringing a few friends with him so he would have an audience for his version of the battle of the Peach Orchard. *Courtesy Library of Congress*

Like Sickles the congressman, and Sickles the general, Sickles the diplomat possessed a tremendous ego. Legend has it that when he came back to Washington he would often drop by the Medical Museum where his leg was "enshrined," bringing a few friends with him. He loved pointing to the severed limb and retelling his version of how and when it was cut from under him.

After his death, Sickles ghost is reported to have continued to visit the museum to admire the severed leg. A long-time custodian I met at the old Medical Museum of the Armed Forces Institute of Pathology wasn't at all reluctant to discuss Sickles's revisitations. The old man, bent with age, but sturdy enough to perform his tasks, claimed that his grandfather had served with Sickles in the Civil War. He took a rather curious pride in working around the leg, and wondered whether all the old stories about the General's ghost still visiting the museum would die out after the museum moved. The old red brick building was being torn down to make room for the Hirshhorn Museum. The Armed Forces Medical Museum was to be moved to the grounds of the Walter Reed Army Medical Center in Northwest. Although the custodian said he had never met the General's ghost, he knew a co-worker who had.

Pointing to the hallway near the glass case containing the General's leg, the custodian told how the co-worker had related his encounter with "a fat shadow with one leg that seemed to float" through the dimly lighted hallway. The custodian learned of the experience when the co-worker came to him threatening to quit if he wasn't shifted to day work. The custodian said that he was sure the ghost his co-worker had seen was Sickles's because there had been others over the years who had described similar encounters—always with a one-legged apparition they described as "fat," "rotund," or "obese." A description that fit the elderly Sickles' shape.

The Hirshhorn Museum has occupied the spot where the old Medical Museum used to be for several years now. So far, I have yet to hear of the old General taking a group of his spectral friends on a midnight tour in search of his leg. There have been no reports of Sickles' ghost showing up on the Walter Reed campus, either. Maybe it's retired to Gettysburg. Who knows, one day we may get a report from Pennsylvania that old Dan's ghost has been seen puffing on one of his infamous cigars surveying the land where he lost his leg.

The sidewalk on the east side of Lafayette Square has changed drastically in the more than one-hundred years since Philip Barton Key was gunned down here by Daniel Sickles. The old Washington Club is long gone, but not so Mr. Key. His ghost reportedly still appears here from time to time. Some even attribute it to helping save the life of Secretary of State William Seward. *Courtesy Lee Shephard*

Ghost of the Washington Club

This is the building that once housed one of the city's most fashionable men's clubs, the old Washington Club. By the time of the Lincoln Administration it had been converted into a residence. It was just across Pennsylvania Avenue from the White House and a block away from the State Department. In spite of whispers that the sidewalk was haunted, the convenience of the house appealed to Secretary of State William Seward and his family. *Courtesy Martin Luther King, Jr. Public Library, District of Columbia*

With the State Department only a few blocks away it was quite natural that Secretary of State William H. Seward would look for a home near his work. He and his family chose a house on Lafayette Square when they moved to town from New York during the Lincoln Administration. The stone structure had once been the quarters of the Washington Club, one of the city's most prominent gentleman's clubs. It had also served as home to such notables as Secretary of State Henry Clay and Vice President John C. Calhoun. It was outside this quaint two-story brick dwelling that Philip Barton Key was murdered. Stories of his restless ghost revisiting the area apparently didn't trouble the Seward family, who quickly settled into their new surroundings.

The State Department, on 15th Street Northwest, is where Secretary of State William Seward worked. The huge building with all those columns is the almost completed Treasury Department, begun in 1839. *Courtesy National Archives*

As the Civil War was drawing to a close dissidents led by John Wilkes Booth were plotting a way to change Union policies. As part of this conspiracy, which resulted in the assassination of President Lincoln, Louis Powell—sometimes known as Payne—was supposed to kill Secretary Seward. However, when this Confederate deserter and son of a Florida Baptist minister broke into the Seward house on the appointed night, Seward's son Frederick and a servant were alerted by noises unlike any they had ever heard. They rushed into the Secretary's bedroom and surprised Powell before he could complete his mission. One thing is certain, if help had not been summoned by the noises, Secretary Seward would have been killed. He was confined to his bed with injuries from a bad carriage accident, and could not defend himself against the attack. Fortunately, the others arrived at his bedside in time to save him from serious harm.

This is Lewis Payne, who attacked Secretary of State William Seward as part of the conspiracy to kill President Lincoln, Vice President Andrew Johnson, and other key members of the Lincoln administration. Loud noises, from just outside the Seward house, are said to have alerted others in the Secretary's household at the time Payne broke in, thereby allowing them to subdue the attacker and save Seward's life. *Courtesy Library of Congress*

Secretary William Seward's spirit is supposed to have haunted his old house on Lafayette Square, where he had known so much tragedy, until it was torn down. Only then did it find eternal rest. *Library of Congress*

Who made the noises that brought help? That depends on what you read and with whom you talk. Some say Powell was clumsy; others insist Philip Barton Key's restless soul sensed another tragedy and raised a ruckus as Powell was breaking in.

The attempted assassination was such a shock to Seward's invalid wife that she died within two months. His only daughter, who had witnessed the assault, never recovered from the "horrendous experience," as one newspaper called it, and died within the year. Seward gradually regained some of his health and managed to put his personal tragedies behind him while he served under Andrew Johnson who assumed the Presidency upon Lincoln's death. Seward retired in 1869 and moved back to his home town of Auburn, New York. Within three years he was dead.

However, the ghost in the old Washington Club continued to frighten off occupants. Several owners tried outlasting the strange, loud noises and other disruptions that awoke them and unnerved them. Not even the YMCA which took over the house in the late 1880s was immune to the haunting. One newspaper article from that time questioned: "What revenant was roaming about? Had Key's spirit come in out of the damp and chilly night air?" Possibly, although another reporter a few years later offered speculation from another former occupant: Secretary Seward's ghost had returned in a most cantankerous state. Certain mediums contended that it was feasible for Seward's spirit to return to the place that had so dramatically affected his life and to make the lives of other occupants miserable.

Whoever the ghost, it soon had to find a new haunt. Since no one wanted to put up with its devilish pranks the old property was torn down in 1895. Since the building was razed the old ghost of the Washington Club has been dormant. If it was Seward's ghost perhaps it is a sign that he, at last, found peace.

The Tragic Major Rathbone

Another house on Lafayette Square belonged to Major Henry Rathbone, still another victim of the Lincoln assassination conspiracy. Because of the tragic way Rathbone died, it is said that people actually were afraid to walk in front of his house

Major Henry Rathbone was an unintended victim of the Lincoln assassination. The thought that he didn't save the President cost him his sanity. He took the life of his wife and then shot himself. Although the incident happened in Germany, people in Washington began avoiding his former home on Lafayette Square because they feared harm from his crazed ghost. *Courtesy Library of Congress*

Clara Harris, daughter of a prominent New York senator, accompanied Major Henry Rathbone to Ford's Theater the night they were guests of President and Mrs. Lincoln. Although Rathbone never emotionally recovered from that night, Miss Harris married him anyway. It cost her life. *Courtesy Library of Congress*

Major Rathbone was a brilliant and successful young officer when he moved into Number 8 Jackson Place. At that time he was hopeful of making Clara Harris, daughter of a New York Senator, his wife. It was Miss Harris who accompanied the Major the night he went with President and Mrs. Lincoln to see *Our American Cousin* at Ford's Theater. Major Rathbone was stabbed in the head and neck by John Wilkes Booth before the assassin made good his escape by jumping onto the stage from the presidential box.

Although seriously wounded, Major Rathbone responded to treatment and physically recovered from his wounds, but his mind was never quite the same. He was distracted and moody. He and Clara Harris were eventually married. She accepted his moods, thinking that someday he would again become the man she used to know. Perhaps that is why she agreed to move with him to Germany.

Hoping to escape his recurring depression, the Major resigned his commission and with his wife set out for Hanover. Another country and another life, however, proved no panacea. He became even more despondent. As his wife and children prepared for the coming Christmas holidays, Rathbone seemed to lose touch with reality altogether. He took a gun, shot his wife to death, and would have killed his children if a nurse had not intervened. He then shot himself. Whether or not Rathbone was reliving that struggle some eighteen years earlier with John Wilkes Booth or whether he was wrestling with other demons is only conjecture. Doctors were able to save what was left of the life of Henry Rathbone, but he spent the rest of his days in an insane asylum far from his former home on Lafayette Square.

The news of the Rathbone tragedy quickly reached Washington. Some of his former neighbors wept at the misfortune, but as they walked along Jackson Place they often took their children by the hand and crossed over into the park rather than walk directly in front of the old Rathbone residence. They seemed to be afraid the web of fate that had entangled so many victims of the Lincoln assassination conspiracy might still hang in the air around the house of the unfortunate Major. A few expressed fear that his deranged ghost would cross the ocean, while others contended it already had. They whispered of hearing a man crying. Tales spun over backyard fences or on porches at night told of heartbreaking sobs drifting from the old home where, for a few brief years, Rathbone had known success, joy, and happiness.

The Grief of Marian "Clover" Adams

The holly bushes and ivy that once sequestered the grave of Marian Hooper Adams in the old Rock Creek Cemetery off North Capitol Street have been trimmed away so that she no longer rests in the shadows. However, in life, the shadows of despair enshrouded "the poor unfortunate Mrs. Adams," as her neighbors referred to her after her untimely death. The gravesite bears no inscription. It bears no date. A statue by Augustus Saint-Gaudens commissioned by her husband, historian Henry Adams, is a silent sentinel. Many who have seen the figure have felt compelled to call it "Grief," although Adams himself never liked that name.

"Clover," as she was called, may have been unfortunate, but she wasn't poor. She was intelligent, well educated, and beautiful. Prior to settling in Washington, Henry Adams had been an assistant professor of history at Harvard from which he had graduated in 1858. Adams was a son of Charles Francis Adams, Sr., a diplomat. Henry Adams grandfather was John Quincy Adams and his great-grandfather was John Adams.

Henry and Clover met in London. It wasn't love at first sight, but they found several mutual interests. However, a letter he wrote to his friend, English nobleman Charles M. Gaskell, three months before the wedding, is rather curious: "She is very open to instruction. We shall improve her. She dresses badly. She decidedly has humor and will appreciate our wit. She has enough money to be quite independent…I don't want you to marry, though. One of us surely should remain single for the good of all."

Sarah Booth Conroy, writing in her 1993 book *Refinements of Love* says Henry Adams wrote several letters to Gaskell before his marriage, and concludes he was anxious to reassure Gaskell that his marriage would make no difference to their relations. In a letter dated four days before his marriage, Adams reassures Gaskell, "You need not be afraid of her coming between me and my friends, for I believe she likes agreeable men as much as I do."

Conroy reports that "Henry's actions and writings may be interpreted in many and varied ways to suggest: homosexuality, bisexuality, asexuality, or impotence." Gossips of the time whispered. Today scholars can only speculate. The fact is Henry and Clover were married for thirteen years. Much of that time she served as his research assistant, while expanding and perfecting her interest in the new field of photography—to which she had been introduced by Henry.

When the couple moved to Washington, they rented a house near 16th and H Street NW owned by noted art collector W.W. Cochran who lived just down the block. John Hay, Lincoln biographer, became Adams's closest friend. Clover got along well with Hay's wife Clara, and together with Clarence King they formed a mock secret society called "The Five of Hearts." For several years their lives seemed uneventful to neighbors who thought the Adamses had a well-adjusted and intellectually compatible marital relationship. They, and most of Washington, were shocked and surprised at the circumstances surrounding the death of "the poor unfortunate Mrs. Adams."

Sunday morning December 6, 1885 Henry Adams went to his dentist with a toothache. When he returned he found a neighbor who had come calling on Mrs. Adams standing at the door. No one was answering. Henry rushed up the stairs to his wife's bedroom. There he found Clover lying on a rug near the fire in her bedroom. She never regained consciousness.

During the last years of their marriage, Clover's upper respiratory condition, exacerbated by Washington's unhealthy climate for allergy sufferers, seemed to worsen. This condition, the death of her father in the spring of 1885, and what some believe was a growing inner conflict over Henry's behavior, could have contributed to a lingering depression that caused her to take her own life.

Did she kill herself by taking potassium cyanide—one of the dangerous chemicals used in her darkroom? Conroy, again in her book *Refinements of Love*, points out that it was Henry who introduced Clover to photography and he, too, had a knowledge of the chemicals. She questions, "If Henry honestly thought his wife was suicidally depressed, why did he take no measures to lock away the poison?"

Adams said very little after Clover's death and his behavior only fueled the flames of the gossips. At the end of the year, only weeks after the "poor unfortunate Mrs. Adams" was laid to rest in Rock Creek cemetery, Henry moved into his part of the new home he and Clover were having built with John and Clara Hay.

Adams himself did much to perpetuate the belief in his eccentricity. When he chose Washington's oldest cemetery as the resting place for his wife, he ordered that no stone, nor marker of any kind, be placed on the grave. He commissioned Augustus Saint Gaudens to create a monument in bronze, but instructed the sculptor that "no…attempt is to be made to make it intelligible to the average mind."

While the statue was being readied, the historian shrugged off the barbs of neighbors and rumors of murder being whispered by town gossips. He continued his work, devoting himself almost entirely to his historical research and writings. He traveled extensively. Meanwhile, the house in which Clover died was apparently difficult to rent. It was dark a great deal of the time, which added to the mystery that was beginning to build up around it. Stories spread that, "Visitors to the house were overcome with uneasiness and would not remain for long." It was said that occasionally, at dusk, the sighs and bitter sobs of a woman crying could be heard from within. There were tales that the house was never warm, that in spite of the hottest of fires there was always a chill around the hearth—where Marian was found unconscious.

The ghost in the Adams house began to receive a great deal of attention in newspapers. An article written in the 1890s related several incidents that had occurred over a period of a few years. There were those who had been awakened in the night by sounds of gentle rocking. Some related encounters with the ghost of a sad-eyed lady "who sits and rocks in a large oak chair" that is as shadowy as she. The woman's unblinking eyes stare directly into the eyes of the person before whom she has appeared.

Those who had such an encounter said they were compelled to stare back but that their initial fears seemed to vanish as they were overtaken by the deep feeling of loneliness and despair generated by the apparition. It is said that some who witnessed the apparition broke into uncontrollable sobbing, and then took weeks to regain their composure. It is as though the woman could transfer her emotions, although she never moved from the rocking chair. The sightings of the ghost seemed to be confined in what was Clover's bedroom. It would sit and rock and stare with never a change of expression until a loud scream, or a frantic motion, would cause it to vanish. The events detailed in this particular article bear a strong similarity to the legend handed down by word of mouth about the statue erected by Henry Adams at his wife's grave in Rock Creek Cemetery.

When Saint-Gaudens's creation was complete and Adams announced he would place it in the cemetery, he met resistance. Cemetery officials took one look at the statue and said no. They felt it was not a fitting memorial, but the persistent Adams insisted on installing it, and won. Adams saw to it that the statue bore no inscription either. It is said that he once referred to it as "The Peace of God," but didn't like people calling it "Grief." Saint-Gaudens must have picked up on Henry Adams penchant for androgyny, for it is expressed quite well in the sculpture for which he used both men and women as models. Some say Adams became obsessed with Saint-Gaudens' creation, and used to sit before it for hours. When Adams was in his seventies he complained to a friend that an "...ocean of sordidness and restless suburbanity has risen over the very steps of the grave, and for the first time, I suddenly asked myself whether I could endure lying there listening to that dreary vulgarity forever, and whether I could forgive myself for condemning my poor wife to it. The grave has become a terror." That was one of the few times since the death of Clover that Adams had ever written or spoken of her.

From the day she died Henry Adams made every effort to obliterate his wife's name from memory, Sarah Booth Conroy told me. The author continued, "After Clover died, he burned her diaries and all of her letters from her father and friends. He burned even his own journals. He destroyed all photographs of her except for two in possession of others, but she's barely visible."

When his autobiography *The Education of Henry Adams* was published in 1918 the gossips started up again, and the scholars were left with a gaping void: Adams wrote nothing of his marriage. The name of Marian Clover Hooper Adams is nowhere to be found in that Pulitzer Prize winning work.

Patricia O'Toole, in her 1990 book *The Five of Hearts: An Intimate Portrait of Henry Adams and His Friends, 1880-1918,* writes of a most interesting transcribed interview with Adams' secretary and a niece. She says it was tucked among papers of the H.D. Cater collection at the Massachusetts Historical Society. The two women found Adams dead in his bed March 27, 1918. Looking through his desk for funeral instructions they reported finding "a partially filled bottle of potassium cyanide, the instrument of Clover's suicide."

Many of those who have visited Rock Creek Cemetery and stood before the statue have said that there is no way to express, or measure, the coldness that enveloped them as they looked upon "Grief." It is described by some as a feeling of "extreme loneliness." Others spoke of being overcome by a tremendous sadness and feeling of despair like none they had ever known.

For years the statue was enshrouded by a brooding grove of holly trees. A cemetery groundskeeper recalled how some who have sat alone in front of the statue felt that the weathered bronzed eyes seemed to come slowly to life. They say the pupils stare back from the shadows of the greenish oxidized cowl that overhangs the forehead and sides of the face.

Another legend told by some is that people who have meditated there have sometimes been joined, at dusk, by the ethereal form of a beautiful but frail woman dressed in the clothing of the mid-1880s. Some say it is the reverberations of her despair that permeate the site, compelling all those who look upon Saint-Gaudens's statue to call it "Grief."

Those who visit the statue that marks the grave of Marian Adams in Rock Creek Cemetery have felt compelled to call it "Grief." Some have said that they have encountered a presence that brings with it a feeling of almost unbearable despair and sorrow. *The Author's Collection*

The White House

Abigail Adams Laundry Room

This is the way the White House appeared in the early 1800s. John Adams, a giant among the Founding Fathers, and his wife Abigail were the first First Family to occupy what was then called "The President's House." *Courtesy Library of Congress*

When Abigail Adams and her husband John moved into the President's House not all of the rooms had been finished. For the highly educated and wealthy family from Massachusetts that included three sons and two daughters, this must have been rather traumatic. It's said Mrs. Adams selected the unfinished East Room as the room in which to hang laundry. It is hard to picture this brilliant woman, who was married to a man who became President and was the mother of a son who also became President, hanging out her own laundry. However, that is an image we are left with. Down through the years folks inside the White House say they have seen the ghost of Abigail Adams carrying loads of laundry to hang in the East Room. *Courtesy Library of Congress*

George Washington never lived in the White House, though he was instrumental in choosing its location. His first presidential residence was in New York, his next one in Philadelphia.

The first family to occupy the President's House was not unlike any other family that has to move into a new home that isn't completed. John and Abigail Adams, Bostonians by birth, had to tolerate all the inconvenience inside, plus a wide, muddy, and unpaved Pennsylvania Avenue. Abigail used to say that even though the East Room wasn't completed; it was the driest area in the house. That's the room in which she hung her wash.

Tricia Nixon Cox, daughter of the thirty-seventh President, said that she was fascinated by the history of the East Room. It included not only affairs of state, but a few weddings, some coffins in state, and even the quartering of troops. Tricia smiled as she recalled the stories about Mrs. Adams's washdays but said that she personally had not encountered Abigail wandering through those East Room doors. Over the years, though, there have been those who have seen Mrs. Adams, with arms outstretched as though carrying a load of laundry. Her ghost passes through the locked doors to the East Room where she spent many hours during her husband's Presidency. Some say that they can tell when Abigail's ghost has been there, for it leaves behind the faint smell of soap and damp clothing.

The White House seems to lend itself to ghost stories. Liz Carpenter, press secretary to Lady Bird Johnson, described it as "a house forever changing, yet always the same." It has been rebuilt a number of times. The British put the torch to it (as well as most of Washington) in the War of 1812 but before the city could burn to the ground rains fell and the fires were extinguished. The blaze did considerable damage, but thanks to the rain enough brick and mortar was left standing to make rebuilding feasible. The foundation and walls were made sound once again, and were repainted to cover the effects of the fire. Although the President's House had always been white, and might have been called the White House before, after this the name stuck permanently.

President James Madison and his wife Dolley escaped the advancing British only by minutes. The President actually headed out of town a little before his wife, riding north toward Brookeville, Maryland, where he spent the night with a Quaker family before swinging south into Virginia. Dolley had grown to love the executive Mansion and its large, green lawn. In the rear of the house, toward the southwest side, she had lovingly planted her own garden. As she prepared to evacuate she could guess its fate. Legend has it that servants and troops found her there, taking one last loving look at her well-manicured garden, when they came to rush her evacuation. Mrs. Madison grabbed up Gilbert Stuart's portrait of George Washington, and a few other White House treasures, and was accompanied by a small detachment of troops to the Madison's Virginia home.

While the re-building was going on, President and Mrs. Madison resided in two locations. From September 1814 to October 1815 Colonel John Tayloe made available to the First Family his spacious town home known as the Octagon, on New York Avenue at 18th Street NW. It was just a couple of blocks away from the White House. The Octagon had not been burned because the French Ministry had been using the house, and the flag of France protected it from British torches. In October 1815 until the end of his term in March of 1817 the Madison's resided in a town home at the Corner of Pennsylvania Avenue and 19th Street NW. It was still close enough so that all during the re-building of the Executive Mansion Mrs. Madison could keep her keen eyes on everything, including the restoration of her garden which she intended as her legacy to future First Ladies.

This painting from the Library of Congress collection is entitled: *A view of the Presidents House in the City of Washington after the Conflagration of the 24th August 1814. Courtesy Library of Congress*

Revisiting the Rose Garden

Almost exactly a hundred years later the second Mrs. Woodrow Wilson, Edith, ordered gardeners to move Dolley Madison's garden. Dolley's ghost, supposedly always on the alert that some upstart first lady might try such a bold move, swooped down in all her nineteenth century magnificence and frightened off the gardeners by flouncing up to them with arms waiving and tongue lashing.

Storytellers say that in order to soothe Mrs. Madison's spirit hundreds of roses were planted in the garden and it was kept just where Dolley Payne Madison wanted it.

The Soldier with a Torch

The burning of the White House during the War of 1812 gave rise to a legend that a British soldier, allegedly killed there with a torch in his hand, still haunts the Executive Mansion. Throughout the years there have been those on the White House staff, and some visitors, who have kept the story alive by reporting encounters with his ghost. One of the best accounts is contained in a 1954 *Evening Star* article. Leslie Lieber told of a former valet for President Franklin Roosevelt who recalled an occasion when he was packing luggage for an obviously upset visiting couple. The woman appeared nervous. The man seemed irritable. He paced and smoked and told the valet why they were cutting short their stay: "Somebody, my wife insists it was a ghost, was trying to set fire to our beds all night long."

The valet also spoke of an omen that sometimes manifests itself inside the White House. On the eve before someone in the White House, or a member of their family dies a painting will fall from the wall. The valet said he was attending to FDR one evening when such an incident happened, and word came the next day that the President's mother had died.

Revisits to the Rose Room

One spot in the White House that seems to be frequented by a ghost or ghosts is the Rose Room, often called the Queen's Bedroom because five queens have stayed there. With its adjacent dressing room and bath, it makes a comfortable apartment. The bed, which probably belonged to Andrew Jackson, the seventh President, has been the source of ribald laughter for more than a century. More than one person is said to have heard the sounds. Their tales have been reported in newspapers.

Storytellers like to recall the scandal involving Jackson and Peggy O'Neil. The beautiful, vivacious daughter of a Washington tavern keeper used to entertain Jackson and a friend of his, John Eaton, at her father's tavern. Her jealous husband apparently couldn't stand it. Rumor has it that he took his own life. The recently widowed Jackson liked Peggy a lot, but he also felt certain presidential responsibilities. He encouraged Eaton to marry the girl, and when Eaton did, Jackson appointed Eaton to his Cabinet as a wedding present.

The appointment caused quite a stir, and the Cabinet wives snubbed the witty Peggy Eaton because they didn't approve of her morals. Secretary of State Martin Van Buren liked her, though. His attention to the "beautiful Mrs. Eaton was obvious"—to quote one ancient article. The scandal was too much. Jackson accepted Eaton's "resignation" and then sent Peggy and her husband to Spain in an attempt to quiet the gossips.

Liz Carpenter, who was closely associated with the White House during the Administration of President Lyndon Johnson referred to the old story of invisible laughter coming from Jackson's bed, and said with a twinkle in her eye, "He was such a salty old character, I've often wondered if it was his laugh."

Death had come to Old Hickory in 1845 at his Nashville, Tennessee, estate, The Hermitage. Within twenty years, however, his ghost was first reported revisiting the White House by none other than Mary Todd Lincoln. The mystical Mrs. Lincoln told friends that she often heard Jackson stomping and swearing.

A White House staff member, Lillian Rogers Parks, in a 1961 book, *My 30 Years Backstairs at the White House,* tells of experiencing what she believed was an actual encounter with Jackson in the Rose Room. She was busily hemming a bedspread in preparation for a visit from Queen Elizabeth II when she felt a presence in the room.

The air directly behind her seemed cold as she sensed someone looking over her shoulder. She could feel a hand on the back of her chair. Her scalp tightened, but fear would not let her look around. Leaving behind her sewing basket and needle and thread, the seamstress quickly left, and it was weeks before anyone could talk her into going back in there. When she had to return to the room, she said that she made certain that she never went alone.

It was in the Rose Room, seen here as it appeared in the late 1890s, that the ghost of Abraham Lincoln appeared before Queen Wilhelmina of the Netherlands several decades ago. *Courtesy Library of Congress*

The bed in the Rose Room is supposed to be the one used by Andrew Jackson. Ribald laughter attributed to his ghost is sometimes heard coming from it. *Courtesy White House Photo*

Revisits to the Oval Office

There was a tradition within the White House to refer to the various rooms by the color of their walls. What is now the Oval Office used to be known as the Yellow Room, or the Oval Room. It has one of the most magnificent views in all of Washington. Looking out toward the Mall, one can see the tall spire of the Washington Monument, the majestic Lincoln Memorial; and across the Tidal Basin, through the Japanese cherry trees, the dome of the Jefferson Memorial.

Thomas Jefferson used the room as a drawing room, and often relaxed by playing his violin there. "My, my," Mary Todd Lincoln once said to a friend, "how that Mr. Jefferson does play the violin." Jefferson had been dead a number of years before Mary Lincoln and her husband moved into the White House. I read in the *Washington Daily News* that she also told some of her closest friends, just after John Tyler died in 1862, that she sometimes heard his ghost returning to the Oval Room to woo his twenty-year old wife.

It is also in that room that Woodrow Wilson proposed to the second Mrs. Wilson; and that Franklin Roosevelt received the leaders of Congress the day after Pearl Harbor was attacked by the Japanese. Noted Lincoln scholar Carl Sandburg spent quite some time meditating in the room a few years ago, then emerged convinced that it was the room in which Lincoln had reached most of his great decisions.

The Yellow Oval Room has had its share of reports of spectral visitors. One tabloid reported Lyndon Johnson, driven from office by the Vietnam War, haunted at least one late night military strategy session during the Gulf War. Thomas Jefferson and John Tyler have reportedly been seen there, too. *Courtesy White House Photo*

During the Truman years, a White House guard related to a reporter that he heard a voice calling out to him, seemingly from the attic above the Oval Room. In a whisper, the voice said: "I'm Mr. Burns, I'm Mr. Burns."

Thinking Secretary of State James Byrnes was upstairs playing a trick on him, the guard rushed to the attic stairs, but found the entrance sealed. The guard told the reporter that he later learned the Secretary had not even been in the White House that day.

The reporter nodded understandingly, shrugged his shoulders, and left. He marked it off as idle conversation until a week or so later when he read something that caused him to change that assessment. It was an article about White House land acquisition. The hairs on the back of his neck bristled and his flesh tingled as he recalled the guard's story. He stared at the name of the man who had owned the land in 1790. His name was David Burns, dubbed "Obstinate Davy" by President Washington because he had not wanted to sell the land. Is it the old Scotsman's ill tempered ghost that is responsible for some pictures crashing off the walls, papers flying off desks, and disturbing "things that go bump in the night?"

The Ever-Present Mr. Lincoln

Abraham Lincoln was fifty-two when he came into the White House, and there were almost as many Presidents before him as have followed him. None has left the mark on the executive mansion that he has. Indeed, many swear that his ghost still walks the halls. More than a few have testified to having seen his form standing at the center window of the Oval Room. During the Civil War he is said to have often stood there, looking out at Virginia with silent concern about the fate of the Union and the miseries of war.

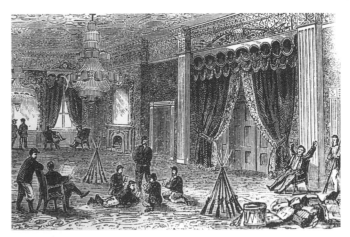

During the Civil War a detachment of Union troops protecting the President and his family occupied the East Room of the White House. *Courtesy Library of Congress*

Lincoln undoubtedly possessed some psychic gifts. Scholars have described him as "introspective," and some said that his periods of silence were trance-like. As a child and a teenager Lincoln was said to have been somewhat moody, yet he always attracted friends.

His personal life was often touched by tragedy. He lost his deeply religious mother when he was four. When his first love, Ann Rutledge, died of typhoid, the trauma thrust him into a profound melancholy, which apparently led to an emotional breakdown several years later.

In 1842 Lincoln married Mary Todd. They had an indisputably rocky marriage. Some have said that it was held together only by their common love for their children. Of those children, only Robert became an adult. Edward died at age four, Willie died of fever in the middle of his father's first term as President, and Tad outlived his father by only six years.

Mary and Abraham Lincoln with their sons. From left to right: Willie, who died during his father's presidency, Tad, and Robert. *Courtesy Library of Congress*

Willie possibly was his father's favorite, and the little boy's unexpected death had profound impact not only on the President, but on Mary Lincoln as well. The family had no gravesite in Washington, but Supreme Court Clerk William Thomas Carroll offered Lincoln a tomb for his son in the Carroll family tomb in Oak Hill Cemetery.

Willie Lincoln died at the age of 12 during his father's presidency and was buried in the Carroll family tomb in Oak Hill Cemetery. Lincoln is supposed to have sat in this chair looking at the crypt and weeping. Willie's ghost has been seen around the White House on several occasions. *Courtesy Lee Shephard*

Lincoln used to spend long hours at that crypt, which is on a narrow path on a hillside overlooking Rock Creek. When I first visited the Carroll family tomb, it was like stepping back in time. There, just inside the locked iron gate were two very old wrought iron chairs. They gave credence to Washington newspaper reports that on at least two occasions while President Lincoln sat inside the tomb mourning, he had the crypt opened so that he could look at his son. He would sit and stare at the dead youth for hours, weeping. Lincoln could not bear to leave Willie alone in that cold, dank, dark tomb.

Members of President Ulysses S. Grant's household believed in the ability to communicate with the dead, and one of them is reported to have conversed with Willie's spirit. More recently, Lynda Johnson Robb, who occupied the room in which Willie died, was "very much" aware of the fact that "it was in her room the little Lincoln boy breathed his last breath," Liz Carpenter told me; but with a smile declined to elaborate. She also said that Lady Bird Johnson encountered what she believed was Lincoln's presence one April evening as she watched a television special on Lincoln's death. "Suddenly, she was aware, conscious of the fact, that the room she was in was special. Someone was compelling her to direct her eyes toward the mantel." It wasn't the mantel that her eyes focused on, however, but a small plaque she had never noticed before. Liz Carpenter said that it told of the room's importance to Lincoln, and that as Lady Bird read it, she felt "a chill. A draft." Mrs. Carpenter recalled that Mrs. Johnson told her later that she felt very ill at ease. "Perhaps she felt his presence."

Lincoln was not much for organized religion, though on occasion he would attend Presbyterian services. As a politician his views on religion had been questioned more than once. When he was running for Congress he distributed a handbill denying that he had ever spoken "with intentional disrespect of religion." Mariah Vance, who did the Lincoln's laundry and cooking in Springfield for ten years, until the Lincoln's moved to Washington, says in her recollections that Mr. Lincoln told her he had been secretly baptized just after he was elected president.

Lincoln did seem to be at least curious about spiritualism. His wife's pursuit of the supernatural was more overt, especially after Willie's death. Mrs. Lincoln confided to a sister that "were it not for the fact that Willie came often to comfort her, she would have drowned in tears." She said Willie came to her every night, and stood at the foot of her bed, with "the same sweet adorable smile he has always had. Sometimes he brings little Eddie with him." Mary Todd Lincoln frequently consulted spiritualists and mediums. There is even a photograph of her seated at a table with a ghostlike Abraham super-imposed behind her. It is thought to be the work of a spiritualist photographer in the 1870s.

Mary Lincoln confided to friends that son Willie sometimes revisited her. She also told a friend that she had heard Mr. Jefferson playing his violin in the Oval office. *Courtesy Library of Congress*

The Lincoln Bedroom as it looked in Lincoln's time. Lincoln's ghost has been seen most often in this room, although it is said to wander through most of the White House. *Library of Congress*

Seances were held at the White House, and there are newspaper records to indicate that Abraham Lincoln attended a couple of these. Mary believed a "very slight veil separates us from the loved and lost and though unseen by us, they are very near." *The Chicago Tribune* reported in 1863 that medium Charles Shockle visited the White House. The levitation and rapping that the President witnessed seemed to impress him. In 1967, Suzy Smith wrote in *Prominent American Ghosts* that she had learned of another time when a medium visited the President. A skeptical Lincoln is said to have ordered a congressman from Maine to sit on top of a piano that a medium was successfully levitating. The congressman's weight made no difference. The President, and others watching, could hardly believe their eyes as the piano and the congressman rose and fell at the medium's command.

A *National Geographic Society News Bulletin* from August 1973 heralding a Library of Congress exhibit on spiritualism, recalled that the medium J.B. Conklin supposedly received a telepathic message from Edward D. Baker for President Lincoln, who was a close friend of Baker's. Conklin received his message for the President two months after Baker had been killed leading Union forces into action at Ball's Bluff, Virginia. Conklin told the President Baker's message was "gone elsewhere" and that "elsewhere is everywhere."

Many of the occupants of the White House seem to have been visited by Lincoln. "I think of Lincoln, shambling, homely, with his sad, strong, deeply furrowed face, all the time," said President Theodore Roosevelt. "I see him in the different rooms and in the halls," he admitted some forty years after Lincoln's occupancy.

Grace Coolidge is said to have seen the specter of Lincoln, too. In a newspaper account I read, she said that he was dressed "in black, with a stole draped across his shoulders to ward off the drafts and chills of Washington's night air."

President Dwight Eisenhower's press secretary, James Haggerty, once said on an ABC-TV news program that the President had told him he often felt Lincoln's presence. President Harry Truman recalled that in the early morning hours a little over a year after he became President he was awakened by two distinct knocks on the door of his bedroom. He got up and went to the door, opened it, but found no one in the hall; just a cold spot that went away as footsteps trailed off down the corridor. Truman wrote in his diary that he wished he had the bravado to summon forth the Lincoln ghost to scare his daughter, Margaret, and a friend who were spending a night in the Lincoln bedroom.

Eleanor Roosevelt, wife of President Franklin D. Roosevelt, denied to reporters that she personally had seen Lincoln's apparition, but she did admit to feeling his presence. She also related a story involving one of her staffers who had an encounter. Her secretary had passed Lincoln's bedroom one day and saw a lanky figure sitting on the bed pulling on his boots. Since Lincoln had been dead more than three-quarters of a century, the girl felt justified in her reaction: she screamed and ran as fast as her legs would carry her from the second floor. An article in the *Evening Star* said on another occasion that FDR's valet ran screaming from the White House and into the arms of a guard, shouting that he had just seen Lincoln.

Visitors also have encountered Lincoln's ghost. When Wilhelmina Helena Pauline Maria (1880-1962), Queen of the Netherlands (1890-1948), was visiting the White House quite a few years ago, she answered a knock on the door of the Rose Room where she was staying. Since the hour was quite late, she felt it must be most important. Standing before the Queen, his large frame taking up most of the doorway, was Abraham Lincoln. A White House staffer said that the Queen shocked her Presidential host and other guests when she re-

President Lincoln's body lay in state in the East Room after his assassination, just as he had dreamed it would. *Courtesy Martin Luther King, Jr. Public Library, District of Columbia*

lated the incident at cocktails the next evening. She told them that when she saw the chilling apparition everything went black, and when she came to, she was lying on the floor.

Winston Churchill never discussed it, but he did not like to sleep in the Lincoln bedroom. It is the room that all visiting male heads of state are quartered in, but the British Prime Minister was quite uncomfortable there. Often Churchill would be found across the hall the next morning. Susan Ford, daughter of President Gerald Ford, shares the uneasiness Churchill felt. She declared in *Seventeen* magazine in the summer of 1975 that she believed in ghosts and had no intention of ever sleeping in the Lincoln bedroom.

Lincoln spent many restless nights in that massive old room, and no doubt suffered through more nightmares than pleasant dreams. *Encyclopedia Britannica* says that Lincoln believed in dreams and "other enigmatic signs and portents" throughout his life. Several of his dreams have been reported, but none is more memorable than Lincoln's vision of his own death.

The President recalled that he dreamed that he became disturbed when he heard weeping, sobbing, and wailing coming from elsewhere in the house. Walking down a White House corridor to investigate, the President said that he saw a coffin lying in state. Inquiring of a mourner, "Who is dead?" Lincoln was told, "The assassinated President." Lincoln said that in his dream, he walked over to the coffin and looking inside, saw himself.

April 14, 1865 had begun rather routinely for President Lincoln. During the morning, and for part of the afternoon, he met with Cabinet officials to map Reconstruction plans. Later that day, he and Mrs. Lincoln went for a carriage ride. They returned home late in the afternoon to dress for the theater. Often, going to the theater or opera took the President's mind off his troubles. General and Mrs. Ulysses S. Grant had been unable to accompany the President and Mrs. Lincoln to Ford's that night, but Major Henry Rathbone and Clara Harris had accepted the President's invitation. The rest of the story has

been retold many times. By the next morning Lincoln was dead, the victim of an assassin's bullet.

The prosecution of the conspirators was vigorously pursued, and feeling ran high about exacting retribution. There is some question, even today, about the degree of guilt of at least one of those convicted of conspiring to assassinate the President. Some believe that Mary Surratt was unjustly punished. On the eve of her execution, her daughter Anna forced her way inside the White House grounds and made it to the front door, where she pleaded for her mother's release. On the anniversary of that night some have claimed to have seen Anna's ghost banging on the front door of the White House and pleading for her mother's release.

Recent Revisits

United Press International, January 26, 1977
Mrs. (Verona) Meeder (Amy Carter's 4th grade teacher) said Amy picked out a book on ghost stories when given a choice of new reading material, and told classmates a ghost story about the White House.

I was flattered that the book she had selected was the first edition of this book, which had just been published. During the years I have continued to gather information for this updated version. I was told that a couple years later, when she was in sixth grade; Amy had a few girl friends in for a sleep over. They took a ouiji board to the Lincoln bedroom but all they conjured up was Amy's mother Rosalynn who made them stop.

Maureen Reagan, whose father Ronald succeeded Jimmy Carter as President, had a ghostly encounter in the White House. An article in the *Wall Street Journal* said that she awoke in the Lincoln bedroom to see "a transparent person."

That isn't much to go on. A cynic might say that her description would fit any one of several people in Washington, none of them necessarily dead. However, I'll choose to interpret her remarks as those of an eyewitness to a White House ghost.

The phantom of Mary Surratt's daughter, Anna, has been seen knocking at the White House door, still pleading for the release of her mother. *Courtesy The National Archives*

Most of Washington turned out to bid farewell to President Lincoln. His body received a military escort in a parade down Pennsylvania Avenue to the railroad station where a funeral train carried it back to Illinois. *Courtesy Library of Congress*

This is the B & O Railroad Station where President Lincoln arrived from Illinois for his inauguration and where his funeral train departed with his body for Illinois. It is said by those who made the trip back home with the Lincoln family that mourners lined the tracks virtually all the way back to Springfield. *Courtesy Library of Congress*

Her father, President Reagan, told a news conference in 1987 that he was not frightened by Lincoln's ghost. "I haven't seen him myself, but every once in a while our little dog Rex will start down that long hall, just glaring as though he's seeing something." Reagan added that the dog would also bark repeatedly as he stopped in front of Lincoln's bedroom door. "And once, early on in this I couldn't understand it, so I went down and opened the door, and I stepped in and turned around for him to come on. He stood there still barking and growling and then started backing away and would not go in that room."

The President smiled at the reporters, whose attention he was holding quite well with his story. He continued: "Funny thing, though, I have to feel, unlike you might think of other ghosts, if he (Lincoln) is still there I don't have any fear at all. I think it would be very wonderful to have a little meeting with him and very probably very helpful."

Several years before, when Richard Nixon's Presidency was under siege, and he was facing impeachment or resignation, there were reports that late at night he wandered the halls talking to the portraits. There were no documented cases of any of the portraits talking back to him, and his behavior seems more related to stress and alcohol than to ghosts.

George Bush assumed the Presidency after Ronald Reagan. He denied ever sensing Lincoln, or any other ghostly presence, while he was in the White House; and he added that went for Barbara and their dog Millie, too. Millie addressed the ghosts issue in *Millie's Book:* "Although this is the room where the White House ghost is supposed to appear the Bush's have not seen it nor do they believe in ghosts. I must confess that I have not seen one either."

One national tabloid asserts, however, that the Bush's may have indeed protested too much to be believed. A 1993 article contends that none other than Lyndon B. Johnson himself paid visits to the Bush White House during the Gulf War.

President Johnson died at his Texas ranch in 1973. He had come into office when President Kennedy was assassinated, and ran for election the next year as a "peace" candidate. Johnson portrayed his Republican opponent Barry Goldwater as someone who would escalate the trouble in Vietnam into a global conflict. LBJ served only one term as the nation's Chief Executive. He is remembered for having presided over the most divisive war since the Civil War. All during his term war protesters followed him. Banner-carrying youth picketed the White House, shouting among other things, "Hey, Hey, LBJ, how many kids have you killed today?"

Johnson aged rapidly as he struggled with the war and with civil unrest and riots at home. Emotions were at a hundred year high inside the LBJ White House, and it seemed throughout much of America, too.

The tabloid reporter quoted an unnamed "White House source" as saying Secretary of State James Baker and Secretary of Defense Richard Cheney were with President George Bush in a late night Oval Office council on the Gulf War when a chill swept the room and papers began flying off the President's desk. Lights allegedly blinked off and LBJs laughter roared through the room.

The writer claims that Bush later joked to confidants of "hearing footsteps at night and seeing a tall, gruff, big-eared ghost resembling LBJ."

To force Iraq to pull back its army that had invaded tiny Kuwait President Bush had put together a coalition army of nations, led by U.S. Commanders, U.S. troops, and most of all, U.S. technology. When the conflict began Bush couldn't have known how quickly and decisively it would end. One can easily imagine him remarking about being haunted by the ghost of LBJ as he took America into its first major conflict since the Vietnam War. However, as we stated earlier, Bush is on record denying, categorically, any ghostly encounters.

As Bill Clinton and his family entered their second year in the nation's most haunted house I began trying to get sources within the new administration to talk about any ghostly encounters Bill, Hillary, or Chelsea may have had. Deep down I guess I knew that with all the experience this administration was getting with alleged cover-ups, even if Lincoln really were to reveal himself to this jittery family fresh from the Ozarks, it too would be covered up. I asked my questions anyway. I spent months trying to get answers. I couldn't even get a straight answer to how Socks the cat reacted when it got near the Lincoln bedroom. "What bedroom? What ghosts? I don't know that the First Family is aware of any of the old stories," said an official spokesman. Even the un-officials with whom I spoke couldn't have deflected questions any better if they had been coached.

When Bob Woodward's book *The Choice* came out with a claim that Hillary Rodham Clinton had invited a psychic researcher to the White House, the press had a field day. Reports of "imaginary" conversations between Hillary and Eleanor Roosevelt kept spin doctors busy and comedians in new material. Not since it was revealed that Nancy Reagan consulted with her astrologer and then advised her husband, President Ronald Reagan, had a First Lady met with such ridicule. I pretty much kissed off any hope of resurrecting ghost stories in the Clinton White House. One cynic (Washington is full of them) noted how the Clinton's growing troubles that began with the Whitewater Savings & Loan scandal continued to haunt them. He confided to me, "There's no doubt the Clinton's are seeing ghosts, but they are all from Arkansas."

For more than one-hundred-fifty years scores of responsible White House employees, members of presidential families, and a few Presidents themselves, have kept alive the legend of Lincoln's ghost still roaming the hallways; still concerned for the nation he fought so mightily to preserve. Several people have run away screaming at the sight of Lincoln's ghost; but none (that we know of) have been Presidents. His presence seems to offer comfort and strength to them.

"Why would they want to come back here I could never understand," President Harry Truman is quoted as having said about the White House ghosts. In her book *Harry S. Truman*, daughter Margaret says that her father was sure ghosts were in the White House, and at one time he wrote "...so I won't lock my doors or bar them either..."

Truman himself had no ambition to haunt the White House. He wrote in a letter to daughter Margaret: "No man in his right mind would want to come here of his own accord."

More Ghosts Of The Lincoln Assassination Conspiracy

A panel of nine military commissioners presided over by Judge Advocate General Joseph Holt administered quick punishment to three of these seven men and one woman. Led by John Wilkes Booth, they were alleged to be mainly responsible for the conspiracy that included the death of President Lincoln at Ford's Theater on Good Friday, April 15, 1863. Most of them had been apprehended before dawn the next morning. Eleven days later Booth was shot, or killed himself, as he holed up in a barn. Washington emotions were at a fever pitch. The conspirators were hastily brought to trial. They were kept chains, with heavy bags over their heads. Some say it more resembled a medieval inquisition than an American legal proceeding. Lewis Payne, David Herold, and George Atzerodt were hanged with Mary Surratt on July 7th.

Mary's son John, also shown in a Zouaves uniform, managed to flee to Canada and later to Europe. He was tracked down, arrested, and brought back to Washington for trial, but later released. Whether justice was served, whether Booth really was the mastermind, whether Mary Surratt knew anything at all of the plot has been hotly debated for more than one hundred years. The widow Surratt's ghost is still supposed to be roaming Washington in her unceasing effort to clear her name. *Courtesy Library of Congress*

Ford's Theater

When I was involved in my initial research for this book Ford's Theater, where President Lincoln was shot, had recently been restored. For the first time in a hundred years there were performances there. I was surprised that I was unable to uncover any stories of ghosts there. It seemed a natural haunt. I examined scores of old and yellowed newspapers down through the years. I talked with old timers who kept up with the Lincoln conspiracy theories. I talked with Park Service personnel and others involved in the restoration of the theater and acquisition of artifacts for the museum. One would think some of them would recognize a ghost, even if it didn't say "boo!!" I found no stories of ghosts haunting Ford's.

However, within a couple of years of *Washington Revisited's* debut and amidst all of the TV and print media fawning over these old stories I'd dug up, sure enough, a ghostly tale or two emerged from Ford's. It made me wonder if people anticipate strange happenings in such places, or if it had just taken a few years of renewed performances at the old theater to awaken a long slumbering spook(s). I guess there's always an outside possibility that since the National Theater had long been known to be haunted, that some creative person decided a ghost at Ford's might be good for business, too.

About 1858 John T. Ford leased the building that had once been home to the 10th Street Baptist Church before it merged with another nearby church. Washington was a growing city; a raw, and wide open, boom town back then. War was in the air. Congressmen were working overtime. The Bureaucracy was growing by leaps and bounds. Businessmen were in and out of town regularly trying to protect their interests. Abolitionists and secessionists were picking verbal and physical fights with each other almost everywhere you turned. Listening to it all, and writing it down with more than a few embellishments, were the newspaper reporters. It seemed as though there wasn't a newspaper in the United States and Europe that didn't have at least a half-dozen correspondents in Washington. Any one of them could solve the country's problems and would be only too glad to tell you how over a drink or two.

These folks all had one thing in common: money to spend. Entertainment, Ford reasoned, was a good way to get them to spend it with him. From 1858 until just after Christmas of 1862 Ford's Theater put on performances that kept the crowds coming. The fact is that when war erupted in the nearby countryside in May 1861 it improved business. The people became more aggressive about seeking out diversions and entertainment that could take their minds off the killing fields surrounding the city. Ford's, and other theaters, music halls, and saloons, flourished.

A gas meter apparently went awry on December 30, 1862, and started a fire that completely destroyed Ford's Theater. Fortunately, it happened when no performances were in progress and no one was there.

Because of his successes the only question in John T. Ford's mind was how much larger the new theater should be. Ford's *New* Theater, as he billed it, opened in August 1863 inside its handsome sturdy brick home. For the next seventeen months it was one of *the* places to be seen in war torn Washington.

This is the box inside Ford's Theater in which President and Mrs. Lincoln sat with Major Henry Rathbone and Miss Clara Harris. As they watched "Our American Cousin" actor John Wilkes Booth slipped into the back of the box and shot Mr. Lincoln in the back of the head at close range. Booth struggled with Major Rathbone and others, but managed to leap to the stage below and flee out a back door. *Courtesy Lee Shephard*

Ford's Theater, on 10th Street, was managed by John Ford's son Harry who lived upstairs in the house to the right of the theater. The Star Saloon occupied the first floor. *Courtesy Library of Congress*

President and Mrs. Lincoln sometimes frequented the National Theater. It was closer to the White House and often featured more popular performers. Mrs. Lincoln, it is said, opted for "Our American Cousin" playing at Ford's Theater because she had heard it was most entertaining. The same night President Lincoln was shot, the manager of the National Theater, C.D. Hess, wired owner Leonard Grover in New York: "President Lincoln shot tonight at Ford's Theater. Thank God it wasn't ours."

The tragic events of April 14, 1865, closed Ford's Theater. There wasn't another performance inside for more than a hundred years. Within a few weeks after the assassination the local YMCA tried to organize support to turn the facility into the *Abraham Lincoln Memorial Temple*, but it couldn't raise the funds.

Later that summer the government purchased the place and hired a Brooklyn contractor, the Dunbar Company, to convert the facility into an office building. The interior was gutted! The stage, balcony, box seats, and even the furnishings inside the Presidential box were either trashed or sold as salvage. The rocking chair in which Lincoln sat when he was shot by Booth wound up in the hands of private collectors for many years, and then in the Henry Ford Museum in Dearborn, Michigan.

About twenty-five years after Ford's was converted into three floors of government clerical offices the entire interior collapsed in on itself, killing 22 government workers and injuring 68. After that, the government used the building as a warehouse for storage of records.

North Dakota Republican Senator Milton Young began the movement to have Ford's restored to a theater in 1945, but his initial efforts didn't get too far. It wasn't until November 1964—one year after President John Kennedy was assassinated in Dallas, Texas—that the Ford building was closed so that restoration, finally approved by the Congress, could begin.

The National Park Service reopened Ford's in 1968. Since then, there has been a theater season every year. Within a decade some folks began insisting that they were seeing more than others. One newspaper report said workmen, guards, and some actors believed John Wilkes Booth was returning to the scene of his most villainous performance. The *Philadelphia Inquirer* reported Hal Holbrook, performing at Ford's as Mark Twain, is among actors who have been chilled as they moved into positions that crossed Booth's escape path across the stage.

Lecturer Paul Tucker told United Press International that he believes he saw Lincoln's face in the darkened President's Box during a performance one night several years ago. "I saw about three-quarters of his face. It struck me that what I saw was a little bit different than pictures I have seen—a human being."

Not all associated with Ford's Theater and Museum are convinced it is haunted. Sue Pridemore, a former supervisor at Ford's said "If you're looking for it, it's going to happen. I'd have to have a ghost sit down next to me to really believe." Michael Maione, a Park Service historian told me emphatically, "There are no ghosts. Ghosts don't exist. If someone wants to believe there are ghosts that is their business, but ghosts don't exist."

In spite of official denials the stories have persisted through recent years. A gospel singer claimed that a light flashing on and off in the President's Box was so distracting that she didn't want to return to the stage after intermission. The President's Box is permanently closed to the pubic so it makes you wonder what the singer really saw, doesn't it?

With so much death associated with the Ford building how can we be sure the reported manifestations are ghosts of Lincoln and/or Booth? We can't, but linking their names to such strange occurrences certainly does add some *zest* to the incidents.

The tales also provide actors with a ready excuse for blown lines and missed cues. I can hear one of them now: "Hey, it was Booth! Booth distracted me. I'll get it right during the next performance, okay?"

The Petersen House

With Ford's Theater now joining the White House in claiming visits by the Lincoln ghost I decided to look once again into the old Petersen House. It's across 10th Street NW from Ford's. After the President was shot it was decided to move him out of the theater. Once onto 10th Street, however, the

crowds proved to be overbearing. The President's men not only encountered those people who had fled the theater; but celebrating Washingtonians, many of whom were shocked into sobriety by what they saw. Those carrying the wounded President tried their best not to aggravate the wound, to shield him and not drop him amidst all the excitement, pushing and shoving.

No one knows where Petersen and his wife were that fateful evening. A roomer inside the Petersen house heard the commotion in the streets and went to investigate. When he saw the difficulty the President's attendants were having he shouted for them to bring Lincoln inside. The roomer showed them down a dimly lighted hallway on the first floor to William Clark's room. Clark, a soldier from Massachusetts assigned to the Quartermaster Department, was out celebrating the Union victory.

Because 10th Street was filled with panic driven theater patrons and jubilant crowds celebrating the end of the war it was determined the President's condition was such that he couldn't be moved far. Mr. Lincoln was carried into the Petersen Rooming House across the street from Ford's Theater. *Courtesy Lee Shephard*

Several of the President's cabinet rushed to his bedside. His wife Mary became so hysterical that a friend had to take her back to the White House. Son Robert arrived at his father's bedside and remained until the President died. It was in this room that Secretary of War Edward Stanton is alleged to have remarked, "Now, he belongs to the ages." *Courtesy Library of Congress*

William Petersen, a tailor from Germany, had come to this country in 1842 when he was in his early twenties. By 1849 he had married a young woman, also from Germany, and they had built the rooming house on 10th Street. Although Petersen kept a tailor shop in the basement at times, his main shop was a few blocks away on Pennsylvania Avenue.

In recent years Petersen had no difficulty in finding roomers. Between the theater across the street, his proximity to government offices, and the troops assigned to various jobs in the city, he usually kept a list of people looking for a place to stay.

An actor friend of John Wilkes Booth used to room at Petersen's and it is said that Booth himself had once napped on the bed where they lay the dying President.

One of the women who greets tourists to the historic house told a newspaper man that she's never heard any stories about the spirit of the dead President revisiting the house. She did wonder, she confided to the reporter; if the ghost of William Petersen didn't revisit his old home from time to time. Petersen was just 51 when he died.

Some theorized that because the President died in Petersen's home, people were reluctant to stay there. Petersen may have had difficulty attracting roomers. Others speculated Petersen was in poor health, and that his tailoring business just wasn't the same in peace time. Whatever the cause of Petersen's financial troubles, we do know that he left behind major debts and a grieving, loving wife who followed him to the grave within less than a year. In October 1871 relatives auctioned off the contents of the house. The bed in which President Lincoln died brought $80.00.

Another Petersen House docent told a reporter she had heard keys rattle and someone walking heavily across the upstairs floor. Petersen, or his wife, still tending to the monotonous housekeeping drudgery of a rooming house that catered to male borders?

A fairly recent contribution to this legend leaves tremendous room for our imagination to work. A reporter quoted one female docent at Petersen House who said that a workman changing his clothes in an upstairs room became so frightened that he fled into the street without his pants!

The Wispy Wanderings of Mary Surratt

Mary Surratt is perhaps the most well-traveled ghost in Washington. Over the years her wispy form has been seen in at least four places: the Old Brick Capitol where she was briefly imprisoned (The Federal government had converted a run down rooming house into a Civil War prison. The building got its name because it was built as a temporary home for Congress while the Capitol underwent major repairs following the British arson of August 1814); drifting around the grounds where the old Arsenal Penitentiary gallows once stood; inside her rooming house on H Street Northwest; and out at her Clinton, Maryland, farm. The troubled ghost of Mary Surratt just can't seem to find a place to rest.

The old Arsenal Penitentiary was located on the grounds of Fort Lesley McNair. It was there in the courtyard on the northern end of the Fort, not too far from Capitol Hill, that she and three of the other conspirators in the Lincoln Assassination plot were hanged. Their bodies were buried near the gallows, and then later moved to permanent graves.

The old Washington Arsenal, now Fort Leslie McNair, is another haunt of Mary Surratt's restless ghost. She and three other Lincoln assassination conspirators were hanged in the courtyard.

As the trap doors sprung the conspirators dropped to their deaths amid the cheers of on-lookers. *Courtesy Library of Congress*

There is an old tale that Mary Surratt's ghost had considerable influence over the sudden appearance of a boxwood tree that seemingly grew of its own accord to mark the site of the gallows. It is claimed that this is her way of continuing to attract attention to prove her innocence.

In the fertile tobacco lands of southern Maryland, just east of Washington, Mary Jenkins married John Surratt. It was 1835. President Andrew Jackson had narrowly escaped assassination during a war with the Seminoles. Mary and John weren't concerned. Politics were in Washington and that was a lifetime away. They were newlyweds and had a twelve-hundred acre farm to run. There weren't many neighbors then, but as the years passed, more and more people seemed to settle in the area. Within fifteen years John and Mary decided that they would turn part of the Surratt house into a country store and tavern. Folks used to drop by often, and they even began calling the place Surrattsville. The area kept that name for more than a dozen years—even after John died and Mary took her children to Washington to escape the memories. She leased the place to a former District of Columbia policeman.

Mary Surratt's former boarding house at 604 H Street Northwest is one of the places her spirit has been seen. *Martin Luther King, Jr. Public Library, District of Columbia*

Ford's Theater wasn't too far from Mary's new home, in the 600 block of H Street Northwest; neither were the other theaters, the White House, or the Capitol—just up the hill. She would have no trouble finding boarders to help her make ends meet. The Surratt house was a convenient place for John Wilkes Booth, an actor from a family of actors, to seek lodging. It offered him the seclusion he sought in directing and casting his real-life drama.

At midnight on the night Lincoln was shot, police and federal troops rousted Mary Surratt out of bed, accused her of being a conspirator, and took her off to prison in the Old Brick Capitol. Her insistence of innocence and her denial that she knew Booth well fell on ears disciplined not to listen.

An article in the *Evening Star*, the newspaper of record in the District of Columbia back then, stated that she was never even allowed a change of clothes. She was "forced to wear the same garments in which she was arrested until hanged July 7, 1865."

Within a few years after her death, there were hints that something strange was going on at her former H Street house. Daughter Anne had sold the boarding house for less than half of its value. After that, the turnover in owners was so rapid that it attracted the attention of journalists of the period, who began to chronicle the tales former owners sometimes told *after* they had rid themselves of the property. Most of the accounts dealt with "ominous sounds," "mumblings," or "muffled sounds." Some claimed "muffled whispers" rehearsed again "the dastardly plot." Boards creaked on the second floor when no one was upstairs.

The Surratt boarding house has been renovated inside and out many times. Washington has changed too. The 600 block of H Street NW is now in a section of the city inhabited predominately by Chinese. When I was researching this book Mary's old place was an oriental grocery store, and had been for several years. The oriental owner had no complaints—that he was willing to voice to a writer.

The old Surratt farmhouse-tavern, in what is now Clinton, Maryland, is under historic properties protection. It is frequented by tourists. John Wilkes Booth is alleged to have stopped by the tavern for supplies and food as he tried to elude his pursuers before crossing over into Virginia. Booth was captured twelve days later in Bowling Green when troopers set fire to the barn in which he was hiding after he refused to come out. Whether he was shot or killed himself can still ignite a good debate; as can the extent of his association, if any, with Mary Surratt. Meanwhile, Mary is said to continue to revisit her old home place from time to time. We're told she would like some answers from the Washington policeman-turned-tavern keeper to whom she sold the place. You see, it was he who turned her in.

The Remorse of the Heartless Judge

The Lincoln assassination conspiracy and its aftermath reached out to touch still another life. Judge Advocate General Joseph Holt, who had been the presiding judge at the conspiracy trial and had insisted on the death penalty for Mary Surratt, was said to have changed dramatically afterward. Holt, a Kentuckian, had few, if any, friends. He wasn't especially liked by other bureaucrats. Once, when he was commissioner of patents, his boss recommended him for promotion to Postmaster General of the United States because "he has no heart." Holt apparently saw no reason to change his personality just because he had a new position. Gerald Cullinan, in his book *The Post Office Department*, says, "He was taciturn, vindictive, and ill-mannered."

The ghost of Joseph Holt, who served as Judge Advocate General in the trial of the Lincoln conspirators, is said to restlessly wander Capitol Hill in search of more evidence of her guilt or innocence. *Courtesy Library of Congress*

Hanging the conspirators was an enormously popular decision with the public, but "doing his job" as Judge Advocate General didn't change any attitudes toward Holt. For whatever the reasons, in the years after the conspirators' trial, Holt became more reclusive. Newspaper articles from that period say he withdrew into the privacy of his home, which was described as decaying, with bars on the windows, and shades that never permitted the sun's rays inside. Neighbor's talked. They wished "the Laws" had never sold the place. It had been such a beautiful and well-maintained home back then. Thomas Law had built the house at 1st and C Streets Southeast for his beautiful wife, the granddaughter of Martha Washington.

One reporter in the late 1880s said that the once-manicured garden of Holt's house had become an "overgrowth of weeds and tangled vines." Children crossed the street to avoid the old house, which stood only a few blocks from the Old Brick Capitol Prison where Mary Surratt was originally incarcerated. Judge Holt apparently spent the remainder of his years in almost total solitude. Infrequently, he would venture out to buy food, but he is said to have much preferred to be sequestered in his shadowy surroundings, among his many volumes. A neighbor, who believed Holt had developed feelings too late, was quoted by one reporter as saying, "His irrevocable decision weighed heavily upon him." Others speculated that he spent his time re-reading the transcripts of the famous trial.

After Holt's death, the new owners of his house worked diligently to make it a cheerful, warm home; but the everlasting presence of the "man with no heart" is said to have chilled more than one room. The sound of someone pacing in the upstairs library is reported to have often lasted for hours. Capitol Hill neighbors were sure they knew who it was. For many years Capitol Hill neighbors used to talk of a remorseful Judge Advocate General Joseph Holt, sentenced to an eternity of unrest that included repetitious pacing; and reading again and again the testimony he had used to hang Mary Surratt.

When the old house was torn down, the stories changed somewhat. The Judge has been seen when the hour is late, walking down 1st Street. The cape of his midnight blue Union uniform pulled tightly about him. According to the legend, he is headed to the Old Brick Capitol to try to learn the truth from Mary Surratt.

This is the house on Capitol Hill where Joseph Holt spent his last years as a recluse. Neighbors believed him to be in deep remorse for having not allowed more time for presentation of evidence regarding the innocence of Mary Surratt in the military trial of the Lincoln assassination conspirators. *Courtesy Library of Congress*

Capitol Hill

Strange Happenings at the Old Brick Capitol

The Jenkins family used to own a lot of the land north and east of the Anacostia River in southern Maryland. It was on Jenkins' Hill that the new government decided to build the Capitol of the United States. Over the years the name gradually changed to Capitol Hill. This area of Washington has provided enough ghostlore to keep storytellers around a campfire well past midnight.

If you are brave enough to venture out at night in the area of 1st and East Capitol Streets, directly behind the U.S. Capitol, do not become alarmed if you encounter an airy figure casting a supernatural shadow over the white marble of the United States Supreme Court building. You certainly won't be the first to do so. Some years ago a congressman who had risen just before dawn, in order to get an early start on a mountain of paperwork that had piled up on his desk, had such a startling experience that he wasn't able to concentrate on anything else for quite some time.

The United States Congress conducted its sessions in this building quickly constructed for just that purpose after the British burned the Capitol in August of 1814. When the Capitol was re-built the Old Brick Capitol was used as a boarding-house. It gradually fell into disrepair, and at the outset of the Civil War its only tenant was said to be a German cobbler and his family. Within six months bars had been added to windows, rooms turned into cells, and prisoners were incarcerated. As you can see in the second photograph taken a year or so later extensions have been added to the sides. A larger mess-hall was needed, among other things. The prison was filled with military offenders, prisoners of state, captured Confederates, and scores of Washington citizens suspected of disloyalty to the Union. *Courtesy Library of Congress*

The nation's highest court has not always occupied that corner. After the British burned the Capitol, August 24, 1814, during the War of 1812 Congress quickly commissioned the rapid construction of a large brick building on that corner behind the Capitol to serve as a temporary home. Congress moved back into the restored Capitol in 1819, and that temporary brick refuge took on different uses. Eventually, the Old Brick Capitol that had stood there for more than a hundred years was torn down in the late 1920s to make room for the U.S. Supreme Court. It had outgrown its location in the basement of the U.S. Capitol. The Old Brick Capitol had survived many threats of demolition over the years. An elderly lady who had grown to love the building told me, "It was the determination of Chief Justice Taft that got it." William H. Taft, who served as 27th President (1909-1913) had always wanted to serve on the U.S. Supreme Court. He got that position and became the only person in U.S. history to head two branches of the federal government when President Warren G. Harding appointed him Chief Justice in 1921. It was Taft who pushed for the court to have a home of its own directly behind the U.S. Capitol, where, he believed the deteriorating old Brick Capitol was expendable.

Once vacated by Congress in 1819, the Old Brick Capitol was divided into apartments and town homes. However, the people on Jenkins Hill kept right on calling the structure the "Old Brick Capitol."

The rooms were quickly let to congressmen, lawyers, and others who were attracted by its convenience to the Capitol. Among those who lived there was famed southern orator John C. Calhoun. The South Carolinian wore many political hats while serving his country. He was a congressman, a senator, a secretary of state, and a vice president. Not too long before he died, Calhoun was visited in a vision by none other than George Washington. The spirit of the Father of the Country warned Calhoun of the growing movement toward secession. It is a matter of record that, before his death in 1850, Calhoun correctly predicted the secession of the next decade. "The dissolution of the Union," warned Calhoun, "is the heaviest blow that can be struck at civilization and representative government."

John C. Calhoun, who some say possessed psychic powers, rented an apartment in the Old Brick Capitol after Congress returned to its original quarters. Calhoun, an ardent supporter of states rights, died in 1850 but correctly predicted secession. It is said his ghost is one of those that frequented the building, grieving over the impact the dissolution of the Union had on representative government. *Courtesy Library of Congress*

Calhoun's ghost continued to roam through the Old Brick Capitol for years. Often-told tales recount how it was most restive when the federal government turned the building into a prison during the Civil War, as if concerned over the treatment of Confederate prisoners. It is a period not many like to remember.

One writer described the Old Brick Capitol complex as having been in a state of decay before the Union decided to take it over and turn it into a prison. It was "a dingy, crumbling structure, with rambling passages, and with quaint rooms where one least expected to find them." When the building was converted into a prison, iron bars were placed in the windows of the upper floors, and some first floor windows were walled up.

The building sat on the corner of two busy streets. Whether in the sweltering humid heat of summer, or in the windy icy dampness of winter, one could often see inmates peering from behind the bars. It was overcrowded with spies and citizens. The slightest rumor linking one to the "southern cause" was grounds for arrest and imprisonment. An investigation and charges could take weeks or months. Unfortunately, not all of the prisoners in the Old Brick Capitol were guilty of crimes, but getting clearance for a release also took weeks and months. There was a war going on and the innocent sometimes suffered too.

Some Washingtonians used to walk by to see if they could catch a glimpse of a wrongly imprisoned loved one; others hoped to spot someone with notoriety. Shouts and epithets would occasionally be exchanged before a Union soldier could intervene. The soldiers served as guards and were also posted on the sidewalks to prevent passers-by from stopping. There was a concern that southern sympathizers or colleague of an inmate might try to communicate, by signs or signals. Long after the prisoners left the Old Brick Capitol, the ghosts of some of the captives and their long departed jailers have continued to revisit the site.

The history of the building at 1st and East Capitol was the furthest thing from the mind of the unidentified congressman in the 1920s who had risen before dawn to get a head start on his paperwork. He was deep in thought about his constituents' problems as he walked along in the chilly, and slightly foggy, morning. His first thought when he saw a man walking back and forth in front of the homes was that he wasn't the only person to brave the chill and venture out before sunup.

His thoughts interrupted by the pacing man ahead; the congressman now began to notice something peculiar about the figure. The cadence of his movement seemed to be a march. There was something long protruding from over his shoulder. He wore a cap with an upturned bill and a saber sheathed at his waist.

The congressman blinked his eyes—several times—scarcely believing what he saw. He never had a chance to question the uniformed sentry, however. At the moment the sun burned a hole through the fog the guard instantly vanished, as though swallowed up by the sun's rays. The apparition had appeared near where the main entrance to the old prison had been.

The congressman just stood there. Finally, he managed to catch his breath, shake the image from his mind's eye, and move on to his office. It had so unnerved him, though, that he simply paced back and forth in his office, doing no work, and talking to no one. Never again would he doubt the whispers he had heard about the Old Brick Capitol.

Many of those whispers about the goings on inside and outside the old structure came from some of the members of the National Woman's Party. The building had been acquired by the suffragettes in 1922—two years after Congress and the 19th Amendment granted voting rights to women, and long after remnants of the old prison had been ripped out. In addition to a headquarters for the movement, the old building—with its cells converted into bedrooms—served as a dormitory for the women. Although it had been over fifty years since anyone had been incarcerated within the building's walls, or executed in the courtyard, some of the tales told by the women would chill the hearts of the most skeptical.

The National Woman's Party workers were well aware of the building's past. They loved to boast of the distinguished Americans who had lived there and of those who had been inside the house when it served as a temporary home for the young nation's legislative branch. More than one woman could guide guests to the rooms of the Honorable Mr. Calhoun. The women also knew there were some not-so-glorious moments in the past, but they had learned to accept the fact that their home had also been a notorious wartime federal prison.

Before her death, former resident Mabel Vernon, a charter member of the National Woman's Party, was reminiscing about the old days of the women's movement. Although she had been retired for a number of years, she had a clear recall not only of the political struggles, but also of some of the unusual events that had taken place in that building. She showed me a scrapbook from her youth. Among other memorabilia it contained clippings of newspaper stories concerning women who had worked there and heard weird sounds and seen strange sights. Matter-of-factly she told me of "unexplainable incidents," as she called them, that she had heard about, but never witnessed.

Some of the National Woman's Party workers quoted in these articles from the late 1920s said that moaning, weeping, and sighing often kept them from sleeping. They never knew when peaceful slumber would be shattered by a maniacal scream or the reverberating clank of an invisible cell door slamming shut or the bitter laughter that drifted through the rooms.

Mable Vernon told me, "We used to talk a lot about the old prison and some of the very notable spies who had been kept there." Some of the Lincoln assassination conspirators were among those incarcerated there. It has been suggested that it was the spirit of accused conspirator Mary Surratt who cried out in agony. On several anniversaries of the hanging of Mrs. Surratt the outline of a female figure was seen against one of the windows. One witness reported that the figure sobbed incessantly while clenching her "ghostly white fists against black iron bars" that were also a part of the apparition.

Some conjectured that the sounds of laughter heard in the building came from notorious Confederate spy Belle Boyd, returning to the place where she had spent many unhappy months. The attractive young woman had used her charms to gain confidence in many circles. She had entertained General Nathaniel Banks, for example, while Stonewall Jackson rode to victory in the Shenandoah Valley. Later Miss Boyd was caught and confined in the Old Brick Capitol Prison.

After the Civil War, when the Old Brick Capitol returned to being a boarding house, occupants reported hearing bitter laughter, which they attributed to the ghost of Confederate spy Belle Boyd, who was imprisoned in the Old Brick Capitol but managed to escape hanging.

Others claimed to hear the sobbing of Rose Greenhow, seen here with her daughter inside the prison, as she agonized about her fate. A zealous supporter of "The Cause," Mrs. Greenhow, who lived in Washington at the opening of the war, alerted General Beauregard by a cryptic message to Union troop movements on Manassas July 16, 1861. It enabled the Confederate forces to repel the Federal advance. However, in just over a month she was tracked down and spent the next eight months in the Old Capitol Prison under the shadow of execution. In June of 1862, however, she pledged not to come north of the Potomac until after the war; and was escorted beyond Union lines and released. It was later learned that even while in prison she managed to correspond extensively with Col. Thomas Jordan of General Beauregard's staff.

Another of the famous female phantoms that allegedly haunted the facility is Mary Surratt. She was kept here only briefly until her trial, but some swear to having heard her pleading voice echoing her innocence. Quite a few of these stories sprang up during the late 1800s and the early part of the twentieth century when the National Woman's Party was headquartered in the Old Brick Capitol, and the former cells were used as dormitory rooms. *Library of Congress*

Some of the women seemed to think the pacing sounds, which were frequently heard coming from one of the former cells, could have been the tormented spirit of Confederate prison camp commander Henry Wirtz. Thirteen thousand Federal soldiers had died while he was in charge of Andersonville prison. Wirtz spent the last days of his life in the Old Brick Capitol before he was led to the courtyard and hanged.

There were executions in the courtyard of the Old Brick Capitol Prison. Perhaps the one that received the most attention was that of Henri Wirtz, the Commandant of Andersonville Prison. Wirtz, who protested his innocence, was tried as a war criminal and hanged. The soldiers at the base of the gallows chanted "Wirtz, remember Andersonville." The crowd shouted and jeered as the trap was sprung. Some fifty years later there were those who lived in the converted cells of the old prison who believed pacing sounds that could be heard in one of the rooms belonged to the tormented ghost of Wirz unable to forget the thirteen thousand Union soldiers who died while he was in charge of their fate at Andersonville. *Courtesy Library of Congress*

It has been more than half of a century since the white marble of the U.S. Supreme Court building replaced the scarred old brick of the building that had been a temporary capitol, a temporary boarding house, a temporary prison, and a temporary headquarters for suffragettes. However, old tale tellers on the hill say that if the time is right, and the moonbeams are glancing off that white marble just a certain way, you may be able to see an apparition of the Old Brick Capitol shimmering before the building that dared to replace it. *Courtesy Lee Shephard*

One incident, Mabel Vernon recalled, involved the violin of a member. The seldom used instrument was kept in the parlor. One evening some of the women in another part of the house heard music coming from that direction. Assuming that the musician had decided to spend a relaxing evening entertaining them, they made their way to the parlor. Imagine their surprise when they discovered no one there.

The violin was resting in its usual place, and the bow still hung on the wall. The women looked at each other silently as the mysteriously produced music continued. They searched the building, but found no violinist. A couple of the young women even checked outside to see if someone was playing a trick on them.

Later in the evening, after their nerves had calmed, Mabel Vernon said they discussed the incident. She recalled how some of the elderly women recognized the melody. They said it was one of the favorites from the war. The Civil War. In early childhood they had heard some of the old veterans humming it, playing it on harmonica, or violin. They concluded that it was also a melody likely to have been a favorite of a homesick prisoner of war, wondering if he would ever be free to live and love again. The women never learned who their musically inclined visitor was, and even though that old melody drifted through the house on several other occasions, Ms. Vernon said its origin was never discovered.

In spite of the ghostly visitors who walked its halls, the members of the National Woman's Party fought gallantly to save their beloved building. However, Chief Justice Taft won and a landmark of more than one hundred years came down.

It has been more than a half-century since the white marble of the Supreme Court replaced the scarred old brick of the building that had been a temporary capitol, a temporary prison, a temporary rooming house, and a temporary headquarters for suffragettes. However, some say that if the time is right, and the moonbeams are glancing off the marble just a certain way, you may be able to see an apparition of the Old Brick Capitol shimmering before the building that dared to replace it. Some say the air even develops a stale, musty odor, and sometimes sobs, cries, and the distant clank of a cell door— or the thud of a trap door—can be heard, *if* you hang around long enough.

The Gaslight Specter

A 1935 *Washington Post* article by Gaeta Wold Boyer told of her investigation of supernatural occurrences at the First Spiritualist Church on C Street. She reported that the minister explained to her how he had received his inspiration to become a minister. It was from a childhood encounter with the ghost of a young woman.

As a young boy, at the close of the nineteenth century, the minister had lived with his family in a house on G Street. The minister recalled how his family happened on the ghost quite by accident. One chilly evening they were enjoying quiet fellowship on their porch when the father, deciding they would need a fire for warmth later that night, went inside to prepare it. Inside the doorway he struck a match to ignite the gaslight. The flame flickered, sputtered, and then caught, suffusing the room with a soft glow. Just about then the father cried out. The minister said the rest of the family rushed in to see their father virtually paralyzed. His eyes were glued to a nearby couch. There stretched out on the sofa with "her hair over the arm rest" was a beautiful, but obviously lifeless young woman.

The reporter quotes the minister as saying that his father began to regain his composure, examine his feelings, and experiment. The father turned the light to a fuller flame and the figure vanished. He dimmed the light and the specter reappeared. He repeated the procedure twice more with the same results. With the presence of the ghost, there also came the strong odor of gas. As the fumes permeated the room, the young woman's complexion and clothing became radiant; she shimmered in the soft light. When coughing broke the silence she vanished. Then, startled out of his trance-like state, the father became concerned about his family's safety and ushered everyone back outside while he searched for the source of the gas fumes.

The minister told the reporter that his family was too shaken to discuss the encounter. They just sat staring into the darkness until their father pronounced the house free of gas. No one slept that night. Most of the family was out of their bedrooms by first light, going over what had happened the night before. They tried to understand what it meant. By midmorning it had been decided that they would question the neighbors, check the real estate records, and do what else was necessary to learn who was the young lady haunting their house. Had other owners before them been visited by her?

The family learned the identity of the ghost from a neighbor. The young woman had lived in the house several decades earlier. She had become so disillusioned with life, and so despondent after her fiancée was killed in the Civil War, that a permanent sleep seemed her only answer. The neighborhood legend had it that she slowly dressed for bed one evening, turned up the gas, and then lay down on the sofa in the parlor to dream her last dream of the handsome young man in the blue uniform whose life had been ended at Manassas by a cannonball. It is said that a smile came to her lips at the thought of rejoining him and then she entered her deepest sleep.

This encounter, said the minister, was the beginning of his lifelong interest in the supernatural, in spiritualism. He spoke with the *Post* reporter in his office at the church. She reported that it was not unusual for those who chatted with him there to be interrupted by a door opening or a chair scraping across the floor of its own volition. Sometimes a book would move across the minister's desk without help from human hands.

The old Spiritualist Church is no longer. It was torn down to make way for a newer structure. The minister is long gone, too—free to join his friends on the other side.

Phantoms on the Stairs

There is another home on G Street around which they spin a tale of an eternal triangle of love, anger and horror. The story was first published in the *Evening Star*, in the spring of 1891. "Other people might have endured such annoyance as we suffered with more patience, but we found it altogether too trying on our nerves," said a young woman whose family had recently moved from the house as she related her experiences to a young gentleman of her acquaintance who wrote for the *Star*.

Her family had rented the G Street house immediately upon their arrival in Washington the previous December. The real estate agent had said nothing about anything disagreeable connected with the house, so no preliminary apprehension on the part of the family prepared them for what subsequently occurred.

The family had lived in the house but a week when they had their first encounter with something out of the ordinary. The young woman was going upstairs after dinner to dress for the theater when she stumbled over something about midway on the first flight. She twisted her ankle and cried out as she fell to one knee. At that same moment she heard a "faint miauow (sic) and perceived that I must have stepped upon a cat."

However, this family's dislike for cats was so great that no cat was ever permitted in their house. The sprained ankle pained the young woman so that she canceled her theater date. Her father and mother immediately began inquiries of her brother and the servants as to how a cat had gotten into the house. No one knew and although the incident had seemed strange, it was forgotten within a few days. Forgotten, that is, until a similar incident happened about a month later. The young woman described it to the reporter:

"My father was coming downstairs from his study at 10:30 in the evening for the purpose of locking up the house before going to bed, when, a few steps below the first landing, he heard close behind him a distinct whisper. Not only did the whisper appear unmistakably a whisper, but as the whisper of a man in anger. He turned, startled, and in so doing, put his foot upon something soft and yielding. The something, which he did not have time to see, uttered a 'miauow,' while he was tripped up by it so as to barely escape a serious fall by grasping the stair rail.

"I don't think I ever saw papa quite so angry as he was on that occasion. He swore dreadfully, demanding to know how it was that a cat had, for the second time, been allowed to get into *his* house, against *his* explicit orders."

The father was also convinced that he had heard a man's whisper on the stairs. His frustration level peaked when a search of the house from attic to cellar revealed neither a cat nor an uninvited male guest. Therefore, as a rational person, the father told himself that the whisper had been an illusion, but he berated the house staff for allowing in a cat—even though he, nor anyone else, had seen a cat. He vowed to fire the entire staff if he ever did see a cat in his house.

The phantom feline became a household joke, the young woman told the reporter; until the upstairs maid had another encounter with it. It was about 10 o'clock in the morning. There was plenty of daylight, when the maid rushed to her mistress in hysterics—still clutching tightly to the dustpan and broom. She called the house bewitched and insisted she couldn't remain in it. Soothing the maid; the mistress learned, in a somewhat inarticulate and disjointed story, of her encounter with the invisible cat. The young woman told her newspaper friend the maid's story.

"It seems that she was sweeping down the stairs when something she did not see got in the way of her broom. She looked to find out what it was, and perceiving nothing, gave another and a stronger sweep. To her astonishment her broom was again impeded, though the viewless obstacle appeared to remove itself once with a 'spit' and 'miauow' very audible. It was the cat again and yet no cat at all."

Although the family was amazed, they figured the maid had overheard talk of the first two incidents and that just stimulated her imagination. Not a superstitious family, nor inclined to believe in ghosts—especially cat ghosts—the family tried to convince themselves and the household servants that the incidents could be explained by natural causes, *if* they just had a little more information. For the next thirty-six hours the family amused itself with speculation. Suddenly, something most unamusing happened that brought the whole matter to a crisis.

"On the evening of Thursday last," the young woman told the reporter, "we were all in the front drawing room downstairs, my mother engaged with her knitting, while my father, my brother, and I read. It was rather later than we were accustomed to sit up, it being about 11:15, as I happened to know, because I had looked at the clock and had made up my mind that I would be able to finish my chapter by half after the hour. I was on the point of breaking the silence of the room by addressing a remark to that effect to my father, when, upon looking up, I saw him place a finger on his lips and assume the attitude of one listening.

"Whereupon, I listened also, and presently I distinguished what he heard—a faint sound of whispering; which seemed to come from the hallway or the stairs. Then my mother dropped her knitting; and looking rather surprised, turned to papa with an exclamation on the point of utterance. My brother Tom erected his ears also, but we all refrained from speaking, in obedience to my father's gesture.

"As we listened, all of us together, the whispering continued, now louder and again not so distinct. There was no doubt that it came from the entry. Papa rose quietly from his chair, laying aside the *Century Magazine* which he had been reading, and, motioning to us not to move, tiptoed without noise to the door of the room. He stood on the threshold for a minute, and then stepped softly outside until he reached the foot of the stairs, where he remained for a brief space in view from where we sat. Presently he turned, and, with his finger to his lips, beckoned us to join him. We obeyed noiselessly, intensely curious to know what the mystery could be.

"A moment later we four stood together at the foot of the stairs, beneath the hall lamp, Papa with one hand on the newel post and the rest of us looking over his shoulder upward toward the landing above. The whispering came from that direction, and it was so loud now and again that the words were

almost distinguishable. A gaslight half turned-up burned upon the landing mentioned, and we could see that there was no one there. My father, apparently actuated by a sudden impulse, started up the steps, pausing occasionally to listen, until he got to the top, then he came down again with more expedition than was habitual with him, I thought. He looked nervous. We raised our eyebrows interrogatorily, and he replied gravely:

"'*I passed the whispers on the stairs!*'"

Although the family was frightened, the young woman said, they felt comparatively safe in numbers.

"Our curiosity, in a certain degree, overcame our fears. None of us had ever come into contact with anything that savored of the supernatural before and the sensation was a novelty. Again we listened and the whispers on the stairs seemed louder than before. They were clearly two voices—a man's angry tones and the pleading accents of a woman. You cannot possibly imagine how fearsome a thing it was to hear all this going on up the very flight of steps we stood at the bottom of and yet to see nobody—absolutely nobody.

"All at once there was audible a subdued exclamation, followed immediately by the startling 'spit' and 'miauow' of a cat and then what sounded like the fall of something heavy on the stairs themselves. We looked at one another, appalled. Mamma's face had turned white as a sheet and papa and Tom half carried her into the drawing room where she was brought around with smelling salts. I nearly fainted myself and even Tom looked a little pale about the gills, as he himself would have expressed it."

The mother and daughter, in spite of the late hour, woke up friends across the street and spent the night there. The father and son, decidedly anxious yet not wanting to admit their fears or an encounter with something supernatural, remained in the house performing a thorough search and totally perplexed by what they had witnessed. The next day the father rented a house on New Hampshire Avenue, Northwest, phoned the movers, and had his family out of the G Street house before sunset.

When the father called upon the real estate agent to turn in his keys the agent waived the customary month's notice because of what had happened. The agent apologized for not letting him know that several previous tenants had claimed the house was haunted. He said he had not bothered to warn the family because there was never anything definite, and he personally thought it to be pure nonsense. As the two men continued to talk, the Realtor sensed he had a rational person before him, so he questioned the father extensively about what the family had experienced in the G Street house. As the story unfolded, the Realtor began to pace the room nervously. His expression became grave. At its conclusion he sat down. Visibly disturbed, he thought for a moment, and then offered to relate to his former tenant a story that his father, now dead, had told him many years earlier. "Perhaps," he said, "you will understand why your words have occasioned me such agitation."

The real estate agent's story was related to the reporter by the young woman the way her father had told it to her, and I now re-tell it to you based upon the reporter's article:

A most beautiful young girl and an outstandingly handsome young attorney of moderate means were devoutly in love. However, the girl's father, described as a temperamental eccentric, had chosen a wealthy old widower for his daughter. He was so determined to force his daughter into marriage with the older gentleman that he never lost an opportunity to bring them together.

One evening, the father invited his wealthy friend to dinner. In those days, it was not unusual for a dinner guest to remain through the night. The daughter was furious when she heard of the plan. However, her good manners prevented her from being unkind to her father's house-guest. A delicious dinner, and perhaps too much wine for one so late in years, brought an early retirement for the old gentleman. He found his way to the guest room well before his host was ready to retire.

The daughter had been polite for as long as she could stand it and flew into her father. Finishing her denunciation of her father's chosen suitor, and repeating her vow never to marry him; the young woman headed for her upstairs bedroom.

The exasperated father followed spewing violent language and threats. He wanted the last word. She paused on the stair landing. Remembering his friend was asleep just above them the old man reduced his remarks to a loud whisper. In the same tone, his daughter fired back at him. Her final words so infuriated him that he either violently struck or pushed his daughter. She stepped backward to regain her balance, but her left foot landed hard on the back of her pet cat which had followed her up the stairs. The animal squealed. The woman screamed as she began to tumble down the stairs. The fall broke her neck. Her pet cat lay dead of a broken spine on the landing.

The cook, who had been entertaining company in the kitchen at a late hour, and against the wishes of her employer, was trying to sneak upstairs without being seen when the commotion erupted. She witnessed it all and told her story to the authorities. However, the old gentleman escaped a trial. He pointed to the cook's notoriety as a liar, and insisted—through his act of grief—that the cat caused his beloved daughter to stumble to her death.

The young real estate agent said he had always been inclined to believe the cook, especially now, adding that his interest in the case stemmed from the fact that "the young lawyer who loved the murdered girl was my own father."

A Murdered Man's Revenge

Throughout most of the late 1800s, there was a dilapidated house in the southwest shadows of the U.S. Capitol that was haunted by the ghosts of a couple that are believed to have lost their lives there. This "house with the ghostly stare," as one reporter described it, was in sharp contrast to the well-cared-for homes in the area and to the manicured lawn of the Capitol. It was in need of repairs and painting. Its yard was overgrown with weeds and vines. A rusted iron fence separated the dismal yellow-brick structure from the sidewalk, yet passers-by preferred the other side of the street.

I have heard that the old house was once owned by a rich young man who, neighborhood storytellers once said, never wanted for female companionship. He is supposed to have dined by candlelight with a young lady late one evening. After the delectable dinner, the charming host lured his companion down into the cellar, where he had stored a remarkable collection of foreign wines—almost all of which he had brought into the country himself from his travels abroad. The host, perhaps he had already consumed too much wine, made advances toward the young woman. She resisted. They quarreled.

How the young man died in that cool, dank, and dimly lighted cellar wasn't preserved as part of the neighborhood legend, and none of the articles I read about the old house answered that question, either. One elderly lady said that she had heard that his dinner companion broke a bottle of wine over his head as she defended her honor.

At this point the story takes two routes to get to the same ending. One version said that she ran from the house screaming and found a policeman. After questioning she was released. The other version says that she slipped out of the house unnoticed.

In both stories she returned the next morning to see whether her victim was dead and never came out again.

That neighborhood legend was the basis for other stories that sprang up over the years as residents moved in and residents moved out rather rapidly. Stories popped up that the shadowy form of a young woman in mourning would unlatch the wrought iron gate, climb the steps, and enter the house. Capitol Hill gossips circulated new stories that the ghost of the host had an "intense hatred" for those of the "same sex and age of his slayer," and it was his actions that were driving people away. One writer in the early 1900s stated, "Few persons have remained long in the house, although it had been variously occupied."

The reporter admitted to having masqueraded as a spiritualist in order to find out about one young woman's experience in the house. However, he confessed in the article, "with remarkable quickness…the lady divined" his profession, but told him of her experiences anyway. She said that her family lived in the old house for a brief time during the 1880s. She was in her late teens. Her father had heard the gossip about the house, but because of the price; he shrugged it off.

Shortly after they moved in, her father was standing "in the house when a woman dressed in deep mourning passed through the hall and up the stairs." Her father pursued the shadow, but found nothing on either the second or third floors. Later, a maid encountered the same shadow, and afterward refused to return to the house.

The Washington Times recorded the young woman's eyewitness story of her encounter with what she believed was the violent ghost of the vengeful young man. She said the frightening episode occurred on an evening when her mother and father were out of town. Since the ghost had not made known its presence before, I assume that, as is true in most ghost stories, this appearance was on the anniversary of his death. She told the reporter who interviewed her that she suddenly became frozen with fear and a numbness permeated her body. Her vocal cords were paralyzed so that she could not cry out.

She recalled, "I felt myself losing shape!" But as she regained the power of motion, she began running around the room in a desperate battle for what she described as the possession of her own spirit. The strong-willed young woman's youthful mind and body succeeded, but the concentration it took to ward off this cunning and violent supernatural attack drained her. She lapsed into unconsciousness.

Workmen coming for some minor repairs the next morning found her lying in her own blood. She told the reporter that the blood came from a wound "right across the bridge of my nose." The article reported the wound was in the shape of "the figure 7."

After that family moved out of the house there were a few others who thought they could brave the turbulence. A few years later the Red Cross made an effort at using it as an office, but moved within a few weeks with no further explanation. Tales of encounters persisted for more than a quarter of a century. The house was so undesirable that no one would live there. It had been unoccupied for several years when it and several other houses around it were torn down for government expansion. In the years since, with that house gone and the neighborhood totally changed, these old stories about it have vanished, too.

Honeymoon House

In the 1840s a handsome home was built on Capitol Hill as a wedding gift to a young couple. Some newspaper articles referred to it as the Honeymoon House. The couple was joyously looking forward to sharing their love and their lives in that home, but when night descended on their wedding day it brought a terrible cloud that was never lifted from the house. That very night the groom mysteriously vanished.

A story in the *Evening Star* said the young man "was reputed to be wealthy," but no one ever found his riches. They searched his bank box, but it contained only some worthless C & O Canal stock. Some believed that the man had simply deserted his wife, but rumors that he had gone to his farm in Virginia were denied by his relatives, who also expressed concern about him. Several years went by, according the *Star* article and then someone found a body on his farm. Word spread rapidly that it was the body of the missing bridegroom, but a doctor who examined it said it wasn't. The skeleton was a good foot taller. "The mystery lingered," said the *Star* account.

The bride could shed no light on her husband's whereabouts. She could offer no reason for his disappearance, only tears and uncontrollable sobs. A *Washington Post* article reported that she once was "a tall, handsome brunette with flashing dark eyes…possessed of an extraordinary mind. She was equally capable of holding her own through scholarly argument or by quick, biting repartee or veiled sarcasm." After her husband vanished she never really ever recovered. The mere mention of her lover's name would send her into a trance-like daze or trigger more sobbing. She refused to believe he would not return, and for that reason, never left the house.

The bride remained inside her honeymoon prison alone. Reportedly, she spent her days polishing silver and cleaning and caring for the many wedding gifts. Some say she spent her evenings preparing for the wedding night that had been interrupted. The house fell into decay, and eventually the health authorities condemned it and set a date when the house could no longer be occupied. A neighbor offered to help her move. According to that *Washington Post* article, "The solitary old soul glanced silently but lovingly at the dingy walls, the threadbare furniture, the big lumbering piano with its dull mahogany boards and yellow ivory keys…and shaking her head sadly but resolutely, she replied 'This is good enough for me.'"

The now frail and elderly woman quietly reassured her neighbor, "So long as you see the shades on my front window up you will know all's well." Within a few days the neighbor noticed that the shades were drawn. He tried to enter, but the door was barred from the inside. Inside he heard moans and groans. Rushing to the corner he hailed a policeman. It was, however, too late.

The woman lay dying on her parlor floor, blood streaming from under her head. She had evidently been stricken with paralysis and had fallen and hit her head while trying to reach the sofa. There were cuts and gashes on her cheek and brow. The woman had lived alone in that huge house for more than half a century. Is it any wonder that tales of her ghosts returning to the old house made good newspaper copy for the next few decades? Until the house was torn down in the late 1930s there were accounts of "a little old lady with a kerosene lamp" who walked through the hallways. One source who was brave enough to enter described the air as "scented and cold." No one wanted the old house. Its decay was a blight on Capitol Hill so it was removed. Where does the restless ghost of the bride now search for her wandering husband?

The Capitol

Seven years later, when the first section of the new Capitol was completed, Congress moved from its temporary headquarters in Philadelphia to the District of Columbia. Since then the Capitol has undergone seven expansions, which have proliferated its narrow marble halls, winding passageways, dank, dark basements, dimly lighted corridors, and infinite rooms and subbasements. The Capitol building now contains about 16.5 acres of floor space with approximately 540 rooms. Almost from the beginning the building became the object of a multitude of stories—not all of them political in nature.

President George Washington laying the cornerstone for the U.S. Capitol, September 18, 1793. *Courtesy Library of Congress*

George Washington, the first President of the United States, laid the cornerstone of the U.S. Capitol building in 1793, with Masonic ceremonies in the southeast corner of the north section of the building. Sixteen architectural design plans had been submitted, but none had as many good qualities as that drawn up by Dr. William Thornton, a versatile physician from Tortilla, West Indies.

By 1862 the expansion of the U.S. Capitol was nearly complete. The House wing had been occupied in 1857 and the Senate wing a couple years later. It would take another year to complete the massive dome. All that was preserved of the original dome is the interior rotunda. Untimely deaths, high stakes debates, intrigue, and imagination have spawned scores of ghost stories. Perhaps not even the White House is revisited more. It was around the time this photograph was taken that the first encounters with the ghost of a workman killed in a fall from the Rotunda scaffolding occurred. Newspapers have chronicled his appearance many times since. *Courtesy Library of Congress*

Building the U.S. Capitol was no easy task. "Congress House" was begun in 1793, not nearly finished when the British burned it in 1814, and then re-built according to the original plans. Congress, in 1820, began moving in although workmen were still around until 1824 finishing off the interior. The dome was completed in 1827. This is the Capitol as it appeared in 1846. Four years after this daguerreotype was made President Millard Fillmore laid a new cornerstone for House and Senate wings, and a larger dome. *Courtesy Library of Congress*

The Workers Who Never Leave

One of the earliest ghosts reported to roam the Capitol corridors belonged to a stonemason who had somehow been sealed into one of the walls while the building was under construction. It is said that the man has been seen—trowel in hand—passing through a wall in the basement on the Senate side of the building. Some say the mason had the misfortune to lose an argument with a hotheaded carpenter who smashed in his head with a brick and used the man's own trowel to seal his tomb.

When the expanded needs of Congress made major additions to the Capitol necessary, President Millard Fillmore laid a new cornerstone for House and Senate wings on July 4, 1851. The new wings would be marble, not sandstone, as the original building. There would also be a new, larger dome to replace the small copper covered wooden dome.

Down through the years quite a few people have sworn that they have seen the silent specter of a workman who fell from the giant new dome scaffolding to the marble floor of the Rotunda. On the anniversary of his fall, the worker, clad in his faded overalls and carrying his wooden tool kit, retraces his journey through the hallway en route to the Rotunda where he made his last climb.

There is a story told by some of the cleaning crew who used to scrub the marble floors of the mammoth building. One of their colleagues collapsed and died one evening with his scrub brush in his hand. They found his body the next morning slumped over the water pail. Legend has it that when the hour grows late and all but the maintenance staff and guards have gone home, water sloshing from an imaginary pail and the sound of incessant scrubbing is often heard.

The Old Man Eloquent: Eternal Orator

Before the House and Senate wings were added to the Capitol, the House of Representatives chamber was in what is now Statuary Hall. Although the hall is dark at night, and the statues of the states' favorite sons are barely distinguishable, some say they have had little trouble seeing an "illuminated transparency" that closely resembles John Quincy Adams.

A couple of years after his term as the sixth President of the United States (1825-29), Adams ran for Congress because he felt he still had much to contribute to the new country. So did his constituents. They elected the former President to nine terms as their representative in the Congress (1831-48). Among his colleagues in the House Adams was known as "the Old Man Eloquent." He frequently raised his voice in defense of free speech and in opposition to slavery. When a congressional majority created a gag rule that ordered the tabling of all resolutions concerning slavery it outraged Adams. Every year, from 1836 until he finally got the rule rescinded in 1844, he rose to lead the fight against it.

Adams had not been in favor of President James K. Polk's War with Mexico. He was eighty-one years old when he stood up once more, February 21, 1848, to let it be known that now that the Mexican War was over he wanted no part of the Congressional plan to bestow special honors on the generals who had won it for them. Adams never finished his speech about what he considered "a most unrighteous war." He suffered a cerebral stroke, fell unconscious on to the House floor, and had to be carried into the Speaker's office. There he died two days later.

John Quincy Adams suffered a stroke in the middle of a speech on the floor of the House. He was eighty years old. He died in the Capitol two days later. However, Adams seems to have be unable to stop making speeches. It is reported that his ghost revisits the spot where his desk stood, and on certain evenings you can hear "old man eloquent" trying to finish his speech. *Courtesy Library of Congress*

President John Quincy Adams left office in 1829, but his Massachusetts constiuents thought so highly of him they sent him back to Washington as their Representative in Congress for nine terms. Some say his ghost is still there.

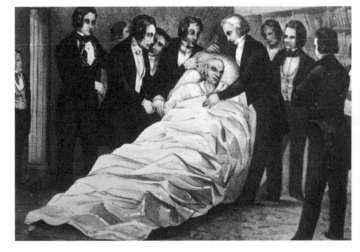

It was only a short time after his death that some of the Capitol workers began telling of colleagues who had seen Adams's ghost revisiting the House chamber. Accounts of eye-witnesses to this occurrence are chronicled in several news-paper articles spanning a century. Those quoted refer to "a figure that appears to be delivering a speech." The place of the encounter is always on the spot where "the Old Man Eloquent" was fatally stricken. For years that spot has been known as the "whisper spot." If one speaks only in a whisper there it can be heard across the room, but those close by cannot hear it. Some old timers claim that too was the work of Old Man Eloquent's ghost—just trying to insure his last speech carried across the room to the opposition.

In the 1890s, several decades after the House chamber had moved into its new wing, an old Capitol guard swore that he stumbled into Statuary Hall late one night only to discover he was once again in the old House chamber and the entire membership was in ghostly assembly. The writer of that news-paper article indicated that the guard might have had a half-pint bottle of liquor in his pocket that night. In spite of ridicule, the old guard stuck to his story. His tale has been told time and again by those who have worked in the Capitol.

It is said that at midnight on New Year's Eve the statues here in Statuary Hall come down off their pedestals and dance with one another to celebrate another year's survival of the Republic. *Courtesy Library of Congress*

This is the original chamber of the House of Representatives—the one in which John Quincy Adams served. When the new House wing was completed in 1857 the Representatives moved over there. It was decided the old chamber would make a great hall for the states to display life sized statues of their heroes. *Courtesy Library of Congress*

Something Ghostly Is Going On In Statuary Hall

In the 1890s, several decades after the House chamber had moved into its new wing, an old Capitol guard swore that he stumbled into Statuary Hall late one night only to discover he was once again in the old House chamber and the entire membership was in ghostly assembly. *Courtesy Lee Shephard*

My favorite tale about Statuary Hall, however, involved another crusty old guard whose name has not been recorded for posterity, but who is remembered, nevertheless, for what he saw. This story dates to a few years after the old chamber was converted to Statuary Hall. It seems that the old fellow began to develop considerable apprehension as various statues were added to the hall. While others around the Capitol expressed fears that the weight of the statues might cause the floor to give way, the old guard was more concerned with the statues themselves. The life-like figures seemed *too* lifelike. He confided to colleagues that he was uncomfortable, uneasy, around them. He didn't like working nights: so many statues, so many shadows.

A few years later it fell on his schedule to work a night shift. It was New Years Eve. As he approached the hall, he was stopped dead in his tracks. In the distance, a clock was striking twelve, and down the corridor in the room washed with soft flickering light; he clearly saw silhouettes float down off pedestals. By his account to a reporter a few days after the incident, "Grant shook hands with Lee."

The guard opened his mouth but could not summon a scream. He was petrified with fear. Where had all the light come from? Or as the newspaper reporter paraphrased the man's question, with some embellishment: "What had illuminated those marble manes?" The reporter said the guard told him that as the reverberation of the clock's last chime died away, he rubbed his eyes, but the vision was still there. Now the figures began to dance. There in Statuary Hall, in the stillness of a New Year's midnight, the guard looked upon a scene like none he had ever witnessed before, or apparently since: statues had come to life and were dancing. Quivering with fright the guard fled the Capitol.

The old man just couldn't keep quiet about what he had seen. The next day, although still trembling and blanched with fear, he told of his nightmare. Well, the story was just too much for the head of the Capitol Police, who prescribed a long, long rest for the guard. In remembrance of the old guard whose imagination brought much pleasure, others inside the Capitol have reported similar experiences. It is said that even today, as guards make their rounds on New Year's Eve they avoid Statuary Hall at midnight. They claim they do so in tribute to their ancient colleague. It sounds good. Would you expect them to say they avoid the area because they secretly wonder if the old man was right, but they're afraid to find out?

The World War I Unknown Soldier lay in state in the Rotunda of the Capitol prior to being placed in the Tomb of the Unknowns at Arlington National Cemetery. In this photograph the casket is being decorated by President Warren G. Harding. A Capitol legend says the unknown "Doughboy" revisits the Rotunda whenever a famous American lies in state there. Witnesses claim that the specter snaps a brisk salute and then vanishes. *Courtesy Library of Congress*

"Fishbait" Miller's Chicken Ghosts

William "Fishbait" Miller was originally from Mississippi, but his adopted home was the U.S. Capitol. Miller served more than half of his life there. When he was still the Doorkeeper of the House of Representatives Miller told me: "Sometimes you sit here and think you hear the funniest things a'going on. You really wonder if you are still here—or what." Among the "queer

noises," with no discernible source, Miller says he has heard are "those infernal clucking sounds."

I couldn't tell whether he was serious, or just trying to lead me down one of those narrow, winding Capitol corridors. His face expressed bewilderment as he spoke of the puzzling sounds that he said he had often heard. His face erupted into a broad grin as he recalled stories that old timers had told him when he was "wet behind the ears, here." There was a time when Congress convened for only a few weeks each year. Some would stay at hotels, others would take rooms in nearby boarding houses, while a few less affluent and more rural representatives might bunk in an out of the way corridor, or office not used at night. Congressmen were not professional politicians. They went back home to their jobs after the session. At least one old congressman of that bygone era used to bring chickens into the Capitol with him. There was also a time during the Civil War that Union troops quartered on the grounds of the Capitol, and some—it is said—ate and slept beneath the unfinished dome. "Wonder," Miller grinned "if those infernal clucking sounds I keep a'hearin' are chicken ghosts?"

Humor is a good tool for dealing with something you don't quite understand, and it was obvious Miller had given the clucking sounds considerable thought and still not resolved in his mind what they might be. He went on to tell me that his most frightening incident came late one night when the House was in session, unable to adjourn because of an important debate. At first, he said, it was a guard who called his attention to some faint noise in the main corridor outside the chambers. As he listened, he said they both looked at each other in amazement. The sounds grew louder. "All sorts of noises. Men yelling. Sounded like a gavel pounding. What all I don't rightly know. I do know that it got so loud that we had to close and bolt the chamber doors to keep the session from being disturbed. They didn't know it inside, but they was locked in!" Miller said the sounds subsided after a while, but apparently were never heard inside the chamber because none of the congressmen, upon adjournment, mentioned them. Miller and the guard just may have heard one of the many loud and ugly verbal corridor confrontations between "Uncle Joe" and "Champ" as they warmed up for a floor fight over how the Speaker should conduct House business.

"Champ vs. Uncle Joe"

The staccato rap of a gavel on the House Speaker's dais is not an uncommon sound when Congress is in session. During the late night hours, however, it can only mean a revisit from Uncle Joe Cannon and Champ Clark. The conjecture is that these former House Speakers keep returning to re-enact their famous confrontation that forever changed the powers of the Speaker of the House.

"Champ" Clark came to the Congress as a progressive during the rule of House Speaker Joseph Cannon. It is Clark's ghost that is said to argue with the ghost of Cannon over just how much power a Speaker of The House of Representatives should have. Their earthly debate over that issue erupted into a powerful partisanship explosion in 1910. When the dust settled, Cannon was ousted. Clark was the new House Speaker. *Courtesy Library of Congress*

Joseph Cannon was a North Carolinian who adopted Illinois as his home state. He became that state's senior Representative in Congress, rising to Speaker of the House in 1903. However, his extreme partisanship and the way he used his power angered many of his colleagues. His ghost is said to still seek out the man who cost him his power and they sometimes meet to engage in ethereal debate. *Courtesy Library of Congress*

Joseph Gurney Cannon, born in North Carolina (1836) and James Beauchamp Clark, born in Kentucky (1850) were both graduates of the Cincinnati Law School. Both men had also moved from their native states—Cannon to Illinois and Clark to Missouri—and it was those states that they represented in Congress. Cannon, a conservative Republican, had already served nineteen years in the House when Clark, a progressive Democrat and former President of Marshall University, was first elected.

When Cannon became Speaker of the House in 1903 he used his thirty years of experience to solidify his power and position. He exercised strong partisan leadership which obviously rankled the Democrats and their minority leader—Champ Clark. As the years passed and the perceived abuses of power accumulated a partisan explosion erupted in 1910. Champ Clark and other progressives in the House engaged in a long, bitter, and often vitriolic fight with Speaker Cannon, but they finally secured enough support to pass an historic resolution greatly reducing the powers of the Office of Speaker of the House of Representatives. The next year, Clark replaced Cannon as House Speaker. Uncle Joe had served eight years. Clark, too, served eight years in that post.

By the late 1920s both men were dead, but by no means forgotten. Guards who have reported seeing the phantoms of the former Speakers revisiting the scene of many of their battles, say they always come at night, and the chamber is always pitch black.

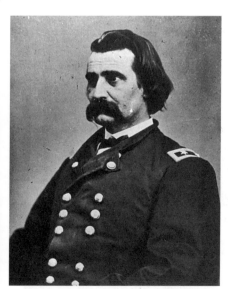

General John Alexander Logan, of Civil War fame, was first and foremost a politician. The Illinois Republican was educated at the University of Louisville, and before his election to Congress in 1859 he had served in the Illinois legislature. When the War between the States came, Logan resigned to fight. He commanded a division at Vicksburg, Mississippi, and when the siege ended, became that city's Military Governor. He led the Army of the Tennessee during the battle of Atlanta. Within two years after the war ended, Logan was back in Congress, and in 1871 was elected to the U.S. Senate. He was a violent partisan, identified with the radical wing of the Republican Party. He was also founder of the organization of Union veterans known as The Grand Army of the Republic.

As the powerful chairman of the Military Affairs Committee, he influenced the policies of the occupying forces in the South during the Reconstruction era. Some say he is still trying to exert his influence. In the years since his death there have been those who have spotted the shade of the vengeful politician eavesdropping outside the old committee room where he wielded most of his power.

A few years after installing air conditioning ducts in the Capitol basement workmen discovered, of all things, a stuffed horse in a room that had been completely sealed off. The Logan legend got another chapter. The old animal bore a strong resemblance to the mount Logan sits astride in the Logan Circle Statue. Someone recalled that when his mount died, the General had it stuffed and displayed for a time inside the Capitol as a reminder of his battlefield exploits. Before long there were folks claiming to have seen his ghost wandering that darkened basement corridor looking for his favorite mount. *Courtesy Library of Congress*

The Garfield Ghost

President James A. Garfield is seen here reading to his daughter. Garfield's ghost has been seen in both the Capitol and the White House. Garfield, it is believed by many, had psychic powers. He confided to a friend that his long dead father revisited him. The day before he was shot he had a premonition that he was about to be killed. *Courtesy White House Collection*

James Abram Garfield came to Congress in 1863 fresh from glory in the Civil War. He was a skilled parliamentarian and negotiator. His work on the House Appropriations Committee helped push him toward the Presidency. A few years after his untimely death, a newspaper reported that the assassinated President had been seen by more than one person silently walking the corridors of the Capitol while his body was lying in state. Garfield, twentieth President of the United States, had only four months in the White House before a disappointed office seeker, Charles J. Guiteau, wounded him at Union Station. The bullet, which entered Garfield's back, eventually killed him, though some specialists today think that if the doctors had left the bullet alone, Garfield probably would have lived. What the doctors could not have known then was that the bullet had lodged in his back muscles only inches from the point of entry. It was harmless, but infection from unsterile medical instruments wasn't. Seventy-nine days after he had been wounded, James Garfield was dead. He left behind a grieving widow and five children.

It was a tragic ending to what had been a long up-hill struggle for this Ohio native who had been born and raised in poverty by his widowed mother. Somehow, by doing just about every kind of frontier work that he could find available, Garfield put himself through college. He was married in 1858 to Lucretia Randolph and a year later elected to the Ohio legislature. When the Civil War came, he found opportunities to develop administrative and leadership skills. Oratory skills that were developed as a lay preacher proved quite valuable when he entered politics. His military record and outspoken position against slavery won him a Congressional seat in 1863. When the 1880 Republican convention became mired in fac-

tional fighting, Garfield emerged as an obvious compromise candidate.

Garfield was a deeply religious man and also quite curious. Darwin's theory of evolution was just emerging in the United States, so he began to study biology and anthropology, in addition to theology. He is said to have possessed certain psychic powers, but to what degree can only be speculation. He did confide to close friends that he had seen and conversed, on several occasions, with the spirit of his father, who died when Garfield was but a child. At least one of these encounters occurred inside the White House while Garfield was President.

President Garfield may have had a premonition of his own death. Two days before he was shot he sent for Robert Lincoln, whom he had appointed Secretary of War, and asked him to recount all his memories of the assassination of his father. Robert Lincoln, who was twenty-two when John Wilkes Booth killed his father, talked for more than an hour that night as the President listened intently.

The day before President Garfield was shot it is said he invited Robert Todd Lincoln into his office. Mr. Lincoln was a member of Garfield's cabinet, but on this day they talked only of the assassination of Robert's father, President Lincoln. Many believe Garfield was seeking answers to a premonition of his own assassination. *Courtesy Library of Congress*

Doctors wrongly believed that if they could only locate and remove the bullet President Garfield could recover from his wound. Even telephone inventor Alexander Graham Bell brought in a special "listening device" in hopes of finding the bullet. He was unsuccessful. Doctors then probed for the bullet. Ironically, had they treated only the wound and left the bullet alone Garfield probably would have recovered. The bullet threatened no vital organs. However, the infection from the probing proved fatal. *The Library of Congress*

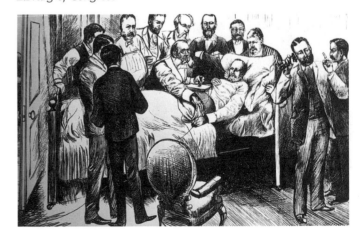

I found no other accounts of Garfield's ghost revisiting the Capitol at any time other than when he lay in state there. I did find an article that quoted a guard as testifying to a reporter that he had seen the assassin Guiteau's ghost on a stairway leading into the basement. The guard said he started to give chase, thinking Guiteau had escaped, but then as he remembered that the execution had taken place the previous week, the figure vanished.

Late at night the sounds of footsteps made by invisible visitors sometimes trail security officers down dimly-lighted corridors like this one.
Courtesy Lee Shephard

The Invisible Guard

Tales are told of elusive footsteps heard in empty Capitol corridors. A skeptical guard was determined to prove that they were simply echoes. Wearing rubber-soled shoes, he set out on his rounds one night determined not to make noise. As he walked, he smiled, and enjoyed the silence. The guard felt an inner sense of accomplishment, thinking how he could boast to his colleagues in the morning of having personally bested one of the Capitol's so-called ghosts.

His smirk was short-lived. The silence was broken by approaching footsteps from the rear. His immediate thought was that a fellow worker was catching up to him and he would be able to share his success. The smile on his lips faded, however, because when he turned around, the hallway was deserted.

The footsteps seemed to move closer, yet the guard saw no one. He tried now to convince himself that someone was playing a joke on him. A good way to prove it would be to corner the footsteps, he thought. So he resumed walking. Entering the next office, he hoped, would cause the culprit to fall into his trap. When he turned to confront the practical joker, no one was there. The only sound to be heard was his own heavy breathing. Then, faintly, from another hallway, he heard ... footsteps. The sound came from the other side of the office wall. How did they get over there? How did the elusive footsteps pass silently through the office wall?

The old guard could never explain it. Many have tried, including some who have had similar experiences. Other guards have said that they too have had "sensations of being followed" and "heard noises." Some describe "sounds like footstep" that sometimes tailed them through the lonely corridors. However, only a few have expressed fear. Most feel that the footsteps are probably those of some ancient Capitol guard who was so dedicated to his job that he still revisits from time to time to walk his appointed rounds.

Whether the stories of "invisible footsteps" inspired a practical joker, or the joker's prank inspired creative imaginations may never be known. However, in the days when stray cats freely roamed the Capitol, a bored guard caught one and tied walnut shells to its' feet. He then tip-toed into a deserted intersection of two corridors where he waited for a colleague on rounds to pass. Giving his co-worker just enough time to get well ahead, the joker released the cat. Staccato echoes of footsteps reverberated down the hallway from the walnut-shell-covered-feet of the cat. The practical joke worked. The other guard, hearing the sound and seeing no one, hastened back to his station, cutting short his rounds. The reporter said he got the story from the practical joker. The victim never said a word to anyone, except his supervisor—and then it was to ask, without explanation, for a transfer to dayshift.

One Less Lawyer

Footsteps roaming the darkened Capitol are but one of the sounds that have been experienced in this historic old building. Moans and groans have been heard. Is it the wind that whips through cracks in the old mortar, or is it a cry from some of the departed souls who wrestled with this nation's problems in life, and have been unable to lay them down in death? It depends on whom you talk to. Some claim that moans heard from the basement beneath the old Supreme Court chamber in the old Senate wing are cries of anguish from a young lawyer who died in a scuffle with a congressman. Back then most members of congress had "real" jobs back home. They spent as little time in Washington as they had too. Since most weren't lawyers, they often consulted with lawyers if complications arose in drafting legislation. Indeed, some say there were congressmen in those days who considered being a lawyer and serving in the legislature a conflict of interest.

The Congress first convened in the new Capitol building, although construction was still going on, in November 1800. The Supreme Court's first session in the new Capitol was the following February. Although Benjamin Latrobe created what some call his crowning achievement, "an umbrella vault ceiling," court members regarded the chamber as a dark musty cavern. It is said Chief Justice John Marshall and the other justices much preferred to meet at a tavern across First Street. The House Chamber wasn't quite ready for occupation until 1807, so members crowded into the Supreme Court section for a while. Then, in March of 1814, along came the British, hell-bent on burning the Capitol and everything else in Washington. They gathered up furniture from rooms adjacent to the High Court chamber, piled it high under the umbrella vault ceiling, and set fire to it.

Latrobe called the Capitol "a magnificent ruin," but was no doubt pleased that the great effort made by the British to destroy the ornate court room had not succeeded. There was considerable smoke damage to the marble, but no structural damage. Some of the columns were cracked from the heat, but not significantly so. The umbrella vault was uninjured. Repairing the damage to the Capitol took some five years. Even after Congress moved back from its temporary headquarters in the Old Brick Capitol, workmen were still trying to finish up. In those days Capitol workmen, senators, representatives, justices, clerks, and secretaries were all trying to make the best of a less than ideal situation. Construction was all around them. Tempers often flared. Fights weren't uncommon. Several congressmen stepped across the District line into Maryland to settle disputes by dueling.

No date has been placed on the argument between the young, unname lawyer and the congressman in what was the old record room of the high court. However, it seems to have been well after Congress re-occupied the Capitol. Legend has it a hot-headed congressman, whose name has also not been remembered, shoved a lawyer against the masonry wall. The lawyer's head split open. The congressman called it an accident, and since no one was around to dispute his word, never faced charges. According to some Capitol Hill storytellers, the moans of the young lawyer continue to reverberate through the ages. His ghost is allegedly eternally locked in that old record room because his slayer was never brought to justice.

This chamber was especially constructed for the Justices of the U.S. Supreme Court, but it is rumored that because it was always so damp and musty they gathered here only for formal opinions, preferring to use a tavern across the street for less formal gatherings. Were they uneasy because the ghost of a lawyer killed during an argument with a congressman haunted the Chamber? *Courtesy Library of Congress*

The Wispy Spy

I'm sure that when this old tale first began to be told around the Capitol there were names connected with it to make it much more interesting. Time has erased the names. We are left with only the titles of those involved and what they experienced.

Legend has it that late one moonless night a Union General whose troops were bivouacked on Capitol Hill in defense of the city saw a shadowy figure sneaking from the Old Brick Capitol prison into the U.S. Capitol. Wondering just what was going on, and fearing the man may be an escaped Confederate espionage agent, the General followed his prey into the building through an unguarded door beneath the Capitol steps. Inside, however, the General lost sight of the man. He seemed to have been swallowed up by the shadows enshrouding the innumerable passageways. So when the General came upon a guard he requested support in his search. Meanwhile, the Union officer remained at the only stairway by which someone could enter or leave that part of the basement. When help arrived, he provided the men with a description of his suspect. A stake out of two days and two nights yielded not a clue. The General relaxed security, but ordered the guards to keep a sharp eye out for anyone matching the intruders' description.

Almost two weeks later a Capitol guard spotted a man matching the description the General had provided. As he rushed toward the suspect with drawn pistol he couldn't help but noticed how pale the man was. The suspect walked trancelike down the east steps of the Capitol, but before the guard could yell halt the figure simply vaporized in the first rays of the morning sun.

These narrow, winding stairs leading to one section of the Capitol basement, are similar to the ones a Civil War General says he watched an escaped spy from the Old Capitol Prison descend. He learned a few days later he had actually tailed a ghost! *Courtesy Lee Shephard*

A Shadowy Serenade

Sometimes, when the hour is late, people have heard the distinctive, resonate voice of Bishop Simms drifting melodically from the Senate barbershop, where he was employed. Simms often worked late putting things in order for the next day. Often he would sing as he worked.

James Ketchum, curator for the U.S. Senate, says that "Bishop" was a nickname, because Simms was "a man of the cloth on occasion." Ketchum adds that little is known of the

Bishop's personal life, including his politics or his church affiliation. Bishop Simms singing had a soothing effect on those who listened; and according to Ketchum, Simms often would break into song during the day, too. Most found it a refreshing change from the talk of politics that usually dominated the Senate barbershop. However, there is one thing that has bothered some of those who have recently heard Mr. Simms in song—he has been dead a goodly number of years.

Ghost of the Gallery Stairs

The Capitol isn't without tales of bloodshed. More than one congressman or senator has physically attacked a colleague. Senator Charles Sumner was so severely beaten by a fellow senator that he almost died. He lived the rest of his life in considerable pain from that crippling injury. Several lawmakers settled their differences by dueling just across the District line. Lawmakers' quarrels weren't restricted to each other; they sometimes involved angry constituents, lobbyists, or reporters.

In the winter of 1890, former congressman-turned minister William Taulbee returned to the Capitol for a visit after an absence of several years. He ran into newspaper reporter Charles Kincade on the stairs leading up to the House Press Gallery. Some say they argued about some articles Kincade had written about Taulbee. The debate grew quite heated and the temperamental Kincade pulled his pistol and shot Taulbee. The former congressman was rushed to Providence Hospital where he clung tenaciously to life for almost two weeks before succumbing to the wounds. Taulbee's life was cut short at age thirty-nine.

There are those who deny the spots on the marble stairs leading up to the House of Representatives Press Gallery are the stains from Taulbee's spilled blood. But some of the older guards and workers just smile. No cleaning agent has been able to remove those stains. Besides, some say they have seen the ghost of the former congressman haunting that very spot. They believe that every time a reporter appears to stumble on those well-worn steps that, in fact, they have just been tripped by Taulbee's ghost who loves to show his eternal contempt and distaste for journalists.

This is the flight of stairs leading up to the Congressional Press Gallery. It is here the ghost of former Congressman William Taulbee is said to enjoy tripping reporters. *Courtesy Lee Shephard*

Revisiting the Tubs

Henry Wilson, a native of New Hampshire, had risen from a lowly indentured servant as a farm boy to the second highest office in the land in manhood. After a distinguished career in the Senate he became Vice President in the Grant Administration. Since the Vice President's office is in the Senate wing Wilson could continue a form of relaxation that he and several other senators regularly enjoyed: tubbing. Few people know it, but at one time in the lower Senate wing there were several hand-carved marble tubs, imported from Italy, for the convenience of senators. Tubbing was a popular pastime. Vice President Wilson, however, apparently caught a congestive chill on one of his tubbing ventures. It proved to be the death of him. That was in November of 1875, but the story only begins then.

Legend has it that these stains on the stairs to the House press gallery are from the blood of former Congressman William Taulbee, who was killed here by a reporter. *Courtesy Lee Shephard*

Henry Wilson, who was Vice President during the Grant Administration, loved to "tub" in the Senate basement. He did so regularly until he caught a congestive chill and died. Some say his ghost carries on that tradition. *Courtesy Library of Congress*

Boise Penrose Catches Up

Republican boss Boise Penrose loved his Senate office. During the 1920s he often worked late at night, reading and researching his subject matter for the next day's debates. Penrose had no one close to him except his office staff, and he preferred the Capitol to his hotel home.

Some say that even now the Penrose ghost returns to the Senator's old office and sits in his favorite swivel chair during the late evening hours catching up on the *Congressional Record*.

This is one of the last of the imported hand carved Italian marble tubs in the Capitol basement. Senators had several installed for their pleasure in the mid-1800s. Indoor bathing with hot and cold running water was a luxury that was not yet available in the White House, although John Peter Van Ness had it in his palatial mansion. Senators called the event "tubbing," and those who indulged in it regularly were known as "tubbers." *Courtesy Lee Shephard*

The catafalque storage area in the Capitol basement is said to be the home of the dreaded Demon Cat, which makes a chilling appearance just before a national tragedy or the changing of an administration. *Courtesy Lee Shephard*

It wasn't too many years later that people who were concerned with guarding the Senate side of the Capitol began to relate how they had seen a diaphanous Vice President Wilson returning from tubbing. They claim also to have heard the Vice President coughing and sneezing.

Several times since Wilson's death, mysterious sneezes have been heard in the corridor leading to the Vice President's office. The unusual thing about it is that no one is ever there. There is just a damp chill in the doorway, and the faint scent of the old soap they used to provide for the senators' use in the basement tubs.

Should you be walking by the office of the Vice President on a Capitol tour and hear a sneeze, but see no one reacting, simply go on walking. The shade of Vice President Henry Wilson may have just joined your tour.

This is the entrance to the office of the Vice President, who presides over the Senate. It was Henry Wilson's office at the time he died. Some say that they have heard his ghost sneezing and coughing in this corridor and a few report they've been enveloped in a damp, "soapy smelling" chill. *Courtesy Lee Shephard*

The area where the catafaulk is stored was originally intended to be the tomb of our nation's first President, George Washington, who laid the cornerstone of the Captiol in 1793. However, when Washington died of pneumonia in December 1799 at age 67, the Capitol was not fully completed. It was also his wish that his final resting place be at his beloved Mount Vernon. *Courtesy White House Collection*

The Continental Soldier Pays His Respects

The lower level of the Capitol, where George Washington declined to be entombed, is the haunting ground of at least two famous apparitions. The empty tomb, beneath the crypt area of the Capitol, is used to store the catafalque on which the nation's great lie in state.

It is said that on certain days, at midnight and occasionally at noon, the locked door noiselessly swings open. Wind stirs the air and a cold spot envelops whoever might be watching as a "fine-looking gentleman in Continental uniform" passes slowly around the bier, through the dark passage, and out the door, which silently closes behind him.

The Dreaded Demon Cat

Perhaps the most infamous apparition in the Capitol isn't that of a man at all, but that of the dreaded Demon Cat—sometimes flippantly referred to as "DC" by those who have yet to learn the Demon Cat is not to be taken lightly. The cat is said to make its home in the catafalque storage area, also.

During the early days of the Capitol the lawmakers, their staff, and workmen would bring their food into the building with them. One might find anything from live chickens to old ham hocks in an office. Bread crusts, apple cores, and other residue wasn't always cleaned up quickly. There developed a severe rat problem. So to combat the rats cats were kept at the Capitol as mousers. As the rat population dwindled, the need for the cats also decreased. Some of them were taken home as household pets and many wandered off into the neighborhoods. Over the years the Capitol cat population dwindled to nothing, except for one highly unusual cat who has stayed.

For well over a hundred years now this phantom feline has roamed the darkened corridors of the U.S. Capitol—carefully choosing just when to appear and just whom to harass. The Demon Cat, as it is unaffectionately called, waits until the victim is alone and the hour is late. Some members of the nighttime protection service shudder at the thought of encountering "DC." They have heard the tales and some have known the victims.

Just seeing a black cat walking toward them is enough to startle many, but an encounter with the Demon Cat is a truly traumatizing experience. One January, not too long ago, a victim retold his encounter. As he walked down a chilly, darkened hallway, he saw a shadowy cat walking silently toward him. It looked as though the creature was swelling. The guard rubbed his eyes. It *was* swelling. He felt paralyzed as he stared into the glowing, piercing eyes that came closer and closer and grew larger and larger. The animal swelled to the size of a giant tiger, yet never lost its unmistakable catlike form. Its purring changed to a ferocious snarl. There was a deafening roar as the monstrous animal leaped—with claws extended—toward its victim. The guard couldn't move. His feet seemed nailed to the floor. He covered his face with his arms as the giant animal seemed just inches away from landing on him. He screamed.

Nothing happened. The Demon Cat vanished into thin air as the man screamed.

The trembling guard stood alone; the corridor deserted; the silence pierced only by his breathing. His limp body was covered in a cold, clammy sweat. He felt drained. The narrow marble hallway now reminded him of a tomb. The guard shud-

dered, tried to pull himself together, and headed back to his desk. For some reason he just didn't feel like finishing his rounds.

Down through the years there have been varied reactions from those who have encountered the phantom cat. Some have fainted. Some have run screaming from the building; others, like the guard, became paralyzed with fear. Years ago, they tell me, old DC's appearance just may have been what brought on one elderly guard's fatal heart attack.

The Demon Cat isn't one of the Capitol's most frequent visitors, but what it lacks in frequency it makes up for in accuracy as a portent. This most famous of all of the Capitol's legendary apparitions always appears just before a national tragedy or on the eve of the changing of an administration. Some cynical veterans of Capitol Hill argue that it is sometimes difficult to tell one of these events from the other, but make no mistake: senators, representatives, staff works, maintenance personnel, and protection staff all walk the Capitol halls in fear of encountering the dreaded Demon Cat—for they are convinced such a meeting is a warning of unpleasant events to come.

Pierre L'Enfant's Sorrowful Vigil

Whenever modifications in the plan of Washington are being discussed within the walls of Congress, French engineer Pierre Charles L'Enfant—or should I say his ghost—is generally at the center of the discussion. A friend of the Marquis de Lafayette, L'Enfant came over during the Revolution. Afterwards, he conceived a grandiose plan for the Federal City in which he envisioned streets one hundred feet wide, and one avenue four hundred feet wide and a mile long. Many of those who looked over the Potomac pastureland and marshes, thought L'Enfant's plan was foolhardy. Nevertheless, President George Washington liked it, and with his endorsement the city began to take shape. There were delays, though, and L'Enfant was not as patient as the politicians.

It wasn't long before his lack of tact and diplomacy got him into difficulties, including confrontations with Congress. He was taken off the job and others completed his work. He died disillusioned with his adopted country, and so impoverished that he had to be buried in a pauper's grave on Digges Farm because Congress still hadn't paid him for his work.

It is said that some have encountered the shadowy figure of a small man, rather seedy in appearance, with a roll of parchment under his arm roaming the musty subterranean rooms of the Capitol. Often he is found pacing and shaking his head. Could it be that L'Enfant still walks the Capitol halls waiting for reparation, and determined to tell Congress how badly they treated him?

The shadowy apparition of Pierre Charles L'Enfant has been seen more than once pacing the corridors of the Capitol, where he still waits to be paid for his part in planning the Federal City. *Courtesy Library of Congress*

This map is based upon a 1798 Plan for the City of Washington as envisioned by Pierre L'Enfant. *Courtesy Martin Luther King, Jr. Public Library, District of Columbia*

The Legendary Library

There was a time when the Library of Congress occupied a portion of the Capitol building. Its early years were marred by the burning of the Capitol by the British in 1814. A few years after the Capitol was rebuilt, the Library became the recipient of a major endowment; albeit the circumstances were unfortunate. An elderly Thomas Jefferson, deeply in debt, was forced to sell his personal library to the Government. It became the heart, some might say the very essence, of the Library of Congress. Jefferson, who devoted the last decade of his life to founding the University of Virginia, had been this country's 3rd President, its 2nd Vice President, and 1st Secretary of State. And he was the principal author of The Declaration of Independence. By purchasing his library a grateful Government enabled this proud patriot to pay off his debts and to die in peace.

In 1851 another fire swept through the Library. Unfortunately, almost half the volumes were destroyed. Damage was repaired and the Library continued to grow and expand. In 1897 when its Capitol home became too small, The Library of Congress moved into an ornate Italian Renaissance structure across the street. However, tales are still told about some of the strange things that continue to occur inside that section of the Capitol which once housed the Congressional Library.

Eternal Dedication: Of the many people who worked for the Library during the years it served only members of Congress, perhaps the most dedicated was a little man who has been remembered only as "Mr. Twine." His sole task was to stamp due dates on the book cards as volumes were loaned to members of Congress.

Because some congressmen came early and some left late, Mr. Twine felt it his responsibility to be at his post from daylight to well past dark. He never grumbled and he seldom missed a workday because of illness. So diligently and tirelessly did he perform his repetitive task that it is said he's still at it. When that section of the Capitol where the old Library was once housed is quiet, if you listen carefully you can still hear the reverberation of the double-click of Twine's stamp. His ghost remains on the job in the corner of the corridor where his desk stood—eternally stamping book cards.

The Librarian's Lost Cache: Years later there was a librarian who became more prominently known after death than he was in life. In life he had been rather miserly, according to his associates. He had no friends, and some say he wasn't especially close to his family. His first love was money. Most of those who worked under him at the Library had heard that he did not trust Washington's banks, but no one knew where he hid his money.

As librarian, the old man had the advantage of knowing which books were not being used. He stashed his wealth in these forgotten volumes. One day he suffered a stroke and died without ever being able to tell members of his family about his cache.

It wasn't until a few years later, when the Library was being moved across the street, that his hiding places were discovered. Workers are said to have found nearly six thousand dollars in various old volumes (that was at least a couple years' pay back then).

Stories still circulate around the Capitol that the ghost of the old librarian comes back to the area just to the west of the Rotunda where the Library was once located. They say his spirit searches for those long-removed shelves and the dusty books in which he hid his savings. Some have sworn that they have heard invisible fingers frantically turning through invisible pages, as though the old man is condemned by his love of money to search in vain throughout eternity.

Long ago a miserly librarian stashed his savings in some of the dusty volumes that were on the shelves of the Library of Congress when it was in the Capitol. Even after the library moved to its own quarters across the street, his spirit continued to return to the library's former site to search for his lost money. *Courtesy Library of Congress*

The Curse On The Capitol

For years there have been debates over the so-called infirmities of the Capitol. Some argue that the building is sinking on less than firm foundations; others that the walls are crumbling. The Capitol has undergone many face-lifts since the day Dr. William Thornton designed it. The only part of the original building that can be seen from the outside is the West front. During the last third of the twentieth century quite visible, too, were the supports that held up the sandstone walls. In the 1980s architects made repairs that they insist have made the walls secure. But for how long?

There are those around Washington who sincerely believe there may be more to the Capitol infirmities than meets the eye. They recall how back in September of 1808, architect Benjamin Latrobe and his construction superintendent John Lenthall argued over the necessity of a particular arch for support. Lenthall contended that it was not only unnecessary, but unsightly. Latrobe felt otherwise. He told Lenthall that the support was designed to prevent stress and a possible collapse of the structure.

The headstrong Lenthall was determined to prove his point. In spite of Latrobe's warning, he pulled out the support. John Lenthall was crushed to death by falling debris, and quite a few Washingtonians believe that his dying words were a curse on the U.S. Capitol.

Beams supported the west front of the Capitol and relieved the strain on some of its crumbling columns for several years. In the late 1980s some new techniques were tried at preservation, and the beams removed. Believers in the John Lenthal curse are skeptical, and fear the worst for the west front. *Courtesy Lee Shephard*

Of Soldiers and Shadows

The Return of the Marine Commandant

The building on the right is the Marine Commandant's home, which is revisited periodically by the spirit of the Corps's first Commander. *Courtesy Columbia Historical Society*

The military quarters of the Federal City are not without their apparitions and ghosts. The Marines, for instance, have some tales that have been passed on through the years. The old Marine Corps Barracks and Parade Grounds have been standing for nearly two hundred years on 8th Street, between G and I Streets, in Southeast Washington.

The Marine Corps commandant's home is exactly what one would expect the quarters of a high military official to look like. The furnishings are sparse and functional, relieved only by mementos of the Corps's long history and by portraits of former commandants. It seems strange that unexplainable events could take place in so regimented a setting. But they do, and some have even occasioned newspaper stories.

Sounds of "rustling papers" fill the house in the darkness of night. Sometimes "the measured pacing of a man, deep in thought" is said to be heard. The shade of a former commandant in the full dress uniform of the Corps's early years has been seen in various rooms.

One reporter of the early 1900s speculated that it is the spirit of the Corps's first commandant, Captain Samuel Nicholas, though no one has ever been able to get close enough to distinguish the features of this ghost. Legend has it that Captain Nicholas periodically returns to survey the home, and perhaps to learn what new glories have been celebrated by the fighting body he once led.

The Faithful Navy Commandant

Call it interservice rivalry if you will, but the Navy's original commandant occasionally surveys his old home grounds, too. Captain Thomas Tingey supervised the building of the Washington Navy Yard from his home, Quarters A. It was also Captain Tingey who personally set fire to the yard in 1814 to keep it from falling into the hands of the advancing British troops; and it was the same Captain Tingey who directed the Navy Yard's reconstruction after the War of 1812.

For some twenty-four years Captain Thomas Tingey lived in the rambling mansion that had been built by Benjamin Latrobe. He and his wife had become quite reluctant to part from it—even in death. Old newspaper articles say that Captain Tingey willed the home to his wife, but the government had other ideas. The Navy fought and won the right to retain possession of the property.

Apparently that bitter battle in the courts didn't sit too well with the ghost of Captain Tingey. The ghost of the harassed commandant has been seen regularly down through the years—looking out from the upper windows of the mansion—surveying the Navy Yard he helped to build, and defying the Navy to evict him. Some say he holds no malice for his successors, and a few of his successors swear he has provided them with inspiration. Captain Thomas Tingey just doesn't seem to want to leave his post.

Quarters A, built for Commandant Tingey, still stands in Southeast Washington and is still revisited by Tingey's ghost. *Courtesy Martin Luther King, Jr. Public Library, District of Columbia*

Old Howard

There is a less famous old leatherneck who is said to revisit the frame house in which he once lived at the rear of the Marine garrison. "Old Howard," as he was referred to in newspaper accounts, lived more than a hundred years ago in a two-story home with his wife and family near 9th and G Streets, Southeast.

Being a Marine was all Howard knew. He joined the Corps as a youth and adopted it as his parents. He spent his time trying to measure up to its tradition as he saw it. However, Howard's life in the service wasn't easy. Howard, you might say, wore his skin too tight. He was argumentative, with a short fuse and a quick, violent release. In other words, Howard had a reputation for being a fighter. Breaking rules and regulations had lost him his sergeant's stripes more than once. His life at home wasn't easy either. He didn't get along with his wife and children any better than he got along with his fellow Marines. An *Evening Star* reporter said in 1871 that he "finally died blaspheming his Maker, and cursing his wife and children."

Legend has it that when "fearfully wicked" Howard died; his ghost dedicated itself to trying to uphold the man's mortal reputation. Over the years there have been several tales, chronicled in newspapers, about the pranks of a poltergeist that certainly sounds like Howard.

From the outset Howard's ghost showed no one mercy. His wife and children couldn't stand to remain in the house. Life was more miserable with him gone; when he was alive they could at least see him when he was around. They sold the house, probably quite cheaply. Over the next several decades the house changed occupants and ownership frequently.

Howard's ghost loved the element of surprise. He would rap loudly when a person least expected it. That was only for openers. The old cuss would shake doors in the middle of the night just so he could watch groggy people stumble across the blackness from the bed to the door. Then he would laugh wildly at their expression when they discovered no one was there. A blind door connecting with the next house, and which had been securely fastened for years, was on several occasions found wide open. No one could account for it. When a family would move upstairs for bed, old Howard would stomp around and make noises downstairs. When the family was downstairs he would thump and knock upstairs. It was enough to rattle anyone's brain.

A few days after another new family moved into the house, Howard decided to have some fun with the couple's older daughter. Even the apparel most young women of the early 1900s wore to bed couldn't hide a shapely body. Never having been accused by any of his brawling buddies of being a prude; Howard sprang into action. As the young lady turned off the gaslight and pulled up the covers, he pulled the covers back and began to pant and sigh. The young woman was so frightened she thought she screamed several times before her shaking hand could re-light the gas. Shivering and sobbing with terror, she cautiously surveyed every shadow in her shimmering room. Her hands tightly clutched the retrieved covers at her neck. The writer said that the family moved within a few days.

On another occasion, a young servant girl living with a family had been up rather late. The family had preceded her to bed. She climbed the stairs to her upper floor bedroom, and after preparing herself for sleep, climbed into bed. Before she dozed off she heard steps softly ascending the stairs and saw the reflection of what was apparently a lighted lamp. Thinking it was a member of the family, she tried to go to sleep. Just then she heard a heavy groan at the door, which was ajar, and as she raised up she saw the ghost of Old Howard. She told a reporter that the ghost immediately extinguished his lamp, but that blue and red streaks of light shot throughout her room. With a single bound she was out of bed screaming and fled the house in her night clothes—the family following.

Old Howard's bawdy ghost seemed unable to resist bedroom pranks. He allegedly pulled a bed with a man and his wife on it, as they lay embracing not sleeping, out into the center of their bedroom. Shock wasn't enough; Howard wanted embarrassment too, so he flung open the shutters on the bedroom window. He made loud moaning sounds. The poor couple was so upset it was easier for them to move than to face their neighbor. He had been sitting on his porch that evening and old Howard had seen to it there was enough light for his entertainment. "The neighborhood is greatly excited over the strange manifestations," declared one reporter.

In recent times, the pranks of the pesky poltergeist have gone unreported. Did "fearfully wicked" Howard mellow? Did his ghost move on? I guess we'll never know.

The Kalorama Legacy

Joel Barlow, born in Connecticut in 1754, was an accomplished New England poet and man of letters when he was first called to serve his country by President George Washington. Barlow became one of a group of young diplomats whose tireless efforts and statesmanship helped to make a young nation strong. During the last years of Washington's Administration, the dreaded Barbary Pirates were terrorizing the ships of all nation's who dared sail the Mediterranean. Many governments paid these terrorists in order to carry on their maritime trade. Not so America. So, when the Barbary Pirates captured one hundred American seamen and tossed them into dungeons in Algiers, it was Barlow who helped to negotiate their release in 1796. He continued to serve within the State Department under Presidents Adams, Jefferson, and Madison.

Although the poet/statesman spent much of his time abroad, Barlow decided to build a home in Washington in 1807. He chose the rolling countryside in northwest, just above Rock Creek—where legend has it Robert Fulton tested some of his boats. On land that is now in the 2300 block of S Street NW Barlow built Kalorama, which means "beautiful view" in Greek. He lived to see his manor completed and rested there frequently in between his diplomatic missions. In 1809 his most famous poem, *The Columbiad*, much of it written at Kalorama, was published.

Barlow's life ended tragically in Poland as he attempted to negotiate with Napoleon who was beating a disastrous retreat from Moscow in the winter of 1812. His comrades in the State Department, and indeed most of Washington, mourned his passing. When Kalorama was put up for sale, General John Bomford acquired it. Bomford was a close friend of Stephen Decatur and his wife, Susan. They were frequent guests in each others' homes. However, when the Commodore's wife was unexpectedly cut short in a duel, his grief stricken widow had no place to bury him. Bomford stepped forth to suggest that his friend be buried in the Kalorama tomb. Susan, quite devastated by the loss of her husband, agreed. She attempted to go on with her life at their Lafayette Square home, but her despair became so deep that Bomford worried for her health. She became a guest of the Bomfords at Kalorama for quite some time. Apparently she was very ill at ease at the home she had once shared with her husband on the President's Square. Staying at the Bomfords enabled her to remain close to her husband, although separated by death.

There is a legend that Decatur's spirit was unhappy at Kalorama and blood from his wound would appear periodically on the outside of the tomb. Some say that is why Susan eventually ordered the body removed to Philadelphia where his parents were buried. She then moved to a house in the 2800 block of N Street NW and lived the rest of her life as a recluse.

During the Civil War, the District of Columbia was virtually surrounded. To keep Maryland from joining her sister state, Virginia, in secession, President Lincoln ordered the military to arrest the Maryland legislature. There were several battles fought in what are now the Washington suburbs, and quite a few of the larger homes near these battlefields became hospitals. The Kalorama manor house was among them. Hundreds of wounded and dying soldiers were cared for on the grounds of the mansion, and the first tales of supernatural events associated with the estate began to be told right after this period.

The war had ended April 5, 1865, but there were many soldiers still recovering from their wounds and unable to return to their homes and celebrate this special Christmas with their families. So, on Christmas eve, 1865, there was a party at Kalorama Hospital. It was a festive affair, but for many of the recovering soldiers it would be their last.

Reporters later quoted fire officials who said that a defective stovepipe turned the evening into a nightmare. The fire spread through the entire east wing of the mansion before it was brought under control. By dawn looters had replaced firefighters and rescuers but they were dispersed by troops who were called in. The old manor house/hospital was severely damaged. Wounded soldiers who had survived were moved elsewhere. Within months tales began to rise from the ruins. People began taking a different path in order to avoid "sinister shadows." One article I read said that the old home never lost the damp and musty odor it acquired after the fire. Cries of anguish are said to have shattered the calmness of many a night on that hillside above Rock Creek.

Some of the visitors to the old hospital ruins have told reporters of hearing the "rustling of silks and satins" from an earlier and happier period of the house's history. Others swore to having seen the shapes of "handsome men and elegant ladies" adorning the halls and rooms that were lighted only by the moon shining through the burned-out roof.

But by far the more prominent phenomena of Kalorama have been moans, groans, and sobs. The *Evening Star*, in June of 1905, devoted considerable attention to the sounds of Kalorama. "The few people who lived in the vacinity were seized with cold tremors when they heard the howls and screeches that came from within the walls." The reporter described these sounds as "enough to freeze the marrow in one's bones."

Occasionally, a visitor to old Kalorama would report a "chill-of-the-spine" accompanied by "goosebumps on the flesh" as he entered one of the many cold spots in the old house. Indeed, several area residents, who often braved the early evening darkness to stroll over the remains of the Kalorama estate, said that they encountered what appeared to be "moving" or "roaming" cold spots. Some of these were described as carrying with them the stench of morphine, blood, sweat, and gunpowder.

Washington's burgeoning population quickly encroached on the Kalorama estate. The grounds became smaller and smaller as the city's quarter of a million people pushed outward. As the twentieth century began, almost all traces of that earlier Washington era were wiped away. We said "almost all traces." From time to time there are still residents and visitors to these historic grounds who encounter a cold spot permeated with a sickly smell. Several of these incidents have been reported in a variety of locations on what used to be the Kalorama estate. Enough for more than one person to wonder if a few former Kalorama patients don't revisit the old hospital from time to time.

A Most Murderous Host

Although Washington itself was spared the battles of the Civil War, there was much fighting in the suburbs. It was there during this period that a bizarre tale of the supernatural had its origin.

Three unsuspecting soldiers were given sanctuary from the enemy and shelter from the elements in an old house just across the District line in Maryland. They had become separated from their group during a skirmish and decided not to try to find it again until morning. Morning never came for these three soldiers.

Their host was of a different political persuasion. The welcome they had received was simply a trap. He bludgeoned all three to death as they slept soundly on the floor by the fire. The host had an easy enough time disposing of the bodies, but removing the crimson stain on the floor proved impossible. The three soldiers were written off as missing. The host placed a rug over the reminder of his deeds.

Whether the murderer died or moved away isn't known, but there were a series of owners down through the next few decades. Although none of them knew for certain what the dark stains on the floor in front of the fireplace were, there is no denying that the strange things that occurred in that room may have led them to suspect the worst—particularly when it was discovered even paint would not permanently cover the stains.

If we accept one reporters account there was another peculiarity of the room: the large oak door to the hallway would never stay closed. As soon as you bolted it and turned away, the creaking of the bolt-action lock and the squeaking of the hinge sent a terrifying message. It wasn't necessary to turn around to know that the door was open again.

According to the story, the three soldiers have continued to keep watch in that room. Perhaps they are trying to atone for their careless mistake of not alternating as lookouts, of not bolting the large oak door, of trusting, in time of war, someone they did not know.

Some think a supernatural occurrence in that house caused the death of one owner. A yellowed newspaper report from the 1920s said that the man was seated in the bedroom where all the mysterious occurrences originated when suddenly the French doors onto the balcony were ripped from their hinges and flung to the ground. They did not break. Neighbors were quoted as saying that the man went into a state of shock from which he never recovered. What else he may have seen or heard was never revealed, for within a few days he died.

One version of this story has it that curious neighbors got to checking the background of the house after hearing the legend. They are supposed to have learned that their recently departed neighbor had the misfortune to have the same last name as the murderous host who had lived in the home during the Civil War. Finding people willing to live in the old house became more difficult. It fell into a state of disrepair, and not too many years ago those owning the property decided the house must be torn down.

Ghosts of the National Building Museum

Although the Old Post Office building, with its bell tower, looms large in the foreground, "Meigs Old Red Barn" is strikingly visible several blocks away. It may be the National Building Museum, now, but its history as the Civil War Pension Building is what gave rise to tales of ghostly horror. *Courtesy National Archives*

The National Building Museum, between F and G and 4th and 5th Streets, Northwest was built in 1885 as the Pension Building. It was a dream of U.S. Quartermaster General Montgomery C. Meigs who had envisioned a place where Union veterans of the Civil War, their widows, and their children could come and have their pensions administered. To most Washingtonians of that period Meigs dream building more resembled a nightmare. They most often referred to it as "Meigs Old Red Barn." At the time it was dedicated the building was described by one newspaper as "the largest brick building in the world."

It is built on the bloodstained ground where the wounded and dying from the Battle of Bull Run were brought, and where the District of Columbia jail stood before it gave way to an asylum for the insane. Is it any wonder that the stories enshrouding it make one's hair stand on end?

Tales of supernatural events and spectral encounters have led to speculation that more than one ghost may revisit Meigs

Old Red Barn. Indeed, a couple of decades ago at least one person who was working on building restoration was committed to a mental institution because he believed he had met up with something not of this world.

Montgomery Meigs fancied himself an architect, although many Washingtonians of that day thought him to be more of an eccentric. One newspaper account compared his design of the Pension Building with the famous Farnese Palace in Rome, and said it was Meigs' strong will rather than good sense that prevailed when the final plans for the building were approved.

One of the few areas in which the General had to compromise was the material for the huge interior Corinthian columns. He wanted to import solid onyx, but the government wouldn't pay the bill. Meigs had to settle for simulated onyx, but only after a worldwide search for a craftsman uncovered a Canadian so talented that few professionals could tell his onyx wasn't the real thing.

Another feature of these monumental columns is their hollow interiors, which Meigs is supposed to have used as an archive. He is reported to have collected secret government documents, letters of state, artifacts of all sorts, along with other momentos of the period, and personally salted them away in one or more of the columns. No one really knows what might be concealed in any of them, or in the various nooks and crannies of the building.

Soon after the mammoth structure was completed, President Grover Cleveland staged his inaugural ball there. Washington papers were filled with stories—among them several about the guest list, which included such notables as General William T. Sherman, Buffalo Bill Cody, and Frederick Douglass. One local newspaper article boasted that the Pension Building was "looked upon as one of the attractions of Washington." Critics called it an "unsightly monstrosity" and loved to repeat the remark made by General Philip Sheridan during a tour of the building. When the guide proudly stated that the fifteen-million-brick structure was fireproof, Sheridan exclaimed, "What a pity."

When Grover Cleveland was elected 22nd President in 1885 he staged his inaugural ball in the newly opened "largest brick building in the world." Over the years there were many gala events in the Great Hall of the Pension Building. *Courtesy Library of Congress*

It was in 1917 that strange happenings were first reported in the Pension Building. One night an old guard sat at his desk and stared in disbelief at one of the huge columns as the simulated onyx began to change its configuration. By the light of his gas lamp, the guard saw the veins slowly shift to form the outline of an Indian, and farther down—a buffalo head! Although he was considerably unnerved, the old man talked himself out of running away. He convinced himself that he had dreamed the whole thing.

By the light of the morning sun, he carefully examined the column. The strange profiles that had been created before his eyes were still there. It was about this time that his relief showed up with the morning paper. There on the first page was a story about the death of Buffalo Bill Cody. Cody had been the center of attention at the first presidential inaugural ball staged in the great hall of the Pension Building. He had died the previous evening.

As time passed some rather strange reports began to circulate about the Pension Building. They seemed to have begun the night "Buffalo Bill" Cody died bankrupt in Denver at the age of 70. He had headlined the guest list at President Cleveland's inaugural ball, thirty-two years before. It had been the first major event in the Pension Building. *Courtesy Library of Congress*

A few months later someone noticed on another of the columns the outline of a skull. Several smaller skulls were also discovered in the imitation marble, but none was like the one referred to in newspaper accounts as the "malevolent, grinning skull." It appeared a short time after the buffalo head incident, and some old guards said it seemed to follow them wherever they went in the great hall.

As the years went by and more and more people visited the great hall, whispers began to develop about other strange swirls that appeared in the columns. A newspaper article in the 1920s said that there were some Pension Building workers who insisted they saw formations resembling the profiles of George and Martha Washington. It also said that anyone reporting such configurations was scoffed at by fellow workers. However, the frequency with which new—and changing patterns—were being noticed in the columns continued to attract attention. Newspapers devoted pages, complete with photographs, to the unfolding drama.

These changing patterns in the columns, along with some startling encounters with shadowy forms, made for short tenure among those who were assigned to watch the building at night. When the District of Columbia altered the building for use by the courts, in the 1970s, the planners—perhaps encouraged by acute personnel problems—covered over the simulated onyx that General Meigs had loved so much. Even though the anomalous profiles are a thing of the past, the renovation has had little effect on the ghosts that come calling from time to time.

It was during that renovation in the 1970s that a night watchman took a prescribed leave of absence to recuperate from an encounter with an ill-tempered man on horseback. Old-timers told me there was a period when one of the upper floors was used to quarter horses. It was there that the guard encountered a rider in military uniform who spurred his transparent mount down the corridor toward the wide stairway. The horse almost rode down the night watchman who fled the building in panic.

I first learned of the watchman's experience from an attorney who practices law in the District of Columbia Superior Court, which at the time was quartered in the old Pension Building. He said he had discussed it with the chief judge and several other lawyers—all of whom expressed concern. Some of the men who were involved in renovating the building at the time were also anxious. They had heard stories about the changing column patterns and about other visits by a horseman. A few who had known the watchman, openly admitted that they would never again enter the place at night—job or no job.

Some believe that General Meigs's ghost is the ill-tempered rider on horseback who comes to the old building, particularly during periods of renovation. They seem to think that a man of such strong will would certainly possess a spirit capable of watching over his cathedral to insure its preservation.

The transparent rider on horseback has not been the only ghost encountered in the old Pension Building. Late one summer night in 1972 one of the security personnel was reading a newspaper behind the information desk on the ground level when he noticed a man in a light colored suit with a peculiar walk moving quietly toward the stairway. Some of his fellow workers told a lawyer that the guard followed the strange-looking man to the third floor. Just as he got close enough to ask the man how he had penetrated the locked doors downstairs, and what his business was, the man turned. The watchman opened his mouth to speak, but out came a nightmarish yell. He covered his face and then ran wildly from the building.

Sometime later that night, I was told, a patrolling police car noticed a man who appeared to be in a daze walking down the middle of Pennsylvania Avenue. Checking his identification, the officers learned where the man worked. Within an hour or so, the watchman's supervisor and a doctor were talking with him. Much of what he said, however, was incoherent. He remained in a state of shock and often broke into uncontrollable sobs. About all the doctor could get out of the watchman was that he had looked at a man with no eyes in his head. He had seen the fires of hell and smelled the stench of death; he sobbed to the doctor.

One of the lawyers, who closely followed the security officer's experience, told me that the man was committed to Saint Elizabeth's Hospital for extensive psychiatric treatment. Meanwhile, no one has yet explained how the man with a peculiar walk was able to enter the tightly locked building—or how he managed to leave it.

Some students of the old Pension Building think the man in the light-colored suit could have been the ghost of one of the first pension commissioners, James Tanner, a famed champion of Civil War veterans. Corporal Tanner had lost both feet in the Second Battle of Bull Run, which would explain the odd gait. After Bull Run, Tanner was re-trained as a shorthand clerk, and he was the Bureau of Ordnance stenographer pressed into service by Secretary of War Edwin Stanton the night President Lincoln was shot. It was Tanner who transcribed the testimony from witnesses at Ford's Theater. In later years, he turned that tragedy into a livelihood. Billed as "Corporal Tan-

ner," he became a celebrated lecturer and public speaker. The job as pension commissioner came in 1889 but lasted only briefly. Tanner was dumped by the administration because he increased veterans' pension payments without approval.

However, those who believe that Tanner is the ghost in the light-colored suit don't believe his re-visitations have anything to do with pensions. They think the appearances are connected with his role as an authority on the assassination of President Lincoln. They recall how Lincoln's son Robert, as Secretary of War in the 1880s, approved the plans for the Pension Building. Robert Lincoln was inclined to think that there was more to the Lincoln death conspiracy than the public was ever told. Some believe that he may have been persuaded by Meigs to hide important documents and secret material connected with his father's death in one of those Corinthian columns. Perhaps he was convinced that if the real truth were known it would shake the public's faith in their form of government. Afterall, the country was only a little over a hundred years old at the time. It was still in the midst of trying to re-unite itself after the War Between The States.

Many who knew Quartermaster General Montgomery Meigs say he had visions of those Corinthian columns standing for centuries—much as the columns of ancient Greece have survived the destruction of most tangible evidence of that civilization. It seems logical, their reasoning goes; that Robert might have given such important material to the ages rather than destroy it.

Some think that Tanner felt he knew the full story but never had the proof. They believe he is sometimes drawn back to Meigs Old Red Barn in his eternal search for evidence of a deeper conspiracy in the death of his President.

The Restless Vampire

As preposterous as it sounds, a vampire once visited the Nation's Capital and left its identifying marks on several victims, or at least that's what I've read. The largest newspaper coverage of this story occurred right after a Washington newspaper article reported that a burial vault, a short distance east of the sprawling Brentwood estate, built by Benjamin Latrobe in 1816, had been "recently dismantled and the bodies entombed there subjected to ghoulish desecration." This was just a few years after the novel *Dracula,* written by Bram Stoker, was published in this country.

Legend has it that a young girl from a well-respected family, living in the neighborhood where Gallaudet College is now located, fell in love with a handsome European prince with piercing black eyes. They had met at a party at an unnamed Eastern European embassy. He concealed the fact that he was a vampire until he got her alone one evening—under a full moon, of course. The young girl's pale body was found early the next morning at the edge of a clearing not too many miles from her home. The mark of the vampire on her neck was obscured by her long flowing hair.

Some say that the fine lace the young woman was laid to rest in had been intended for a wedding dress. She was sealed in her family's burial vault, and flowers were laid over the stone slab; but having once received the bite of the vampire, she too would rise again as a vampire. Apparently finished with his recruiting in Washington, the prince was never reported to have been seen again.

In the 1920s, Gorman Hendricks was given considerable space in the *Washington Post* to tell of some highly unusual reports. A few folks in Northeast Washington had seen a "white-clad beautiful girl" whose face was "distorted by a pair of wolf-like fangs." Hendricks said that a vampire had bitten her in the 1850s. He then proceeded to tell what had happened to her since.

The first chilling encounter apparently occurred within weeks or months of the young girl's death. The article says that a woodcutter making his way home by cutting through an old family cemetery "spotted a white-robed figure of a woman floating through the sealed vault." Nobody believed him until a stable groom's lifeless body was found a few months later. This time the mark of the vampire did not escape detection. Remembering the woodcutter's tale, people became panic-stricken. Out came the garlic bag necklaces to ward off vampire attacks. The neighbors were terrified that the creature might return, so they put a couple of heavily armed men in front of the burial vault around the clock. Hendricks said that the watch was maintained for many nights before the night stalker put in another appearance.

Although Hendricks didn't say so directly, the incident he described took place on April 22ⁿᵈ. He reported it to be the "eve of St. George," and that a thunderstorm was raging (of course). St. George was a 4ᵗʰ century Christian martyr on whom sainthood was bestowed in 1222. April 23 was set as the date on which he should be honored. George became a saint for slaying a dragon (representing the Devil) to rescue a Princess (representing the church). His article reported two dozing guards were awakened by what sounded to them like the squeak of rusty iron hinges. According to one eyewitness, a figure crept out "and glided through the woods in the direction of the mansion." Apparently the men didn't stick around to see if she went in. They seemed eager to get back to the neighbors with their news.

Next morning, well after the sun brightly lit the way, a small group of brave but frightened people cautiously ventured back out to the old estate to investigate. At the tomb they found that "the huge stone slab over the coffin had been displaced." Hendricks said that the girl was in the coffin, but "sharp wolf-like fangs" that parted her blood-red lips sent a ripple of shudders and gasps through the group. He said that they thought to fasten the coffin lid before running, but he made no mention of anyone driving a stake through her heart. Perhaps that is why reports of her stalking the neighborhood persisted.

Gorman Hendricks described another encounter a few months later. A man ran into the creature as it floated through the trees near the vine-covered and "half-forgotten vault." The man told the reporter that the thing was emitting a maniacal laugh and claimed that he caught "the foul odor of the charnel house and saw the gleam of hell-fire" in the creature's eyes. The man must have been in terrible shape after that encounter. Hendricks says he died a few weeks later.

Legend has it that the neighbors didn't want the family in the neighborhood, so to avoid possible violence the family moved away. News of the vampire spread throughout the area and nobody would buy the house of a vampire's family. It remained deserted for quite a while. According to Hendricks, decay had set in before someone unfamiliar with the old stories moved in.

Fresh blood in the old house was apparently something the vampire couldn't resist. The new occupants reported a horrible figure "gazing in the window of an upper room," and then moved out. Neighbors, who several times in the past had thought they were rid of the vampire, found themselves reaching for the garlic again. Petrified, they shunned the property day and night, and when it stormed no one ventured outside. When Hendricks wrote the article in 1923, he described the vault's door as hanging on "rusty hinges," adding that "the hand of time has obliterated the name." He said "large sections of broken sandstone that once covered the tombs of the dead lie about the dank vault given over to the creatures that creep and crawl."

The legend spanned a century, and the last reported victims seem to be those mentioned in Hendricks's story. If there have been none since, the vigilantes succeeded, but I suppose it could be argued that in a bustling international city more than twice the size of Hendricks's town, not many people are going to take the time to raise a question about two tiny red perforations on a few necks now and then.

The Phantom of the National Theater

The National Theater on Pennsylvania Avenue NW opened in 1835. This photograph is believed to have been taken about 1868. The ghost of a long dead actor, allegedly murdered in the basement of the theater, still revisits the stage from time to time. *Courtesy Historical Society of Washington, D.C.*

The oldest continually operating theater in the country stands at 1321 Pennsylvania Avenue Northwest. The National Theater opened December 7, 1835. Ten years later, the night after President James K. Polk's inaugural ball was held there; it burned but was quickly rebuilt. Its illustrious history includes many of this country's most notable theatrical events, including an 1850 performance of "the Swedish Nightingale," Jenny Lind, before President Millard Fillmore. The National experienced at least three other fires and the partial collapse of a wall. Through all of these, and other hardships, there has been a strong determination by theater owners and managers that "the show must go on." Many of America's finest Thespians have strutted and fretted their hours upon that stage. Yet, to my knowledge, only one actor regularly revisits the theater to play a role he has performed for more than a hundred years.

The story dates back to 1885. It seems that the actor was slain by an insanely jealous fellow actor who buried his body in the unexcavated area under the stage by a small creek that

flowed through the basement. Whether they had argued over a pretty young actress or over who would have the most lines in a new play cannot be answered. Supposedly, the actor had not been a terribly reliable one, and so when he didn't report for that night's performance, an understudy took his job. The legend also says that in spite of the fact that a grave was found a few years later the body was never removed.

Several years ago some workers beneath the stage, where the basement gives way to unexcavated dirt and near the area where the old actor lies buried, found some parts of an old gun. Smithsonian Institution experts identified them as parts of a gun in common use during and after the Civil War.

A former stage doorman, who worked at the National Theater for some fifteen years, apparently holds the record for the most number of sightings. "He was just kind of floating, very peaceful," the doorman told a former manager, who told a reporter.

The old basement is off-limits except to certain key theater personnel. I tried, unsuccessfully, on several occasions to gain permission to have a look downstairs, and to question one stage watchman whom I had learned actually had an encounter with the ghost. I did manage to talk by phone with the watchman, but he became edgy and upset when he learned that I knew he had once spotted the apparition. Under no circumstances would he discuss the encounter.

According to the legend, the old actor—dressed in Shakespearean costume—generally makes himself visible near the prompter's table whenever a new show is being readied. He is said to look around, inspect the sets, indicate his approval or disapproval—and vanish.

The old thespian has never spoken to anyone as far I could learn, but one thing is certain: those around the National Theater have virtually adopted the ghost as a mascot and are very protective of him.

The Poltergeist and the Musician

People will sometimes go to great lengths to remain in a house they have grown to love—even if it is haunted. There is a story told of a family who bought an old house at 6th and N. Northwest that once belonged to Richard Bland Lee, uncle of Robert E. Lee.

The house apparently had no known history of a poltergeist; but nevertheless, one plagued this family almost from the very day they moved in. There were accounts of dishes being tossed through the air. Pictures would slam to the floor. Furniture would move across the room. Bedspreads would be ripped from beds and left crumpled on the floor.

The family was at wits' end. So far, the incidents had just been costly. No one had been harmed. The family did so love the old house. The father reluctantly confided his dilemma to a close friend who told him he had read somewhere that one could charm the spirit with soothing music, and just maybe that would quiet their ghostly intruder. It was worth a try; the father reasoned. The next day, according to the account I read, the father contracted with one of the most famous musicians of the day. It was for a most unusual request, but the old German maestro was intrigued by the desperation in the man's voice—and in the amount he was willing to pay. The maestro was to arrive at the home for an intimate solo concert at precisely 11:30 P.M. He was to play his favorite compositions for one hour. The father rushed home to tell his family what he had done. They all prayed that the music at midnight would exorcise the ghost.

It was reported that the German maestro arrived on time and was prepared to give the concert of his life. His finest performance was also a brief performance. The newspaper account lacked details of what happened as the clock struck midnight. It simply said it was the musician—not the ghost—who left at the stroke of twelve.

Evil at 11ᵗʰ and D Streets Northwest

The attempted exorcism of a poltergeist with music is unique. Most consult a priest when they want the ancient rite performed. In September of 1907 the *Evening Star* carried a story about another, more conventional, attempted exorcism in a house at 11ᵗʰ and D Streets, Northwest. If we are to believe the article, the owner had a great deal of trouble renting the property, described as "a fine old home." The writer says that the owner was reluctant to believe the many stories of ghostly occurrences his tenants had told, but he was finally convinced that something had to be done. When all attempts at ridding the house of the unwelcome presence had failed, he consulted his parish priest. The writer was quite vague about the exact nature of the troubles that caused the owner to seek an exorcist, yet the details of the attempted exorcism, and who attempted it, are carefully spelled out.

The reporter said that the owner talked with "Father Boyle and an assistant priest of St. Patrick's Church" about performing the ancient rite of exorcism. The reporter says that the priests, though at first reluctant, gave in because of the desperation of the owner of the house. Father Boyle and his assistant arrived at the deserted home, just off Pennsylvania Avenue, at precisely 11:00 P.M. They went through the house turning on all the gaslights, and closing and bolting the heavy wooden shutters, windows, and doors. We are told that they established themselves in the exact center of the house. I would have been disappointed if the reporter had not noted that "the hallway timepiece chimed twelve" as they prepared to begin the exorcism.

Suddenly, locked windows flew open, shutters banged against the side of the house, and doors opened and closed. The writer says, "the iron bar across the front door was lifted by invisible hands" and slammed to the floor. Wailing and screaming began to fill the rooms.

Like most articles of the period, this one is melodramatic, but it conjures up a picture of the priest and his assistant trying to shout the words of their ritual over the sobbing and wailing that echoed through first one room and then another as the distraught demon searched for those who threatened it. The priests apparently saw nothing, yet from what they experienced they knew they had encountered something not of this world. Strong winds "of gale force" and maniacal laughter shook the inside of the house, and according to the reporter created such a tempest that pieces of furniture toppled over and were blown about as though made of cardboard. It is possible that the priest and his assistant were overcome with a feeling that the wind was actually compelling them through the doorway and out of the house.

The writer said that they were unable to complete the rite that evening, but had sufficiently recovered the next day to apologize to the owner of the house and to promise to return the following evening to try again. The reporter inferred that the owner, being a reasonable man, decided that anything capable of defying men of God must be truly evil. So rather than risk the lives of the priests by further attempts, he decided to have the house torn down—hoping to put an end to the horrifying events for all time.

The owner was no doubt relieved that his decision restored calm to the neighborhood. No one has heard anything more about strange happenings from 11th and D Northwest.

Does H Stand for Haunted?

Down through the years I haven't found any street in Washington that has more haunted houses than H Street Northwest. In the Lafayette Square area, the Decatur, Madison, and Adams houses are adjacent to H Street. Mary Surratt's boarding house was on H Street, and a benevolent poltergeist is said to have haunted an H Street house near 18th Street. That story, from the late-1800s, concerned a family that endured the antics of an old servant's pesky ghost for several months.

It seems that the servant had worked for this particular family for years. She had her own room and kept to herself. Little did the family suspect that for years the woman had been stashing most of her pay beneath her mattress. This most kindhearted woman was making sacrifices so a cousin, with whom she had grown up in the south, could one day come to Washington and re-join her. She died without being able to tell anyone of her dream. Within days, however, unexplainable things began happening in her former room.

The newspaper article I read described "stomping sounds that would awake the soundest of sleepers," chairs that rocked mysteriously, blankets and quilts that flew off the bed whenever someone tried to sleep on it. If we are to believe that old article, the servant was so determined to help her relative that her ghost kept coming back to lead someone to her treasure.

The owner of the haunted house decided that the room was of no value as a bedroom, and decided to see what would happen if it was converted into a sewing room—using it only in the daytime. In dismantling the bedroom, one of their first steps was to remove the mattress from the bed. An envelope bearing the name and address of the servant's cousin fell onto the floor. Everyone lived happily ever after, according to the reporter. The money was forwarded to the needy relative, the servant's ghost rested, and the family was overjoyed at the return of peace and quiet.

The Tailor's Slain Bride

A tale of passion, violence and death concerned a home on I street, Northwest—just off Connecticut Avenue and yet still near Lafayette Square. The tale goes back to the 1870s, when, legend has it, a rather successful tailor moved into the home with his bride. The writer of one of the articles said that the tailor seemed quite proud at having been able to afford such a home so near to where some of the city's notables lived and worked. It wasn't too long after the couple moved in that neighbors began to notice that the bride never came outside. Even when people called on the couple, they were greeted only by the tailor, who seemed distant, though cordial.

Inquiries about his bride drew casual remarks and a quick change of subject. "Visiting relatives," was the excuse that he used most often as to why his wife was unavailable to socialize. Busybody neighbors spread rumors that the bride had left her husband. They amused themselves by speculating why. Meanwhile, the tailor moved out of his house, never to be seen in the neighborhood again. Neighbors talked for a while, but the gossip eventually died down.

However, as a series of new occupants came and went from the house, some neighbors began to gossip that the house was haunted. Although they had no evidence, they suspected the tailor probably killed his bride and her ghost was ever-present. That is how some gossips explained the moans and the rapping sounds from within the walls that they had been told of by occupants and former owners. Sometimes the house would stay vacant for months. It no longer was in the best of condition.

One determined occupant felt that all the house really needed was a good clean-up, which he undertook as he did some remodeling. The new occupant, said the reporter, was a skeptic and not at all convinced that a ghost was at the root of the problems in the house. He explained to neighbors that the moans were from a brisk wind blowing through loose window and door frames. Tapping sounds were possibly squirrels, nesting in the walls, and trying to crack nuts. You can imagine his surprise when he knocked down one of the walls and as the plaster dust settled, found a skeleton. A wedding ring encircled one finger bone, and there was a silver letter opener, stained a deep crimson, lodged between two bones in the rib cage.

One article on the old house said that the uncovering of the skeleton of the tailor's wife unleashed an awesome volume of stories, which only served to keep the house unoccupied over even longer periods. A new story evolved of a shadowy woman, dressed in white, who often floated through the rooms—mumbling a name no one could understand.

No harm had ever come to anyone in the home since the tailor moved out, so Benjamin Tracy and his wife decided that their attraction for the house transcended any ghostly legends. In the 1890s just after he was appointed Secretary of the Navy by President Benjamin Harrison, Tracy and his wife moved in. Within months the old house was consumed by a fire that killed Mrs. Tracy. Although fire officials claimed otherwise, gossipy neighbors contended the ghost of the tailor's bride burned down the house following decades of discontent at being unable to find her slayer. Legend has it that the fire was her way of freeing her frustrated soul to continue its search for the tailor elsewhere.

Winters' House

"Winters' House"—a somewhat appropriate name for a home said to be chilled by the vision of a lovely young woman. The home that once belonged to Harry Winters, of Prevost-Winters & Company—the firm that supplied the marble for the new wings to the U.S. Capitol, is reported to be kissed with the breath of the supernatural.

Winters built his home sometime in the mid-1800s in what was then the outskirts of a growing District of Columbia. It was just south of the arch that spanned the canal at New Jersey Avenue, on the east side of the street. Because much of this area was reclaimed wetlands, the soil was fertile. Winters saw to it that much of his estate was sculpted into a fine garden, lush with greenery and a virtual rainbow of color in the spring. The trails were punctuated with fine pieces of marble statuary. Such beauty was a showcase in Southeast Washington.

Neighbors were apparently surprised when the Winters family moved away. The writer of the article I read didn't indicate what persuaded Winters to uproot his family and essentially abandon the large home, nor why it remained vacant for a goodly number of years. However, it wasn't long before stories began to circulate throughout the community that the house was really not empty. There were reports of a "lovely young vision" gazing out of one of the windows. Her appearance was said to mystify those walking along New Jersey Avenue, Southeast, looking up at her. At first it appeared that the beautiful young girl peering out from a window was bathed in moonlight; but a closer look revealed that the illumination was coming from around her!

Another newspaper report quoted a person who claimed to have "communed" with the girl briefly, sensing that she was deeply depressed. The reporter said the person was so emotionally sensitive that she had to break away and flee because the intense loneliness and pain of isolation she felt was unbearable. A male witness to the apparition said the girl beckoned him to draw closer. When he did, he told the reporter, he stopped dead in his tracks before reaching the house because "this nocturnal vision of loveliness" evaporated before his very eyes! Engulfed in a cold, clammy chill, he fled.

Olivia's Ghostly Gift

In a newspaper article from 1927, Maple Square was described as a "stately house of distinguished occupancy." Good way to begin a ghost story, I thought. Maple Square was built by wealthy tobacco planter W.M. Duncanson on South Carolina Avenue quite early in the nineteenth century.

After the Civil War a relatively well known newspaper correspondent, Emily E. Briggs, who used the name "Olivia," bought the house. Much to her surprise she found the master bed chamber was the "abode of a most gentle and benign female ghost" who roamed the property and wept considerably. Sometimes at midnight soft sounds of strange music, from an instrument with which Briggs was unfamiliar, would waft through the old house.

Briggs claimed she was more fascinated than frightened by the ghost. Although she tried, she never learned just who it may have been, or why it chose to haunt mainly the master bedchamber. There was some speculation in the old newspaper article that the ghost was that of a young and jealous wife who became despondent and embittered over her husband's gallantries toward an older woman, and took her own life.

Several years passed with Briggs and her ghost co-existing with neither causing the other problems. Then one morning Briggs seemed to be drawn to a spare bedroom. She entered and was astonished to note a depression in the pillow. It was as though someone had lain down upon the bed and left an imprint. Briggs went closer. A tiny pearl lay in the hollow of the pillow.

Briggs insisted that with the appearance of the pearl her ghostly resident departed and never returned. Briggs chose to interpret the appearance of the pearl as a symbol the woman's despondent spirit had found peace at last. However, for the rest of Briggs' life she was haunted by three questions that her research never answered: who was her ghostly house guest, how had she died, and what had happened to put her at peace?

— —

This article published in the *Washington Star*, April 18, 1891, is typical of newspaper articles of that period in their coverage of ghost stories.

Drips of Gore
A Horrible Sort of Ghost That Haunts a House on 19th Street

WASHINGTON IS THE GREATEST TOWN for ghosts in this country. The city is dotted all over with haunted houses which remain unrented year after year on account of the spooks that are supposed to inhabit them, all the way from the great empty Tayloe mansion at the corner of 17th street and New York avenue to the humble and deserted negro hut in Swampoodle, regarded by neighborhood superstition as the abode of bogies most horrible and frightening.

But perhaps the most thoroughly original of Washington ghosts is located in a house on nineteenth street northwest between E and R. The dwelling has been for rent and unoccupied nearly all of the time for several years past, notwithstanding its situation in the fashionable quarter. The last tenants were induced to take it by the extremely low rent, although the real estate agent for security's sake, would only let them have it on a year's lease. How they got out of the bargain I don't know, but they moved away at the end of the fifth week. That was six months ago.

It seems that eight years ago a man committed suicide in this house with a razor. The deed was done in cold blood apparently. He stood in front of the mirror which overhung the marble mantelpiece and deliberately cut his throat from ear to ear. Then, as appeared from the condition in which things were subsequently found, he clung with one hand to the mantelpiece, while his blood poured out on the hearth, until he fell and died.

That was the story, as the tenants here referred to understood it afterward. Their notion of the ghost when they took the house was altogether indefinite, and they only laughed at it, considering it rather in the light of a joke than otherwise. It so chanced that what, as they found out later, was reputed to be the particular haunted chamber, was occupied by the two daughters of the family—fifteen and eighteen years of age respectively.

From first to last there was no such thing observed as an apparition. The girls slept well, save for the fact that they were annoyed on occasions by a sound of dripping, which they at first supposed was caused by a leak of some sort. But their surprise was awakened by the continuance of this dripping during a long spell of dry weather, and more particularly did they find reason at length for wonderment in the circumstance that the dripping began invariable at about 11:15 p.m. and lasted for perhaps twenty minutes, but not longer.

The dripping sound seemed to come from the mantelpiece and they carefully investigated that fixture and its surroundings, but without result, save for the discovery of a slightly hollowed area in the stone underneath, which had apparently been made by scraping away its substance.

Inquiry developed the fact that the stone had been scraped away for the purpose of eliminating the spot where a pool of the suicide's blood had formed. Also it was learned that the hour at which he killed himself was about 11:15 p.m.

The tenants moved out.

— —

The Gambler

During the middle part of the last century, one of Washington's legendary gamblers was Colonel Beau Hickman. Local lore has it that he was easily recognized by his beaver hat, cane, and diamond stick pin. One article I read said that Beau was about twenty when he left his Virginia home in 1833 to come to Washington, seeking fame and fortune. His good looks and his gift for handling a deck of cards convinced him that he would succeed.

This is the strip of Pennsylvania Avenue where Colonel Beau, the legendary gambler, practiced his skills during the late 1800s. *Courtesy National Archives*

This is the corner allegedly revisited by Colonel Beau for decades after his death. The National Hotel, owned by Alexandria tavern owner John Gadsby, stood here on the northeast corner of Pennsylvania Avenue and 6th Street NW for almost one hundred years, before being torn down shortly after this photograph was taken. The hotel was said to have been a favorite of the gamblers because it attracted so many famous and powerful guests.
Courtesy National Archives

For some forty years, Hickman lived in Washington—spending most of his time in the old hotel that once was located at 6th Street and Pennsylvania Avenue, Northwest. The Colonel provided many men of the city with pleasurable ways to lose their money. When the cards didn't fall just right for his friends, the Colonel seemed most adroit at soothing their losses with good liquor and beautiful women. Gamblers seldom have friends, but Colonel Beau proved to be the exception, and nothing more illustrated this fact than his death.

Newspapers tell us that in 1873 some of his card-playing friends were startled to learn of the Colonel's sudden death through a small obituary in the newspaper. They were even more shocked to read that burial was in the pauper's graveyard. Never in their wildest dreams had his friends imagined the Colonel penniless.

After the initial shock passed the group gathered in the saloon of the hotel where the Colonel had lived. They reminisced about the many hours of pleasure the Colonel had provided them. None expressed any bitterness toward the old gambler, which may help to explain why he died broke. The Colonel never fleeced his friends.

With moist eyes and spirits warmed with alcohol the gentlemen decided that their long-time host deserved a more prominent resting place. It just wouldn't be right for such a fine fellow to spend eternity in a pauper's grave. Such a noble person should be buried in Congressional Cemetery they reasoned. So, after one last drink for the road, the men set out for the pauper's field. Dusk was settling as they arrived at the deserted cemetery on the outskirts of Washington, but there was enough light for them to see that body snatchers had been at work.

It was a particularly disreputable occupation—as a matter of fact it was illegal—but a good living could be made selling cadavers to "no-questions-asked" medical schools. Shuddering with fear, the men saw the Colonel's body lying half in and half out of the freshly re-opened grave. Someone had frightened off the body snatchers. The Colonel's friends went quickly to work. Turning their faces into the wind, taking a deep breath, and closing their eyes, the men grabbed up the body in its shroud and tossed it into the back of their wagon. With the crack of a whip, and an obscene shout, they were off to a greener and more respectable gravesite in Congressional Cemetery. The Colonel's body bounced around in the buckboard as it flew along G Street. It looked as though that old wagon was being chased by the devil himself. It nearly tipped over as the horses galloped through the gates of Congressional Cemetery and around the curve to where the Colonel would be reburied. The grave was dug; the Colonel was lowered into it, prayed over, and covered up in less than an hour. One chronicler of the tale says that one of the men even produced a thin marble tombstone with no markings on it. With a piece of burned wood, he scribbled the Colonel's name and the date of his death. Tipping their hats in one final gesture of respect, the men jumped onto the wagon and in a cloud of dust headed back for the bar in the old hotel on Pennsylvania Avenue. Reportedly, Colonel Beau never forgave his friends for their cowardice and their mockery of such a solemn occasion. That is said to be part of the reason why he revisits the area of 6th and Pennsylvania Avenue, Northwest.

Not long after the Colonel's death, people began to tell tales of wild things happening in some of the card games at the old hotel—particularly card games involving Beau Hickman's old friends. Apparently the Colonel's ghost liked a practical joke as well as the Colonel had. He even got to one of his friends at a most tender moment with a beautiful young woman. Yes, Colonel Beau was dead, but his ghost was dedicated to making sure that his friends wouldn't forget him.

The old hotel that had been a favorite of the Colonel and his cronies was torn down in 1892 to make way for the new Atlantic Coastline Railroad Headquarters, but that apparently had little effect on the Colonel's ghost. Once a gambler, always a gambler. It is said that the Colonel has been seen standing on his corner just after dark, wearing a rather lonely expression, as he searches for his friends and just one more card game. Those claiming to have spotted Colonel Beau Hickman say you can't mistake him. He's still wearing his beaver hat, and carrying his cane. His diamond stickpin glistens in the light from the street lamp.

Congressional Cemetery

Seventeen blocks east of the U.S. Capitol, on the banks of the Anacostia River, sprawls Congressional Cemetery. It's an almost forgotten place because most of the Congressmen originally buried there, along with three Presidents, were long ago dug up and re-interred "back home."

In the early 1800s, when a congressman was just as likely to die in a duel as to die from disease, Congress purchased hundreds of lots at the Washington Parish Burial Ground of Christ Episcopal Church. Over the years it became known as Congressional Cemetery. *Courtesy Lee Shephard*

I had looked into the possibility of ghosts haunting the old burial ground during my original research for this book. I found no such stories, or at least no one willing to tell me what they knew. However, with the renewed popularity of these old tales, I am discovering that people are becoming more aware of good stories, and if they discover one they send it to me. It's possible, too, that some of these old stories just weren't known by the folks with whom I originally talked. I do know that the art form of spinning a good ghost story isn't dead. It's a thriving pastime. Of course, there is always the possibility that a lot more dead folks in Washington have become restless.

Back in the very early 1800s, when a congressman was just as likely to die in a duel as to die from disease, Congress purchased hundreds of lots at the Washington Parish Burial Ground of Christ Episcopal Church. It was too much of a problem, back then, to ship bodies home. A special marker was designed so that all Congressional graves would be uniform in appearance.

When corpse transportation became easier most of the famous, and even some of the infamous, buried in Congres-

sional Cemetery were claimed by their families, dug up, and sent home. The distinctive markers thus became cenotaphs, rather than headstones. A cenotaph is a monument erected in honor of someone whose mortal remains lie elsewhere.

Above, opposite page top left and bottom left: A special marker was designed so that all Congressional graves would look alike. However, when corpse transportation became easier, most of the famous and even some of the infamous buried in Congressional Cemetery, were claimed by their families, dug up, and sent home. That included the mortal remains of Presidents John Quincy Adams, Zach Taylor, and William Henry Harrison. A couple of Vice Presidents were uprooted and returned home, but apparently Henry Wilson has remained along with a considerable number of other notables. *Courtesy Lee Shephard*

Now that is the case with the mortal remains of Presidents William H. Harrison, John Quincy Adams, and Zachary Taylor. Vice Presidents George Clinton of New York and Elbridge Gerry were also uprooted and returned home. However, a considerable number of notables still call Congressional home and at least one of them is said to serenade us.

John Phillip Sousa

March King John Phillip Sousa is still buried in Congressional Cemetery. Washington has always been home to him. Although he traveled throughout the country, and to Europe with his famous bands, he always returned to the city he loved.

Sousa was born in Washington, D.C. in 1854. Music was the most important thing in his life. The number thirteen was anything but unlucky for the march master. By the age of thirteen his family apprenticed him to the Marine Band, the official band of the President of the United States. Thirteen years later he was appointed leader of that most distinguished band. It was during this period of Sousa's life that a great many of his most famous marches were composed, including *Semper Fidelis*, *The Washington Post March*, and his most popular march, *The Stars and Stripes Forever*. As he was about to begin his thirteenth year with the Marine Band, Sousa resigned to form his own concert band.

Sousa was a perfectionist. He established new marks of excellence in performance and instrumentation to which other concert bands could only aspire. He also was an inventor of sorts. Sousa redesigned the tuba into what he called the "sousaphone."

The sousaphone is a large bass tuba with circular coiling and an upright bell. He felt its big bold bassy sound added an additional zest to his stimulating marches that the old tuba just couldn't match.

Sousa's tomb in the southwest corner of Congressional Cemetery overlooks the bridge that bears his name and spans the Anacostia River. Some old-timers who still love to tap their feet to Sousa's robust marches claim those deep bassy sounds emanating over the cemetery on foggy moonless nights are, in fact, the March King still trying to perfect the sound of the sousaphone. Others point out that the river is only a few hundred yards away, and more than likely it's just the fog horn of a boat.

Phantom Photographer

Mathew Brady, seen here in his seventies, was still trying to win compensation from the War Department and Congress for their use of his extensive war time photographs. He never did. When he died Brady was buried, not in Arlington National Cemetery among those heroes whose exploits he had so bravely documented, but in Congressional Cemetery among some of the very congressmen who had refused to reimburse him. *Courtesy Library of Congress*

Famed photographer Mathew Brady, (there is no second "t" in the spelling of his first name) who preserved the images of eighteen U.S. Presidents and has been called "the chronicler of an epoch and the delineator of the manners of his time" is another who still resides in Congressional Cemetery.

Brady was at the height of his career when Civil War erupted. He had fashionable photography galleries in New York City and in Washington, D.C. His reputation as an excellent portrait photographer was world wide. When rumors reached Washington that there was going to be a battle just south of the city, Brady hastily outfitted a wagon with equipment and supplies and, like so many other curious Washingtonians, set out for Bull Run.

Over the course of the war Brady invested his own money in documenting the devastation. He financed up to twenty-two photographic teams in every theater of the war, but instead of bringing him success it brought financial disaster. By the time of Lee's surrender at Appomattox Courthouse Brady had spent his entire fortune and had run up debts for supplies long since used. Sale of war views had been less that successful. The War Department, although it had made much use of the photographs, balked at paying for the ones that many officers thought the government should preserve as a record of the war. Congress wasn't much help either when it came to reimbursing Brady for expenses.

The great photographer was near exhaustion. He denied he was bitter, but it was obvious to those around him that he was disillusioned and depressed. His beloved wife, Julia, whom he had been away from during much of the war, was in poor health. He attempted to rebuild his business, but couldn't. His life was in shambles. Much younger, more energetic photographers, competed for clients. Misfortune continued to stalk Brady for the rest of his life. Julia's illness got no better. She died in 1887. Brady grieved, but continued working in his Washington gallery. He never gave up hope that one day his war views might win wider acceptance.

In the summer of 1895 he began to talk of a New York exhibit that would feature his Civil War photographs. The following winter he packed up and moved to New York to prepare for that showing. However, a kidney ailment bothering the photographer continued to grow worse. In January 1896 Mathew Brady died of complications from that illness. He died alone, and in poverty, in a small room of a New York rooming house.

"After life's fitful fever he sleeps well…"
The New York Globe, January 1896

Brady was to suffer one final humiliation. His body was returned to Washington and he was laid to rest *not* in the National Cemetery at Arlington among so many of the statesmen, military officers, and soldiers whose portraits he had taken for posterity; but in out-of-the-way Congressional Cemetery—among some of the very members who, when alive, had fought against the government reimbursing the photographer for his wartime expenses.

In the years that have followed a few people claim to have seen the frail, bearded little man, still dressed in his wrinkled overcoat and slouch hat, reading names on the cenotaphs. Names of those whose likenesses were made immortal by Brady. However, I am told that a better place to look for Brady's ghost is in what is called the old Executive Office Building. It's a somewhat gothic structure that stands next to the White House, and was for years The War Department. It was inside those walls that a tremendous amount of Brady's time and emotion poured out in his bid for reimbursement for the most vivid and explicit documentation of war that had ever been achieved.

Death In The Land Of Strangers

Famous Choctaw Chief Pushmataha, who sought only peaceful co-existence with the government of the United States and led his own warriors into twenty-four battles to help secure the southeastern frontier from the Creek, Seminole, and British, is buried in Congressional Cemetery.

PUSH-MA-TA-HA.
A CHOCTAW WARRIOR.

Pushmataha was a famous Choctaw Chief who dreamed of living in peaceful co-existence with his white brothers. He organized his warriors into an efficient fighting force and proved himself over and over again in battle. He even earned the respect of old Indian fighter Andrew Jackson. Pushmataha died in the land of strangers. He was in Washington to negotiate a treaty when he died. He was laid to rest, with full military honors, in Congressional Cemetery. *Courtesy Alabama Department of Archives and History, Montgomery, Alabama*

Pushmataha was born in 1764 in what is now southern Mississippi, but back then it was just a small part of the vast Choctaw lands that included Georgia, Alabama, and Louisiana. The Choctaw were most able farmers, and considerably less warlike than their traditional enemies the Chickasaw,

Cherokee, and the feared Creek. They developed their own horse breeds.

Pushmataha was about twenty when he first demonstrated the qualities that would make him a leader of his people. He was part of a Choctaw raiding party that ventured to the west bank of the Mississippi River to engage the Osage. He disappeared early in the conflict that lasted all day, and on rejoining the Choctaw, was accused of cowardice. He produced five scalps which he threw on the ground exclaiming "Let those laugh who can show more scalps than I."

Pushmataha, translated 'the sapling is ready,' had performed single-handedly an onslaught on the enemy's rear. It won for him a chieftaincy. This young man had an exceptionally strong eagerness to revenge himself upon his enemies and did so whenever opportunity presented itself. To his friends, however, Pushmataha was loyal and trustworthy. Those virtues were the ones exploited by the U.S. Government. When he was about forty and with much influence among other Choctaw leaders, the U.S. government persuaded him, in 1805, to cede Choctaw lands in Alabama and Mississippi for $500.00 and a small annuity. The Choctaw had much land, Pushmataha reasoned, and the money could help educate his people in the ways of the newcomers. He worked hard to maintain a good relationship between the whites and his people.

A few years later, when Tecumseh and his brother, The Prophet, were trying to organize a broad alliance of Native American tribes—with the help of the British; Pushmataha resisted formation of a southern confederacy. Pushmataha liked the Americans and believed an association with them could help his people prosper. So when Tecumseh succeeded in getting the Choctaw's bitter enemies, the Creek, to join his cause it seemed natural to Pushmataha to ally with the Americans.

Pushmataha was so rigid in his discipline that he gained the respect of U.S. military officers who witnessed his ability in converting his warriors into efficient soldiers. At first they called him "the Indian General," but as he proved himself in battle, he became "General Pushmataha."

Ironically, famed Indian fighter "Old Hickory" owed his rise to national fame to two Indian chiefs—Pushmataha and Junaluska. Were it not for them and their highly disciplined Choctaw and Cherokee warriors, Andrew Jackson might have been killed at Horseshoe Bend or New Orleans. Instead, he lived to become President, defy the Supreme Court, and evict all southeast tribes of their homelands.
Courtesy Library of Congress

It is ironic that Andrew Jackson, a militia leader from Tennessee, owed his widespread fame to Pushmataha, 500 Choctaw warriors, and Chief Junaluska's fierce fighting Cherokees. Jackson was known as a hot-headed, ill-tempered, ambitious soldier who was no Indian lover. Wiley Neal, a historian in the Waxhaws of North and South Carolina, where Jackson was born, told me Jackson used Indians in a disgraceful way. "If he were alive today taking those actions he would be court martialed."

Pushmataha had no quarrel with the way Jackson used the Cherokee or with the harsh terms he imposed upon the Creek. Both tribes were enemies of the Choctaw. Pushmataha went on with Jackson to New Orleans where he helped defeat the British. Five years later his Choctaw soldiers fought under General Jackson again in the Pensacola Campaign against the Seminole who were part of the Creek family. The Choctaw name for the Seminole is translated 'runaway' because in earlier times they had once been part of lower Creek towns before migrating to Florida. Pushmataha saw Seminole war as an opportunity to avenge ancient wrongs against his people that were still a vivid part of the tribes oral history.

During these campaigns the Choctaw chief earned the respect of "Old Hickory," but when the fighting was over he learned a sad lesson about the U.S. Government's attitude toward Indians. With the Creek defeated and dispersed west of the Mississippi River; and the Seminoles pushed deep into the Everglades, the federal government (under pressure from the states and their people) turned its attention to the more peaceful tribes. Gold had been found in Georgia and North Carolina and that added impetus to the removal effort.

Although Pushmataha could neither read nor speak English he wanted his people educated in the ways of the Americans. By affixing his mark to the treaties of 1805 and 1816 he felt he was furthering the cause of peaceful co-existence. In the negotiations at Doak's Stand, and the treaty of 1820, one observer wrote that Pushmataha "displayed much diplomacy and showed a business capacity equal to that of General Jackson, against whom he was pitted, in driving a sharp bargain." Rough translation: Jackson didn't get all he was looking for.

Four years later, as the old chief turned sixty, he and other Choctaw chiefs were invited to Washington. He knew they were summoned because Jackson didn't get all he wanted at Doak's Stand. The U.S. Government wanted still another treaty that would take more of their lands.

It was the winter of 1824. Pushmataha knew that his old commander, Andrew Jackson, was engaged in a contest to be the leader of all of his people, and he hoped to see him once again. The negotiations consumed much time because of the language problems, but Pushmataha seemed to be in good spirits.

Upon the occasion of a visit by the Marquis de Lafayette to Washington, D.C. it was decided that negotiations could be put on hold for a day or so. Perhaps, it was reasoned, these Indian warrior chieftains would like to meet a warrior from across the sea. Pushmataha agreed. The stories of Lafayette's exploits during the American Revolution were known to the Choctaw, too.

Through an interpreter Pushmataha boasted to a reporter, "I am an American. My hand is white. It has never been stained by the blood of Americans, but it is red with that of their enemies." The interpreter smiled at Pushmataha's next remark. "What did he say?" quizzed the reporter.

"He said that he feels the Great Spirit loves him today."

Pushmataha met the aging Lafayette, expressed his admiration for his abilities as a warrior, and predicted they would not see each other again. That night the old chief collapsed from what was described as the croup. Apparently, he had been ill all day.

That evening the chief summoned some of the other chiefs to his bedside at Tension's Hotel. He gave them some directions regarding his affairs, his family, and the treaty. *The National Journal*, December 28, 1824, provided an account of Chief Pushmataha's last hours.

"I am told," he said, "that I am better. It is a mistake. I shall die…at about 12 O'clock tonight. It has always been in my heart that I should die in the land of strangers. When I am dead, let the big guns be fired over me."

The newspaper also said that the dying chief had requested to see General Jackson, but the wish had not been conveyed. The writer of the article said he informed General Jackson of the request the next day. "I deeply regret it. Had it been midnight, I would have risen and gone to see him," the General is quoted as saying to the correspondent.

"The big guns" were fired over Pushmataha's burial, but not simply in compliance with his last request. He had endeared himself to many Americans, and it was the wish of the U.S. Government that "this noble man be laid to rest with full military honors among the great and venerated of our land" in Congressional Cemetery.

It is also possible that the government reasoned such an elaborate burial for the Choctaw Chief would so impress the other chiefs that concluding the treaty negotiations favorably would be easier. Although saddened by the loss of their leader, the other Choctaw chiefs concluded the treaty in January 1824. The U.S. Government had a monument placed above Pushmataha's grave and said it was "erected by his brother chiefs who were associated with him" in the delegation. It read in part, "He was wise in council, eloquent in an extraordinary degree; and on all occasions, and under all circumstances, the white man's friend."

Later that month the House of Representatives chose John Quincy Adams as the next President of the United States. Jackson was furious. Jackson had won the popular and electoral vote in the election of 1824, but because none of the five contenders had a majority, it was up to the House to choose the next President. Jackson accused Adams of buying the Presidency by rewarding Henry Clay the post of Secretary of State after Clay helped persuade the House to elect Adams. Jackson resigned as Senator from Tennessee and began organizing a campaign that would put him in the White House in 1828. Most historians still call it the most vicious campaign in U.S. presidential politics. "Old Hickory" won a smashing victory, and by mid-term had succeeded in ram-roding through Congress the Indian Removal Act.

It called for the removal, by force, of *all* Indians east of the Mississippi River, including Pushmataha's Choctaw people and the Cherokee who were perhaps the "most civilized" of the tribes. They had their own democratic government, school system, and newspaper. They also had gold on their land.

Not all Americans believed in a genocidal approach to the Indians. Many were against removal, and considerable numbers in government and within the U.S. population believed in peaceful co-existence, as had been Pushmataha's dream. Jackson's views cannot be said to have represented frontiersmen or old Indian fighters, either. On the issue of removal, Tennessee Congressman Davy Crockett was a most determined and outspoken opponent.

Some say that when Pushmataha was negotiating across from Jackson at Doak's Stand he sensed the destiny of "Old Hickory," and began to sense the cruelty, and underlying hatred driving Jackson. Was Pushmataha's death bed request an attempt for one more meeting with Jackson to try to change Old Hickory's course?

In spite of what he told the reporter, there are those who believe that Jackson would not have inconvenienced himself for a dying old Indian. As proof that Jackson frequently said one thing and did another, they cite his remarks at his first inauguration:

"It will be my sincere and constant desire to observe toward the Indian tribes within our limits a just and liberal policy, and to give that humane and considerate attention to their rights and their wants which is consistent with the habits of our Government and the feelings of our people."
—*Andrew Jackson, 1829*

Within the year President Jackson had dispatched troops to forcibly remove the southern tribes from lands guaranteed them by federal treaties and upheld by a decision of the U.S. Supreme Court. An example of Jackson's arrogance and dictatorial tendencies is his total disregard of the constitutional restraints and the rule of law. When told the U.S. Supreme Court ruled Georgia had no right to expel the Cherokee from their land, Jackson bellowed: "John Marshall has made the decision, now let him enforce it." It was the beginning of the Trail of Tears.

Was Pushmataha's spirit aware of this betrayal? Well, at least one person thinks the old chief is all too aware of what happened after his death. His spirit has been blamed for some of the overturned and broken headstones and cenotaphs in Congressional Cemetery. "Revenge. That's what it is. Revenge against them guys what cheated his people out of their land," said a cemetery worker as he spat tobacco juice on the mound of earth he was piling up beside a new grave he was digging. I loved the twinkle in his eye and the seriousness of his expression as he embellished his story.

"I think he's tryin' to break outta this place and get to ole Andy Jackson."

The grave digger had an attentive listener and he knew it. "What about vandals?" I asked. "I thought most of the stones were defaced, broken and overturned by vandals over the years."

"Vandals?" The man thought a minute. "Vandals?" He repeated. "Hey man, this is Washington, D.C., the Nation's Capital. We got police and more police. Probably more policemen than any other city in the country. Don't you think if it was vandals that did all this, them police would've caught 'em? No sir. Nosiree. It's that Indian. He's what did it."

He kept a serious face, but the twinkle in his eyes was still there. He went back to his work. The marker on the fairly recent stone beside the grave he was digging said "HOOVER." It was 1972. I really didn't want to think about where J. Edgar stories might surface in the coming years. It was almost dusk. It was time I moved on.

J. Edgar Hoover's grave is being dug next to that of his mother's in Congressional Cemetery. Hoover died in 1972 at the age of 77. He had been the director of the Federal Bureau of Investigation for forty-eight years. *Courtesy Lee Shephard*

These photographs were taken in Rock Creek Cemetery, Washington's oldest burial ground. An investigator who probes ghostlore more deeply than I, once wrote, "The popular notion that ghosts are likely to be seen in a graveyard is not borne out by psychical research." He contended that, "A haunting ghost usually haunts a place that the person lived in or frequented while alive." He concluded, "Only a grave digger's ghost would be likely to haunt a graveyard."

Well, maybe; but on a dark and stormy night you won't find many visitors in any cemetery. I'd always been told that if you must cut through a cemetery at night, "don't forget to whistle to let the ghosts know you're coming and that you're not afraid." Most people can't whistle when their scared, so they just stay out of graveyards at night. *Courtesy Lee Shephard*

I left the worker to his task, and headed out of Congressional Cemetery. I walked past a life-sized statue of Marion Ooletia, aged 10; hit by a bakery truck in 1904. She was the first motor vehicle traffic fatality in Washington, D.C. By the old grave digger's reasoning, I thought, we should blame all the city's traffic problems on the ghost of this poor little girl.

I turned a corner and went through a row of heavily damaged gray sandstone cenotaphs. On some of the markers the names were so obscured they couldn't be read. Others were split into several pieces. The dome of one was missing. There was a pile of sandstone dust at its base.

"Powerful ghost," I thought, and couldn't help but smile as I remembered what I had read a few years ago in a United Press International article. Dick West had written that several years after the Civil War the practice of placing cenotaphs in Congressional Cemetery was stopped, largely due to the efforts of Massachusetts Senator G.F. Hoar. He thought the taxpayer provided cenotaphs were an eyesore. As Senator Hoar put it "They add a new terror to death."

A Few More Prominent Places With Revisitations From The Past

The Old Post Office

The second tallest structure in Washington, D.C. is an imposing granite building sporting a 300 foot clock tower at Pennsylvania Avenue and 12th Street Northwest. It's the old Post Office Building and it is now used by several other federal agencies. The building has also been revitalized with a thriving shopping mall under a glass roof, but none of the renovations seemed to have stopped stories that the building is haunted.

The project seemed cursed right from the start. Construction began in 1892. That was the year iron and steel workers went on a major strike throughout the country. The following year a "financial panic" gripped the country for the next four years. President Grover Cleveland exerted tremendous pressure on the builder to complete the project. The federal city, and the whole country, was growing. Five new states were admitted to the Union in 1890: North and South Dakota, Montana, Washington, and Idaho. The following year Wyoming was brought in, and in 1896 Utah was added. That was also the year that Rural Free Delivery began.

The Post Office had its work cut out for it and it needed more space. In fact, the government began moving the Post Office into the facility two years before completion. I am told that on the day it opened the Postmaster General stepped into what he thought was an elevator car on the fifth floor only to find no car. He fell to his death at the bottom of the shaft.

The architecture of the building was soon out of style and many people considered it an eyesore. The Federal Post Office turned the building over to the District of Columbia postal department in 1934. Reportedly, the old Post Office building was scheduled to be razed at least three or four times, but somehow managed to escape demolition. It definitely stood out among those neo-classic structures in the Federal Triangle. Apparently surviving to be old and ugly counted for something, and in 1978 the old Post Office Building was designated a National Historic Building.

Down through those turbulent years there have been reports of a ghost in the building. There have always been elevator problems. Doors open between floors. Sometimes a car goes to a floor unsummoned. Alarms have gone off when no one has been inside a car. I am told that more than once since English bells, a bicentennial gift from England, were installed in the Old Post Office tower, they rang of their own volition.

I received a letter a couple of years ago from someone who described an incident involving the bells and the night manager. It seems that on this occasion the bells started ring-

ing during his shift, so he rushed to see who was pulling the ropes in the ringing chamber. The ropes were moving, but no one was pulling them!

During another night time ringing episode I'm told two employees rushed into the ringing chamber just in time to see what appeared to be a man clad in a very old long coat and black boots. He vanished in the shadows. The pair of postal workers ran down the stairs but the doors were still locked. No one had come in or out, according to security.

The old Post Office was built back in the days of President Grover Cleveland. Many people considered it an eyesore, but it survived several attempts to tear it down, and is now designated an historic building. An historic *haunted* building, according to some.
Courtesy Library of Congress

The Inconsolable Woodrow Wilson

It was 1924 when President Woodrow Wilson died, yet according to some Washingtonians he still revisits his old home in Northwest Washington.

Wilson, born in Virginia in 1856, was the son of a Presbyterian minister. During his boyhood Wilson's father served several churches in southern cities. When time came for college, Woodrow Wilson began at Davidson, a small Presbyterian college in North Carolina but had to drop out briefly because of family illness. When he returned to school it was to Princeton where, in 1902 that school chose him as its President. Wilson resigned in 1910 to run for Governor. Three years later he was elected President of the United States. Wilson considered himself the steward of the people. He proposed many reforms during his first term, but the shadow of war in Europe kept getting larger. During his second term Wilson was reluctant to abandon neutrality but when it was required he led the United States on a crusade to "make the world safe for democracy." Wilson also played a major role as peacemaker, but the U.S. Senate declined to ratify the treaty ending World War I because it contained a clause establishing a League of Nations. It seemed to break Wilson's spirit.

President Woodrow Wilson in happier days. He is being welcomed by his predecessor President William Howard Taft. *Courtesy Library of Congress*

Former President Woodrow Wilson is shown here leaving his S Street home. The stroke he suffered before his term expired left him unable to walk without assistance. Some claim to have heard his shuffling footsteps and the tapping of his cane inside his home long after his death. *Courtesy Library of Congress*

The President began his physical decline in the fall of 1919 after suffering a stroke. However, his wife, Edith, and those close to him shielded Wilson from the press—and the public—keeping his disability a secret. When he left office in 1921, President Wilson and his wife moved into an elegant house just off Embassy Row, at 2340 S Street Northwest.

Looking old, worn, and haggard, Wilson the citizen lived out the remainder of his years in a quiet routine at his new home. He moved about with an ever-present cane from the large collection he owned. An elevator helped him get upstairs to the bedroom.

Wilson never quite recovered from the country's rejection of his dream—the League of Nations. Some newspaper accounts from that era indicate that he brooded. Sources close to him were quoted as saying that he had periodic lapses of memory and what still other friends described as "unpredictable crying spells."

Woodrow Wilson died about three years after leaving office, but several old-timers say that he hasn't left his beloved home. Legend has it that the former President has been heard more than once climbing the stairs to his bedroom. Some who used to work in the home have sworn to hearing sounds that remind them of a man sobbing, and they speculate that it's Wilson's ghost still unable to cope with the shattering of his dream for the League of Nations.

An article in the *Washington Post* in 1969 focused on a caretaker at the Wilson house who had had enough of the "slow shuffle." He told the reporter that it sounded like someone walking with a cane. I talked with a carpenter and a gardener who also indicated that they had heard some strange noises in the house when they had been around late. However, the hostesses who now staff the house for the National Trust for Historic Preservation, insist that the sounds are caused by an aging house, not the ghost of a former President.

This is the rear of the Woodrow Wilson house. The window on the second floor illuminates the bedroom where "the slow shuffle" of a man having difficulty walking has been heard. It was also President Wilson's bedroom. *Courtesy Lee Shephard*

This stairway leading up to the second floor of the Wilson house is also where sounds have been heard of someone having difficulty walking. There are those who believe that President Wilson has never left his beloved home, although he died in 1924. *Courtesy Lee Shephard*

In the 1980s a cleaning woman at the Wilson House reported to her supervisor that she had heard the sound of a typewriter, only to see no one else in the room. Patricia Sullivan, a former Wilson House administrator, told writer Susan Gervasi in 1989 that she had been working alone in the house only to have her thoughts disrupted by the sounds of the piano being played in the parlor.

Gervasi, in her *Washington Post* story, describes another incident related to her by a docent who was working a wedding party at the house. Knowing the former President's love of small children (he is said to have kept cookies on hand for them) the docent remarked to the six-year-old flower girl that President Wilson would have been pleased to see her.

"Oh, he is glad. He told me," replied the little girl to the startled docent.

The Smithsonian Castle

I grew up thinking that every castle had its ghost. Imagine my disappointment when I discovered, during my initial research for this book, that America's favorite castle—The Smithsonian Institution—appeared ghostless. Although I had searched through archives, and made inquires of Castle staff and guards, I found no stories of James Smithson's ghost haunting the Institution named for him. Well, over the years it would seem that the bones of the old scientist just couldn't take being slighted. If we are to believe some of the stories that have surfaced during the last twenty years, Smithson stirs again!

James Smithson was a British scientist who was born in France in 1765 and christened James Lewis Mace. However, his mother had been widowed before his birth. Several years later, James learned his real father was Hugh Smithson, Duke of Northumberland. When a student at Oxford, young James began signing his papers "James Smithson." By the age of 22 he had become a fellow of the Royal Society—an independent body, founded in 1660, to promote and encourage scientific research and its application.

During his lifetime James Smithson, best known as a mineralogist, presented more than a score of scientific papers before the Society. A zinc carbonate, *Smithsonite*, was named for him. Smithson died most wealthy in Genoa, Italy, in 1829 at the age of sixty-four. Why a man who had never visited the United States and apparently never corresponded with anyone in this country would leave a fortune to it is a major mystery. Yet Smithson left a substantial endowment to found an American institution "for the increase and diffusion of knowledge among men."

The Smithsonian Institution is seen here from the top of the Washington Monument in 1890. John Quincy Adams had sponsored the legislation in Congress that set in motion the acceptance of an endowment from the estate of minerologist James Smithson. Why Smithson gave so much money to found a scientific institution in a country he had never visited remains a mystery. Smithson finally got to the United States, however—his bones were brought over and re-buried in the Smithsonian Castle. Now, some are convinced, Smithson's ghost has walked its halls. *Courtesy Library of Congress*

It took eight years of wrangling in Congress before the Smithson gift was accepted and another nine years before the Smithsonian Institution became a reality. The Castle was its first structure.

It probably would never have occurred to Congress to bring Smithson's bones to this country and re-bury them inside the Castle had not an Italian marble drilling company bought the Genoan-English Cemetery in which he was interred, and began moving graves so it could excavate marble. The guard's room, just inside the Castle doors, was redesigned as a tomb. Apparently for more than half-a-century Smithson slept soundly in his new surroundings. Then, sometime in the late 1970s, watchmen and guards began to whisper about some strange happenings. The tower elevator would jam without cause. Sometimes, the alarm would go off—even with no one inside.

Sarah Booth Conroy, writing in the *Washington Post*, November 1, 1981, said, "A pesky phantom pulled back the necklace of one woman visitor and let it snap to her neck." She also wrote that books have been pulled out and left all over the floor of the Woodrow Wilson library. The Wilson Center is a relatively new addition to the Castle. The special events coordinator sometimes works late. "If the castle isn't supposed to be haunted, somebody better tell the ghosts." She gets to hear all the latest stories from the cleaning crews and tales from the guards who work all night.

An administrative assistant to Smithsonian Secretary S. Dillon Ripley told Conroy "we often feel as though someone unseen is there." Conroy reported that when the third floor was divided horizontally to create the Wilson Center, guards claimed that Smithson "rocked in his grave."

The commotion and turmoil was apparently so disconcerting that Castle historian James Goode had the tomb opened. Much to his puzzlement it was empty. Goode had workmen drill into the base. There, in a tin box, were Smithson's bones—all jumbled together. Scraps of his original coffin with his name in brass tacks were also inside the box.

Conroy concluded her article by writing that apparently there have been no further disturbances inside the Castle since Goode had the bones reassembled in proper order and re-installed inside the crypt.

Marcia Burns Van Ness and Her Husband's Mausoleum

As thousands of Washingtonians and tourists alike pass by the Pan American Union Building at 17th and Constitution daily; few are familiar with the mansion that occupied the land for almost one hundred years. It was owned by a famous family around whom District storytellers spun ghostly tales.

General John Peter Van Ness, was a very popular mayor of Washington. His mansion rivaled the White House in design and beauty. *Courtesy Martin Luther King, Jr. Public Library, District of Columbia*

John Peter Van Ness was a well-liked New York politician and protégé of Aaron Burr. Both men came south at about the same time. Van Ness was elected to the 6th Congress that convened in December 1799. In the Presidential election of 1800 Burr had received the same number of electoral votes as Thomas Jefferson, but the House of Representatives named Jefferson President and Burr Vice President—largely because

of the influence exerted by Burr's old rival Alexander Hamilton, the Federalist leader.

Van Ness liked the rustic boom town atmosphere that was the new Federal City. During his tenure in Congress he met the lovely Marcia Burns, daughter of David Burns who sold the government much of the land on which the District of Columbia is built. In those days Congress convened an average of just under eighteen weeks a year, so when Van Ness began spending most of his time in Washington, his constituents began to take it personal. They voted him out of office in 1803. Van Ness was in love. He didn't mind. He married Marcia and moved in with his father-in-law, David Burns. "Obstinent Davy," as George Washington labeled him because of the hard stance he took in selling his land, may have had accumulated wealth, but Scotsman as he was, he continued to live in an old log house—not far from where the Washington Monument is now located.

Van Ness had many influential friends and no one enjoyed entertaining and talking politics more than he did. For a while, he contented himself with being entertained and managing his wife's estate. When he decided to build his own house, the only man he considered capable of designing a mansion suitable for the style of entertainment he envisioned was the noted Benjamin Latrobe. The house was finished a few years after the War of 1812 ended, and most of Washington was still in a festive mood. Newspaper articles written at the time the Van Ness home was completed say that few homes in any city could rival it. It was asserted to be the first house in America to have indoor plumbing that supplied hot and cold running water. The north portico of the house was modeled after the White House, right down to the same number of pillars. The south front faced the river, and looked out on an immense fruit orchard, according to an article in *Washingtonia, The Nation's Weekly.*

John Van Ness had wanted his house finished by the time his only daughter, Ann, returned from school in Philadelphia so that she would have a suitable place to entertain young gentlemen callers. Another reporter called it the "city's finest" home, and remarked that the cream of Washington society visited there often. Over the years most of the city's elite—including Vice President Aaron Burr, recent war hero Commodore Stephen Decatur and his lovely wife Susan, Congressman John C. Calhoun, Attorney General William Wirt, House Speaker Henry Clay and others from the legislative, judicial, and executive branches of government could be seen coming and going at the Van Ness mansion.

It is said that one of the most lavish affairs at the Van Ness mansion was staged in celebration of daughter Ann's marriage to Arthur Middleton of South Carolina. Middleton's father was one of the signers of the Declaration of Independence. One of the saddest days in the Van Ness home was when Ann died in childbirth in 1822. The baby was stillborn.

John Van Ness tried to overcome his sadness by plunging himself deeper into his work. He was now Mayor of the District of Columbia, and served as General of the local Militia, too. One writer said that the deeply religious Marcia, mourned for her daughter and attempted to find solace in her charitable activities. However, the grief manifested itself in failing health, and within a few years she died. Newspapers of that day said she was given a public funeral as a testimony of how well she was loved by her city. Apparently she was the first woman in the United States to be so honored. It was reported that children from the orphan asylum, where she had devoted much of her time and energy, walked beside her bier.

It was difficult for a man like Van Ness to survive the loss of his family. There was absolutely nothing that he loved more. He vowed that his wife, his departed daughter, and her infant would have a final resting place befitting his love. Van Ness personally supervised the construction of a mausoleum, which was of the finest brick and marble, and cost about half what it had cost him to build his mansion. Another reporter described it as "an exact replica of the pillared temple of Tivoli." The mausoleum sits on top of the highest hill in Oak Hill Cemetery looking down on picturesque Rock Creek.

Having provided his family with an eternal resting place, Van Ness began to slowly increase his activities once again, though some who knew him well said it was obvious the sparkle had gone from his personality. Van Ness was becoming legendary. No one in Washington rivaled "His Honor," Van Ness in entertaining at home. One of his most talked-about and anticipated events was an annual banquet for the members of Congress. It is said people lined up along the streets to catch a glimpse of some of the more famous statesmen as their carriages turned into the great circular drive leading to the Van Ness Mansion. As his age advanced, his body grew weaker; his mind returned more and more frequently to the days he had spent with his wife, and to the days he had been denied with his daughter and a grandchild. Servants said they sometimes overheard him talking to his family as though they were still with him.

An increasingly despondent Van Ness began to withdraw into the shadows of his home, not only losing contact with his friends, but with reality as well. Reports from that period say he didn't care that the mansion was decaying and his staff was dwindling. Whispers circulated about certain rooms in the old mansion that no one entered, and that more than one ghost haunted its corridors. Allegedly, laughter from his departed daughter evaporated into bloodcurdling screams; similar to those she had made just before dying in childbirth. One article mentioned "footsteps unattached to human bodies." Another brief story focused on a small lady "in quaint costume and wearing an old-fashioned bonnet," who had been seen wandering the hallways upstairs.

Van Ness was portrayed by the newspapers as having been so caught up in his despair that he paid the tales little, if any attention—that is, if he was aware they were circulating. Even when the staff dwindled, he made no effort to replace them, hastening the decay of the estate and the house in which he died in 1846.

When death called John Peter Van Ness to join his family; his body was placed on a bier that was pulled to Oak Hill Cemetery by his six most cherished white horses. The United States was at war with Mexico, and yet Washington took time to mourn more than just a former Mayor. Van Ness had been a man who had been loved by many. One writer recalled that "many private houses on the route of the funeral procession were draped in mourning."

During the graveside ceremony on Oak Hill, the white stallions were observed munching grass by the mausoleum. When they lowered their heads behind a mound, one mourner sobbed, "They've buried their heads with their master." In a few days most of the mourners put John Van Ness out of their

minds and resumed the routines of the living. However, for some others it wasn't that simple. His decaying mansion was a reminder to some of his happier years. They wanted it restored as a memorial to the man. The opposition believed it could produce only nightmares, for ghostly tales had increased since the funeral, and now included new and strange reports of activity on the mansion grounds. So the mansion continued to decay and to be the source of incredible stories.

As John Peter Van Ness advanced in age, his thoughts returned to happier times with his wife and daughter. He became more reclusive. Some of his staff said it was as though he just sat around waiting on death. *Courtesy Library of Congress*

The ghost of Marcia Van Ness, who sought consolation by helping orphans when her only child died in childbirth is said to have haunted the Van Ness mansion after her death. *Courtesy Columbia Historical Society*

During the Civil War Thomas Green owned the old Van Ness mansion for a while. Green, described as an "inoffensive old gentleman," lived there with his wife. In the wild excitement which followed the assassination of President Lincoln a story was set afloat that Booth conspirators had originally planned to kidnap Lincoln and hold him in the wine cellar of the old Van Ness mansion until they could spirit him across the Potomac to be tried in the south as a war criminal. Green and his wife were arrested and locked up in the old Capitol Prison for six weeks before the authorities finally decided the couple were victims of just another story that swirled around the old estate.

There was a time when sounds of gaiety radiated from the mansion of General John Peter Van Ness. Even after the house was vacant, sounds were heard, not all of them happy. *Courtesy Library of Congress*

In the early part of the 1900s a writer interviewed some of those who had experienced supernatural manifestations associated with the ruin of some fifty years, now being torn down. The reporter said some who had dared to cut across the deserted, expansive grounds during the late night hours, heard sounds of laughter and gaiety float from the old house, as though still carried on the winds that swept through the once beautifully manicured lawn, shrubs, and trees. Another reporter recalled an incident that had happened to the wife of a caretaker. The woman swore that a wispy woman appeared before her bedside late one night and attempted to give her a message to relay to someone in another part of the city. The message was lost, however, because the woman's husband awakened and rolled over—causing the ghost to vanish.

One newspaper article quoted several witnesses, unnamed, who claimed to have seen specters of six headless white horses galloping around the mansion grounds. One of them told the reporter that the moonlight was "so bright their gleaming coats looked like silver." Stories about the six headless white horses have persisted down through the years, even though the mansion of John Peter Van Ness is long gone. More than a century after his death a newspaper article retold the legend, declaring that the phantom horses are almost always spotted on the anniversary of the General's death, retracing that journey to Oak Hill Cemetery and circling the grounds of the Pan American Union Building at a gallop—frantically searching for their master.

John Peter Van Ness loved horses. A short time after his death a newspaper article quoted several witnesses who claimed to have seen specters of six headless white horses galloping around the mansion grounds. The moonlight was so bright, said one witness, that their gleaming coats looked liked silver. *Courtesy Library of Congress*

The ghostly shapes of the six white horses that pulled the coffin of John Van Ness to Oak Hill Cemetery have been spotted circling the family mausoleum, too. *Courtesy Lee Shephard*

Just a few years ago a motorist tried to explain to police why he had run his car off Rock Creek Parkway. He told an officer it was because he had seen the shimmering forms of six headless white horses up by the Van Ness mausoleum. His excuse may have kept the legend alive, but it did nothing for the man's reputation for being able to hold his liquor.

Ghosts of the Octagon

The Octagon, one of Washington's oldest houses, was visited by all the leading figures of the new government, some of whom still drop by from time to time. *Courtesy Martin Luther King Jr. Public Library, District of Columbia*

The Octagon, at New York Avenue and 18th Street, Northwest, is perhaps the District of Columbia's most handsome haunted home. It was used by President and Mrs. James Madison while the White House was being rebuilt after the fire of 1814. Dolley Madison's ghost revisits there from time to time, and there are tales of other phantom visitors, too.

Encounters of several types have been reported in newspapers for more than one hundred years. Some involve the great spiral staircase in the entry hall, others have their origins in the dank cellar or subterranean kitchen. Only the U.S. Capitol and the White House seem to be revisited more than this elegant and sturdy home built for Colonel John Tayloe, a close friend of George Washington.

Work on the Octagon began in 1797, and the retired President frequently rode up to the District of Columbia with his friend, Col. Tayloe, to inspect the progress. Dr. William Thornton, who had not yet submitted his Capitol building design, was Tayloe's architect. Even though the President's Mansion was under construction just two blocks away, the area still had the look of being in the countryside. Major Pierre Charles L'Enfant, President Washington's choice to draw up plans for the Federal City, had already plotted the streets. New York Avenue and 18th Street formed an acute angle and thus presented Dr. Thornton with a design challenge that resulted in the unique shape of the house. Thornton was a remarkable man, with an apparent natural ability when it came to building design. The West Indies born Thornton had earned his medical degree in Edinburgh, Scotland—coming to Washington in 1793. His intelligence, charm and wit made him a most popular gentleman, and a much sought after guest. Medicine wasn't his only interest, Thornton had published papers on astronomy, philosophy, finance, art, and language. It's believed he had only a couple of weeks of formal study in the field of architecture.

The Octagon is considered a fine example of the Federal style. To fit the unusual shape of the lot, Thornton designed the house with six sides. It took two years to build. Why or how it became known as "The Octagon" isn't known.

Except for the period during the War of 1812, the Tayloe family occupied the Octagon from the time it was completed in the early 1800s until Mrs. Tayloe's death in 1855. The Colonel and his wife had fifteen children, seven sons and eight daughters. One article from a nineteenth century newspaper said that the Tayloe girls were as famed for their grace, charm, and beauty as for their wealth.

According to the stories that have survived, some of their love affairs were turbulent and involved dramatic denouements on the huge oval staircase. A striking bell lantern hanging down the stairwell from a twenty-two-foot chain casts a shadowy light on the large statues that occupied niches in the wall of the main stairs. That gave the entry hall an ominous air that set the stage for the arguments and violence that are part of the Octagon's history.

The ghostly presence of the Tayloe sisters have been heard re-enacting their tragic deaths on this stairway. The hanging lantern sometimes sways for no discernible reason. *Courtesy Lee Shephard*

The interior of the Octagon House is unique. Some of the rooms are positioned at angles that result in odd corners. Closets go into other closets. Doors are said to sometimes open with a squeak and shut with a slam—of their own volition. *Courtesy Lee Shephard*

Early in the 1800s, one of the Tayloe girls was supposed to have fallen in love with a British officer, but feelings between the United States and Great Britain were so hostile that her father would have no part of such a relationship. His refusal to allow the Englishman to set foot in his house sparked several loud arguments. It was just after one of these heated battles, on a dark and stormy night, that the girl grabbed up her candle and stomped up the stairs. As she neared the top, there was a scream and her body plunged down the stairwell and landed in a crumpled heap beneath the swaying bell lantern.

One reporter recalling the story decades later, quoted some who speculated that the clash with her father proved too much and she chose to end her life. Nonsense, said others who believed she tripped and fell over the rather low railing. That daughter's restive ghost is said to still haunt the stairway on certain stormy nights. A flickering candle may be seen casting the shadows of the railing against the opposite wall as it moves upward one step at a time. According to those who have witnessed it, the drama always ends the same way. There is a shriek, followed a second later by a sickening thud.

The death of a daughter, particularly in such a horrible manner, grieved the Colonel and allegedly hardened his feelings toward the British. Storytellers say that he was haunted by his daughter's ghost and sought to stay away from the Octagon after her death.

When the War of 1812 erupted, Tayloe reasoned that flight to his Mount Airy plantation would offer the family safety and provide him an escape from those terrible nightmares. So he arranged with the French Minister to the United States to make the Octagon his official residence, and then escorted his family to their Virginia plantation. It wasn't long before the British overran the Americans at Bladensburg and moved into the city with little resistance. Many historians believe the Octagon would have gone up in flames from British torches had not the house been flying the French flag.

When Colonel Tayloe heard of the plight of the President, he wrote to Madison at Montpelier, Madison's Virginia estate; offering the Octagon as a temporary home until 1600 Pennsylvania Avenue was rebuilt. Eager to return to Washington so he could better prosecute the war and conduct affairs of state Madison accepted the generous offer. The President and Dolley moved into the Octagon during the fall of 1814. The Madison's kept up a round of Washington social functions and tried to bolster the spirits of the war-weary citizens. The war was not a popular one, and the charred ruins in the city made the dark cloud hanging over Washington even darker.

Five months after the Madison's moved into the Octagon a courier from Ghent brought the President the treaty that declared the end of the war the previous December. Madison ratified the treaty at this desk in a room at the head of the stairs on the second floor. *Courtesy Lee Shephard*

Colonel John Tayloe, who had the Octagon built, couldn't bear to live there after tragic accidents claimed two of his daughters. Some say their dying screams haunted him and kept him from sleeping. *Courtesy The Octagon*

When the war ended the parties began in earnest. The first social event at the temporary Executive Mansion was an informal open house, but after that the guest lists for the celebrations at the Octagon included foreign diplomats, congressmen, local politicians, military leaders, and the cream of the Federal City's society.

If anyone in Washington knew how to celebrate the end of a war, it was Dolley Madison. Well-known for her social grace, she generally greeted her guests dressed in the latest fashions topped by a plumed turban that made her appear taller. She was quite conscious of her shortness.

President James Madison, and his wife Dolley, lived in the Octagon while the White House was being rebuilt after the British put the torch to it. Although they lived in the Tayloe Mansion for just over a year, Dolley loved the Octagon so much that her spirit is said to revisit from time to time. She manifests her presence as a cold spot scented with the fragrance of lilacs. It is the scent she almost always wore. *Courtesy Columbia Historical Society*

Parties were an almost daily affair at the Octagon while the Madison's lived there. They seemed to be equally relaxed entertaining forty or so friends, or four hundred or more guests. Some say that it was during one of Dolley's lavish parties that she slipped away for a rendezvous in the garden with Aaron Burr. Burr is supposed to have scaled a ten-foot wall just to see the President's wife. Apparently it was a "welcome back" encounter. Burr had spent several years in European exile, following his controversial duel with Alexander Hamilton. Burr had been Dolley Payne Todd's suitor some twenty years before when she "a vivacious widow." That was before she met and married James Madison, sixteen years her senior, in 1794.

Years after the Madison era, in the second half of the nineteenth century, newspapers were writing accounts about apparitions of footmen dressed in the full uniform of that earlier period, hailing the carriages of guests. They quoted some who said they had heard the sounds of wheels rumbling over gravel roads, the opening and closing of carriage doors, and the fading sounds of carriages rolling away.

This was just one of several phenomena associated with the Octagon that the press has chronicled. Dolley Madison's ghost has been seen standing in front of the mantelpiece in the ballroom, where she used to receive her guests over a century and a half ago. One article quoted a witness to "the wispy form of the turbaned hostess," who was seen dancing through the entrance hall.

Concerned that they may be taking advantage of the generosity, hospitality, and patriotism of Colonel Tayloe, the Madison's moved from the Octagon in October 1815 into a town home a block away on 19th Street, NW. From there the Madison's continued to conduct affairs of state, host lavish parties, and oversee the re-building of the President's Mansion until President Madison's term ended in March 1817.

Meanwhile, Colonel Tayloe moved his family back into the Octagon from their Mount Airy, Virginia, plantation, but their second attempt at living in that house was to be tragedy-marred as well—if we're to believe the legends.

One of the Tayloe daughters, who had eloped against the wishes of her father, had returned to beg his forgiveness. Legend has it that they met on the stairway. The Colonel couldn't bring himself to forgive his daughter for not marrying the gentleman of position he had chosen for her. The Colonel, in an ill-tempered mood, hardly glanced at his young daughter as he continued down the stairs. The girl was in his path, and not wishing to continue the discussion, he tried to move past her. The girl either lost her balance or fell trying to escape her father's touch. She tumbled past the Colonel and fell dead of a broken neck at the foot of the stairs.

It is difficult to imagine what must have gone through the Colonel's mind as he saw a second daughter become a victim of the oval stairway. Some think that the shock of losing two of his girls contributed, in part, to his own death at the relatively young age of fifty-seven.

The ghost of the second Tayloe girl also is alleged to return to the scene of her accident. Some people who have never heard the tale walk around the spot at the foot of the stairs where the young woman's body once lay in a crumpled mass. Perhaps they sense a cold spot or pick up other vibrations.

After the death of Mrs. John Tayloe in 1855, the mansion changed hands several times and was allowed to deteriorate. The constant acting out of its violent history during late night hours was enough to keep most people away.

Sometime after the Tayloe's moved out and before the outbreak of the Civil War, an old gambler and his retinue of women supposedly occupied the upper floors of the decaying old mansion. It was a more than suitable place for the activities of the gambler. He became fascinated by the intricately designed bellpull system used to summon servants, and used to position himself at his card table so that he was within reach of the rope. He pulled it frequently to summon food or drink, a new deck of cards, or one of his female cohorts.

This staircase inside the Octagon was used only by servants when the Tayloes lived there. In a later time, it provided an unseen way for a farmer evicted from the premises by a gambler to re-enter the Octagon and kill the man who had cheated him at cards. *Courtesy Lee Shephard*

One night the gambler was assaulted by a hard-drinking farmer he had cheated. As the farmer slammed the gambler against the wall, the card shark grabbed the bellpull for support and reached for his gun. The farmer's gun exploded first and the gambler crumpled to the floor frantically clutching the bellpull.

It is said by the best of old D.C. storytellers that the gambler's ghost, on revisits to the Octagon, has often grabbed for the bellpull since that fateful night.

Reporters have frequently filed stories about screams of agony, sobs, and moans of despair, echoing through the Octagon. A writer in the later part of the 1800s said "the spectral

goings on there are so extraordinary that no one will live in the house." The article attributed the moans and sobs to a slave who had been whipped or otherwise tortured to death by "the former proprietor of the establishment."

This is what the Octagon's neighborhood looked like in the early 1860s. The trees make it difficult to see the Octagon, but it stands just beyond this storage area for the marble being used in construction of the new Treasury building two blocks away on 15th Street. Long mule teams were used to pull the huge marble columns. *Courtesy National Archives.*

The Octagon was deserted, for the most part, during the Civil War. Tunnels at the rear of the house are supposed to have led to the White House and to the Potomac River. Abolitionists allegedly used the old Potomac tunnel as they helped runaway slaves. They would then hide them for a while in the cellar of the Octagon until they had regained their strength. Another legend has it that southern enemies of President Lincoln once planned to abduct him, and via the tunnel system, spirit him from the White House to the Octagon to the Potomac where a boat would be waiting to take them to Richmond. There the Confederate States of America would put the President on trial for war crimes.

During the latter part of the Civil War, the Union Army used the house as a war records office; and temporarily, as a place for treatment of wounded and dying soldiers. One reporter speculated the sounds of sobbing and moaning could be from the souls of runaway slaves crying out in nightmares of previously endured tortures, or they could be the agony of men wounded in battle.

On April 18, 1891, a story in the *Evening Star* told about how the Sisters of Charity moved into the house "after purifying it from top to bottom with holy water." It didn't work. When the Sisters of Charity fell victim to the bizarre goings on and had to move, it was time for something to be done. Another newspaper article told of how a dozen men took it upon themselves to investigate. Determined to put the ghost talk to rest once and for all, the men gathered up their bed rolls and went inside the Octagon to spend the night. They vowed to capture anyone responsible for generating the "ghosts."

Shortly after midnight, the reporter said, "female shrieks, the clanking of sabers, and thumping sounds in the wall" drove the twelve men to seek slumber elsewhere.

In 1902 the American Institute of Architects acquired the Octagon. Almost a half-century of deterioration was stopped. Restoration work was begun. One day as workmen were repairing a wall they may have inadvertently solved the riddle of those "thumping sounds" that plagued residents for years. They came upon the skeleton of a young woman. Her finger bones on both hands were clenched tight, as though she had died knocking on the wall. She was taken out of the wall and given a proper burial. The thumping sounds were never again heard in that part of the house.

The Octagon was saved when the American Institute of Architects managed to acquire it in the early 1900s. Dr. William Thornton had designed the unusual home just a few years before he submitted plans for building the Capitol. The AIA had a dream of restoring the fine old mansion to the luster of the Tayloe era.
Courtesy Lee Shephard

At the time, one of the Colonel's descendants said that she seemed to recall a tale her grandmother had told of a soldier and a slave girl when the French Ministry occupied the Octagon. They were lovers, but in a jealous rage, the soldier killed her and somehow managed to seal her body inside a hollow wall.

Restoration was a costly struggle, but the AIA persisted. It was their dream to one day restore the majestic old structure to its original state. Meanwhile, more strange events occurred and new stories arose. A caretaker told a newspaper reporter in the 1950s how he returned after a night out with his family to find all of the lights on. Because of faulty old wiring, the watchman insisted, he *always* turned the lights off anytime he left the house. It was locked up tight, just as he had left it. Everything inside seemed normal. However, the edge of the carpet at the foot of the stairs was turned over—right at the very spot where death had claimed one the Tayloe girls.

A physician admitted to an encounter of a different kind a few years later. Back then, doctors still made house calls. This particular doctor had received a call from Caretaker James Cyprus, whose wife was ill. As the doctor prepared to leave, he mustered up enough courage to ask Cyprus if there was a costume party going on in the Octagon that evening.

"No, no there isn't," Cyprus replied. The doctor looked perplexed and described to Cyprus a man in colonial military uniform he had seen coming down the stairs as he was going up. The doctor told Cyprus that he had to move over to let him pass.

John Sherwood described that incident in the *Evening Star* in August 1965. He also wrote that "Velma May, curator of the house, has seen the big chandelier that hangs down the stairwell swing of its own volition. Another time she found tiptoeing tracks of human feet in the undisturbed dust on the top floor landing."

Even quite recently there have been reports of encounters with Dolley Madison's ghost, which often manifests itself surrounded by the fragrance of lilacs. Apparently she still visits often, for I have had several encounters related to me. One came from an official with the American Institute of Architects. He did not want to be identified, but said that on two separate occasions when he was showing people through the house during a major renovation in the 1960s; the guests had mentioned walking through a pocket of scented air. In neither case were those who made contact aware of the legends. The AIA official swore that no flowers were in bloom. He told me he stood within a few feet of one of the people in the pocket of perfume but he never got a whiff. On another occasion, a person walked into such a pocket, walked out of it, and then stepped back into it.

An assistant secretary for the Institute related a few years ago how she had sensed the presence of someone with her in one of the Octagon rooms. The woman told of hearing a very deep sigh while waiting for someone to come down from the third floor, which has now been converted to offices. She didn't think too much about the sound; but was surprised to turn around after hearing it again to find no one there. The presence she felt made her ill at ease. She never put the experience out of her mind, especially after learning that the room was a favorite of Dolley Madison's.

When the American Institute of Architects was preparing for the Octagon restoration, an architectural photographer was commissioned to provide material for the renovation committee. He took interior and exterior photographs, and the AIA had them processed. One picture turned out to be highly unusual. Without knowing it, the photographer had caught on film the apparition of a woman slipping into the house from the rear garden. She was passing through the locked rear doors. The AIA official who told me the story said the form wasn't clear enough to determine whether it was Dolley Madison. "Of course," he said with a smile, "it could also have been one of the Tayloes." The AIA would not release the photograph for publication in this book.

Many who visit the three-story brick structure have claimed that it is not uncommon to encounter the aroma of food being prepared in the kitchen. When they investigate, they find the kitchen deserted and the food displayed there made of wax.

When I first visited the Octagon in 1970, the curator, who had been there for about six months, was reluctant to discuss the old tales. The house was just being reopened to the public after extensive restoration work and she said that the Octagon board of directors was more interested in publicity about the historical significance of the house. She confessed a personal interest, even an inquisitiveness, about the ghostly manifestations, but steadfastly maintained that since she had been there, she had neither seen nor heard anything unusual.

"Yes," she said, "the floors creak very nicely. Some of the doors also have squeaks." She rightly insisted that that wasn't evidence of ghosts. She also related how she had often worked late into the evening but had encountered no apparitions or supernatural phenomena of any sort.

In December of 1972 I had occasion to return to the Octagon on another assignment. As I sat by the curator's desk, the phone rang. It was her husband; apparently telling her he would be working late. As she discussed other methods of transportation home, she told him, "You know I don't really care to stay in this house alone after dark."

The curator would not discuss that remark with me. She seemed edgy. I soon left, but I couldn't help but wonder what caused such a change in so short a time. Within a few months the Octagon had another curator.

The smell of food cooking sometimes drifts from the kitchen in the basement of the Octagon. When the source of the odors is investigated, however, the room is always deserted. *Courtesy Lee Shephard*

The Curse of the Hope Diamond

The specter of a nude woman, "of unparalleled beauty and form," is said to occasionally grace the imposing stairway inside the palatial Indonesian Embassy at 2020 Massachusetts Avenue, Northwest. Those who keep alive the lore of Embassy Row like to think "the nocturnal nude," as one reporter labeled her, is a youthful Evalyn Walsh McLean visiting the home she first occupied upon coming East—a home where she had known only happiness. All of that, of course, was before she and her husband, Ned, acquired the infamous, and some say diabolical, diamond so strangely misnamed Hope.

Evalyn Walsh McLean was the daughter of a Colorado miner who moved east and traveled in wealthy circles after her *Father Struck It Rich*. However, it wasn't until she was on her honeymoon with the *Washington Post's* Ned McLean that she spotted and coveted the legendary Hope Diamond. It became hers within a few years and tragedy followed. *Courtesy Father Struck It Rich, (Brown, Little and Company, 1936)*

Evalyn Walsh first met Edward McLean in Denver when he was covering the Democratic Convention for his father's newspaper. The 1908 election went to Republican William Howard Taft, but politics was the farthest thing from the minds of Evalyn and Ned. Evalyn Walsh was the daughter of a western miner who had struck it rich; Edward McLean was heir to the *Washington Post*. They were married that year, and celebrated by leaving the country for "a happy whirlwind of worldwide travels," as one newspaper article described their honeymoon.

Ned McLean took his new wife Evalyn Walsh McLean on an exotic honeymoon. It was while they were in the mid-east that Evalyn first saw the brilliant blue sapphire diamond that she would own within a few years. *Courtesy Library of Congress*

It was while the McLean's were in Turkey that Evalyn first saw the most seductive gem she had ever laid her eyes on. She was totally captivated by the shimmering blue diamond on the neck of a sultan's harem favorite, and never really put it from her mind. In 1922 when she heard that the sultan had been dethroned and his favorite wife murdered, she set out to acquire the stone.

The fact that the sultan's life had fallen apart when he came into possession of the Hope Diamond didn't seem to bother Evalyn McLean. She told reporters shortly after acquiring the stone that she never believed any of the stories of tragedy and death connected with it. There were whispers, however, that she discouraged her friends from touching it and never allowed her children to. For one who did not believe those sinister stories, many thought it strange that Evalyn arranged a ceremony in which a priest blessed the stone. One reporter said that the guests at the ceremony became rather unnerved when a storm broke out and lightning flashed through the windows as the priest performed the rites.

Centuries before, the Hope Diamond was supposed to have been part of the 112-carat eye of an Indian idol. The idol's eye had been stolen and sold to a man named Tavernier, whom some have described as a French adventurer. He smuggled it into Paris, but not long after, he met a slow and horrible death as the victim of a pack of wild dogs. Later, the stone turned up as part of the French royal jewels, although Louis XIV probably wished that he had never acquired the diabolical diamond. Legend has it that his eldest son, his eldest grandson, and his great-grandson fell victim to the curse within a year. History documents that his trusted confidant, Nicholas Fouquet, who had once worn the stone, fell from grace and was executed. The Princess de Lamballe, who had dared to wear it, was murdered by a mob.

Stanly Loomis theorizes in *The Fatal Friendship*, written in 1973, that the diamond was used to bribe the commander of a foreign army to leave France after he had brought his troops near to Paris to save the imprisoned Louis XVI and Marie Antoinette. The royal couple lost their heads. The stone was lost for quite a while, too. It later surfaced in Amsterdam, where a jeweler named Fals recut it. Those who believe the legend say the diamond's new shape and size did not affect the curse. They relate how Fals's own son stole the diamond from him, and years later when Fals died poor and broken in spirit, the son took his own life out of guilt for what he had done to his father.

In 1830, Henry Thomas Hope, a London banker, acquired what was reported in one newspaper article to be a "45-carat sapphire-blue diamond." From this point on the stone bore Hope's name. The curse spared him, but not his grandson. After inheriting the diamond, the young man soon found his own marriage to American actress Mae Yohe on the rocks. He died poor and his former wife eventually fared no better. Her career collapsed and she too died after several poverty-stricken years. According to the legend, the Hope Diamond next made its way into Russia, where it was acquired by Catherine the Great. Her life of turbulence, marital woes, and death by apoplexy is well known.

As a new century dawned, the curse of the Hope Diamond remained strong. A merchant in gems and precious stones acquired it in Turkey for a wealth sultan who sought to impress his harem favorite. The merchant delivered the goods but never lived long enough to enjoy his share of the sale. He, his wife, and their children were killed in a terrible accident in which their car crashed down a deep precipice.

Now, Evalyn Walsh McLean had the diamond, and when the priest concluded his blessing, a collective sigh of relief

This house at 2020 Massachusetts Avenue once belonged to Evalyn Walsh McLean, before she and husband Ned moved into "Friendship." It is now the Indonesian Embassy. Even today a nude apparition, said to be the ghost of a youthful Evalyn searching for the happy days she spent there, is seen on the stairway. *Courtesy Martin Luther King, Jr. Public Library, District of Columbia*

could be heard from the few guests present. The Hope Diamond was returned to its place of safekeeping, and some even say the storm quieted down.

Two of the first people to handle the Hope Diamond after Evalyn acquired it were her mother-in-law and a friend of her mother-in-law, Mrs. Robert Goelet. In her book *Father Struck It Rich*, Evalyn McLean says, "Within a narrow space, just about a year or so, both women died."

As the years passed, Evalyn Walsh McLean continued to insist to reporters that she was not a believer in the curse, yet the press was filled with stories about how protective she was of her young son, Vinson. Often there were photographs. One article featured a young Vinson in a goat cart being pulled around his mother's elaborate new estate, Friendship, just off Wisconsin Avenue at R Street Northwest.

In spite of the constant protection Evalyn gave her son, Vinson, he died in an accident at age nine. An out of control automobile struck and killed him in front of his home, Friendship, on Wisconsin Avenue NW at R Street. *Courtesy Father Struck It Rich (Little, Brown and Company, 1936; Library of Congress*

One writer said that the boy had six automobiles assigned to him, and he was always driven by a chauffeur "in order that he might not run the risk of accident or contamination that might result from riding in other persons' cars." There was a complete staff to protect Vinson. Some speculated that Evalyn lived in fear of a Lindbergh-type kidnapping. It was widely reported in the Washington press when she hired the entire circus to come to her estate rather than take the little boy to the circus.

Vinson had always been showered with everything money could buy. The year after his mother acquired the Hope Diamond, one newspaper reporter wrote that his Christmas presents cost $40,000, and that "they included a working model of the Gatun locks on the Panama Canal and a miniature steam yacht." Money, however, could not give Vinson a long life. When he was nine years old, the curse penetrated the protection: an out-of-control automobile struck Vinson McLean in front of his home.

Evalyn McLean's marriage was becoming stormy. The couple's bickering at parties attracted attention and often made the society pages, but Evalyn and her husband continued to entertain often and lavishly. One society reporter wrote about friends "close to the McLeans" who privately expressed opinions that the pair liked crowds because they had grown to dislike each other's company so much.

The parties gave the town's newspapers something—other than politics—to write about. Often, reporters listed the scores of notables present; several tried to pin down rumors that some of the garden parties featured nudes on pedestals; a few concentrated on the political aspects of the affairs.

Tragedy also touched the life of Edward McLean, seen here (on the right) with good friend Warren G. Harding. Ned, who had acquired the Hope Diamond for his wife, became a victim of the stone's curse. His marriage fell apart. He developed a severe drinking problem. He was declared insane and hospitalized for eight years before he died of a heart attack. *Father Struck It Rich (Little, Brown and Company, 1936)*

Warren G. Harding was a good friend of the McLeans, and Ned worked on the Harding Inaugural Committee. The two had a lot in common. Before Harding got into politics he was a prosperous publisher in Marion, Ohio. When he delivered the nominating speech at the Republican convention for President Taft it proved to be a springboard to the U.S. Senate. The election of 1920 awarded the Presidency to Harding, who had opposed U.S. membership in "Wilson's League of Nations." Trying to ease the social and economic problems created by the end of World War I, he advocated a "return to normalcy." Harding looked backward to simplicity and quietude, to an America that once was.

The legend surrounding the Hope Diamond would have us believe that Harding's life began to change after he came in contact with the stone. The President's health declined and he began to suffer from heart, lung, and stomach trouble. In 1922, two men in his administration died violently. One shot himself to death, the other either killed himself or was murdered—amid charges that they had fattened their bank accounts at government expense. In 1923, Harding left Washington for a western tour. It was an exhausting excursion. On August 2, he died in San Francisco of what was diagnosed as a blood clot in the brain.

Several months after the President's death, the Teapot Dome scandal broke wide open. Ned McLean's name was brought up in connection with a $100,000.00 check to Interior Secretary Albert Fall, who had been accused of selling government oil supplies to Harry Sinclair and Edward Doheny. The stress apparently pushed Ned into excessive self-medication with alcohol.

Edward McLean's drinking problem grew, and press reports indicate that his wife became less and less tolerant, often berating him in public. A decade of newspaper headlines from the mid-1920s to the mid-1930s chronicled the McLeans'

public fights and separation. Ned tried to divorce Evalyn in Mexico, but she filed a countersuit in the country. According to a *Washington Herald* article in November of 1930, she charged that he had lived "for protracted periods with an unnamed woman; that he drank excessively; and caused Mrs. McLean bodily suffering by beating and striking her, cursing and calling her vile names."

Two years later, when the press reported that Ned had obtained a divorce in Riga, Latvia, Evalyn issued a statement through her attorney that Ned had been hospitalized in Paris for three months "as a result of a complete breakdown," and that the divorce was probably illegal. "There's something decidedly irregular about the whole thing," her statement said.

While Ned was trying to divorce her; she was moving to have him committed to an asylum. **"Mrs. McLean Wants Husband Adjudged of Unsound Mind,"** *Washington Daily News* headlines proclaimed on October 4, 1933. Before the month was over, that newspaper and others in town reported the verdict of twenty jurors: Ned McLean was insane. He remained hospitalized for eight years before a heart attack added his name to the roster of those whose wrecked lives and premature deaths can be traced to contact with the Hope Diamond.

Edward McLean's death didn't prevent him from trying to get back at his wife. In July of 1941, the *Washington Daily News* reported that McLean's will "disclosed that in a last dramatic gesture he had cut off his wife with only dower rights and similarly disposed of his children in order to leave $300,000.00 to Rose Davies...his companion in cheerier days."

During that same time, the McLeans' daughter, named after her mother, was making news of her own. One Washington newspaper featured a picture from a few years earlier of North Carolina Senator Robert Rice Reynolds kissing Jean

Harlow, and ran another photograph along with it of twenty-year old Evalyn McLean, with her comments on whether or not the fifty-six-year old "kissing Senator" would marry her.

Although Evalyn Walsh McLean was concerned for her daughter's happiness; she had troubles of her own, which seemed to get worse not better. Newspaper stories were focusing on her willingness to put the Hope Diamond up as collateral for a quarter-of-a-million dollar loan she needed to help bail the *Washington Post* out of trouble. Evalyn's daughter went on to marry the flamboyant Senator Reynolds, more than thirty-years her senior. On September 20, 1946, newspapers carried a story that the fifth wife of the former senator from North Carolina was dead. She had overdosed on sleeping pills.

Evalyn Walsh McLean had survived her husband, her son Vinson, and her only daughter; and like so many of those who have fallen victim to the curse of the stone, her own death was not quick. She fell and broke her hip, and while suffering from that she contracted another illness from which she never recovered.

On April 28, 1947, only days after her death, the *Washington Daily News* asked: "Who'll Be the Next to Risk Wearing 'Unlucky' Diamond?"

The Hope Diamond became the property of diamond merchant Harry Winston of New York, who professed that he did not believe in the curse. As the United States entered the 1950s, however, the Hope Diamond was placed on what Winston called "permanent loan" to a branch of the U.S. Government: The Smithsonian Institution. One article inferred that he decided to get rid of the stone because his wife kept nagging him to let her wear it.

There was a column in the *Washington Post* not long after the diamond was turned over to the Smithsonian. The columnist said that the diamond merchant used registered mail to ship the stone from New York to Washington—much to the misfortune of the unsuspecting mail carrier. Soon after delivering the Hope Diamond to the museum, the columnist reported, the thirty-five-year old letter carrier's leg was crushed by a truck. The 1959 column went on to describe a series of horrible events that were allegedly traced to this man since his contact with the diabolical diamond: his wife had died of a heart attack; the family dog hanged itself by jumping from the lawn through an open basement window while still tied to a leash; and nine months after he delivered the diamond, the mailman's suburban Washington home was gutted by fire. Still, said the columnist, the man held a philosophic attitude about his misfortune. He insisted that he did not believe in the curse of the Hope Diamond: "If the hex is supposed to affect the owners, then the public should be having all the bad luck," he was quoted as saying.

Cynics make a good case daily that our country "has gone down hill" since the 1950s. They point to the social unrest, riots, and assassinations of the sixties, the political betrayals and resignation of a President for wrong-doing in the seventies, followed by what they perceive as drugs, greed, and general moral decay since then. So, is the satanic stone concentrating its powers on its largest victim yet?

Maryland Suburban Ghosts

The Bloody Bladensburg Dueling Grounds

Above left, right and opposite page top left: If these ancient trees could talk, what stories they could tell. They grow on one of America's bloodiest dueling grounds. It was here that Commodore Stephen Decatur was fatally wounded in his duel with James Barron; here that the youngest son of Francis Scott Key breathed his last breath; and here scores of congressmen and senators came to settle what they could not settle on the floors of the House and Senate. *Courtesy Lee Shephard*

Just across the District of Columbia boundary, in the state of Maryland, along the old stage coach route from Washington to Baltimore, stands an historical marker on the side of Maryland State Route 450. It commemorates a killing field used so often that the stream running beside it was called Blood Run. The famous and the not so famous were among the antagonists who faced each other. Some men hired professional duelists to fill in for them. There were more than fifty fatal face-offs here; all in the name of honor. Death seemed to hover permanently over the grounds—not too far from the tavern that was Bladensburg. It is on this field that James Barron mortally wounded Stephen Decatur.

Survivors had looked into the face of death and sometimes their lives were drastically changed. One *Evening Star* writer of the 1890s recalled how some "appeared to be as walking corpses." This seemed particularly true in cases where the duels were fought at close range.

The stage from Washington to Baltimore went across this small creek called by some "Blood Run," and by others "Dueling Creek." More than fifty duels were fought alongside the creek before a public outcry finally forced laws to outlaw "the manly art of defending one's honor." *Courtesy Library of Congress*

One of the shades that haunts the Bladensburg dueling grounds is suspected of being a party to a tragic encounter that occurred in February of 1819. A former Virginia senator, General Armistead T. Mason, was challenged by his cousin Colonel John M. McCarty. Some accounts said the cousins quarreled over a woman; some attributed it to a dispute over Mason's right to vote in a Leesburg, Virginia, election.

Colonel McCarty felt the only way to settle the feud was by a means that allowed neither to escape. What more sure-fire way than to leap from the top of the new Capitol? Mason would have no part of it. The Colonel importuned Mason to join him atop a lighted keg of powder. Mason told McCarty he was insane. McCarty countered with charges of cowardice. At the same time, he tossed out an offer to fight at ten paces with muskets filled with buckshot. Mason liked the odds better, but felt they could still be improved. He suggested that a single ball replace the buckshot, and that the duel be held at twelve paces. McCarty hurried home to prepare his musket.

The sun's first rays were shining through the barren trees as the men met at the Bladensburg Tavern. It was a familiar scene on the mornings of bloodletting: the two groups of adversaries were gathered at opposite corners of the tavern, seconds and friends filling the ears of the combatants with encouragement and advice. Finally, it was time to venture out into the cold. It was a bleak morning. No birds could be heard, just Blood Run trickling along a narrow winding gully by the edge of the field. The men positioned themselves. A second barked the count.

Two shots rang out.

Mason fell dead.

McCarty was struck in the hand, and the bullet traveled up the muscle of his arm and out his shoulder. McCarty had his "honor," but he had lost the ability to use his right arm. In the years that followed, he tried to put that February morning out of his mind. Friends said that the pain would not allow it. Over and over in McCarty's mind he replayed the scene, heard the shots, and felt the pain as it moved up his arm. Repeatedly he saw Mason fall dead.

Some fifty years later, a newspaper writer looked back on the aftermath of that duel. He wrote that McCarty's behavior became erratic, causing him to "become a wanderer." His deep depression made him apathetic about his appearance. The article said that he often was seen in wrinkled clothing, looking "unkempt."

Some wonder if one of the wispy corpses seen walking in a trance-like state over the old dueling ground is not McCarty's tortured soul still searching for the honor he thought would come with the death of his cousin, now resting in peace.

Another of the shades often silhouetted against the moonlight as it roams the old grounds could be that of young Daniel Key, son of Francis Scott Key, the Washington lawyer who wrote "The Star Spangled Banner." Key had educated his older son Philip to be an attorney, and was preparing Daniel to be an officer and a gentleman by schooling him at the new Naval Academy in Annapolis,

Maryland. It seems that young Daniel argued with a midshipman friend, John Sherburne, over the speed of two steamboats. Some say it was the tension of a long sea voyage that led the two students to argue, but nevertheless they could hardly wait to be put ashore to settle their discord on the field of honor.

After visiting their families, the young men met at Bladensburg. Young Key never celebrated his twenty-first birthday. A brilliant and promising career in the Navy was snuffed out with a single shot under the June sun in 1836.

As more and more blood was shed in the name of honor; the public became aroused about dueling. Stories about the moans and groans and darkened apparitions stalking the fog-shrouded grounds began to spread. Gradually, people started to show concern over the continuation of this legal murder.

One of the main drawbacks to outlawing dueling was the lack of uniformity in the laws. The Maryland anti-dueling law did not cover residents of the District of Columbia or other states; and in the District, so many congressmen believed in the dueling code that they were reluctant to outlaw what they considered the manly art of self-defense. An incident in February of 1838, however, finally caused such a public outcry that Congress was forced to act.

Popular Member of Congress Jonathan Cilley of Maine was shot to death by Representative William Graves of Kentucky, who was a stand-in for New York newspaper editor James W. Webb. Cilley had called Webb corrupt. Graves was a good friend of Webb's and took the charge personally. He felt that a remark against Webb was a remark against him.

Graves knew weapons and was an experienced marksman. Cilley knew nothing about guns, let alone dueling. The

Representative Jonathan Cilley from Maine, a reluctant participant in a fatal duel, is just one of the victims whose spirits revisit the old dueling grounds. *Courtesy Library of Congress*

thirty-eight year old congressman had a wife and three children. He took his work seriously and tried to serve his district well. He seemed to try to put the challenge from Graves out of his mind. Some said that he never really expected it to come down to two grown men actually firing shots at each other. Graves, on the other hand, engaged in target practice for weeks before the duel.

On the cold winter morning agreed to by both parties, Graves showed up with a rifle much more powerful than the one Cilley brought. He was allowed to use it, though. The seconds helped position the pair eighty paces apart. The count was shouted. Shots were exchanged, but no one was struck.

The bizarre scene was repeated, but again the results were the same. The seconds wanted both to agree they were satisfied, but Graves would not consider the request until they fired one more round.

In the third round, Cilley's left leg was shot out from under him. The bullet from Graves's high powered rifle tore into a large artery in Cilley's left leg and within ninety seconds life ebbed from the body of the young, likable congressman from Maine. Several members from the House and Senate watched…in silence.

Congressman Cilley had not yet been laid to rest in Congressional Cemetery when the public protest began. The tragic end of Jonathan Cilley so outraged Washington citizens that the next session of Congress was forced to make dueling—or accepting or giving a challenge—a criminal offense within the District of Columbia.

The law appeased the public but unfortunately did not put an end to dueling. The challenges were made less openly, and the "meets" became more clandestine. Finally, the outbreak of the Civil War brought an end to the deadly dawn ritual so often staged at Bladensburg. After the war, things were not the same. The carnage of war had taken the sport out of dueling.

The old Inn located near the dueling grounds saw only a fraction of the business it had enjoyed in earlier years when men of courage would stop in for a toast, and men without courage would come by for some of it out of a bottle. The stage business wasn't enough to keep the old Bladensburg Tavern going and it too became a relic of the past. The fields around the old grounds have been overtaken by sprawling urban growth that has choked off all but a tiny corner of those infamous grounds. When I last visited there a few towering trees shaded what was left of the grass, but an asphalt playground covered the rest of the open space. "Blood Run," or "Dueling Creek" —forgotten names that belong in the past, was nothing more than a contaminated trickle inside a high chain-link fence that kept the

children from contacting its polluted waters. Not too many children play there after dusk. You don't see too many adults crossing the site at night, either. Those who have had occasion to walk across the field, or be parked by the road, and staring into the early morning fog, have sometimes seen into the past and glimpsed shadows of men of another era. One youth who reported a dramatic encounter with one such spirit described it to his father as "dark, but not really transparent. Like a man dressed in black, an old man, whose back was bowed and head cast downward," the boy said. He saw it only a few seconds before he stepped on a twig that snapped. The noise apparently caused the apparition to vanish.

There is no answer to what causes these doomed men to revisit the field where they died in defense of honor, for at the slightest sound they fade, leaving no time for questions—should anyone be brave enough to try to ask one.

Avalon

Sandy Spring is a quaint old Maryland community founded by Quakers. Avalon is a beautiful residence, built in 1855 on almost thirty acres. Avalon also apparently remained home to the ghost of one little Quaker lady for many years after she died.

Several owners reported the sound of footsteps through the house. Sometimes the sound would go up the stairs. Sometimes the sound came through the front door even though it was closed. No one seemed to have a clue as to what, or who, was causing the noises until a visiting uncle proved to have a little more sensitivity to the phenomena. The man came down the stairs one morning and announced "There's a little old lady that walks through your house. She wears a long gray dress and steel rimmed glasses. Her hair is tied back in a bun."

The startled niece was amazed. She and others in the family had many times heard the footsteps, but no one had actually seen who was making them. Asking around the neighborhood, the family learned that the person described by the uncle was Rachel Gilpin, whose husband Alban, built Avalon.

Avalon, built in 1855, is haunted by a little Quaker lady. She has been described by those who have seen her as wearing a long gray dress and steel rimmed glasses. Her hair is tied back in a bun. *Courtesy Montgomery County Historical Society*

Cousin Rachel, as the family started calling her, was like a relative that didn't know when to leave. After a while, her noises and tampering with clocks wore thin. The family loved Avalon and weren't interested in moving. The owner's wife had read an article that said to just tell the "earthbound" to leave and they will. Well, she did. It worked. She told writer Hank Plant in *The Montgomery County Sentinel*, October 26, 1972, that "the children were very unhappy. They liked her around."

Clifton

The oldest brick home in Montgomery County, built on what is now New Hampshire Avenue, in Sandy Spring, is said to still be home to Aunt Betsy. John Thomas built the place almost thirty-five years before the War for Independence from the British. Legend has it that Aunt Betsy was one of Thomas's house servants who has stayed around to keep an eye on things.

One version of the tale says she went insane and was confined to the basement. That's where the moans and sobs have been heard late some nights. She is also said to stalk the house shutting off the lights and slamming doors at no particular time and for no particular reason.

A decade or so ago, *The Montgomery County Sentinel* reported Mrs. T.R. Wellens was taking a picture of her husband and father outside of Clifton. They lived there at the time. In the finished picture, in addition to the two men, there is a white form at one of the attic windows. Aunt Betsy?

"Ive heard Aunt Betsy rock in the rocking chair up in the garret of the house, Sandy Spring Postmaster William Thomas III told the newspaper. Clifton has been in his family over 200 years. "She was always completely benevolent from all the stories I've heard." Nobody has seen Aunt Betsy, but she certainly makes her presence known by noise.

Annington

This Germantown, Maryland, estate was built approximately two hundred years ago by Congressman Major George Peter who had served in the War of 1812. Legend has it this lusty old soldier-politician who married three times not only loved a toddy before bedtime, but after draining his glass he relished smashing it against the fireplace. That is the sound subsequent owners claim startled them awake time and again. *Courtesy Montgomery County Historical Society*

This is the oldest brick home in Montgomery County, believed to have been built by John Thomas in the 1740s. Clifton is still home to a ghost known as "Aunt Betsy." *Courtesy Montgomery County Historical Society*

Fair Hill

Colonel Richard Brooke, the Revolutionary War hero for whom Brookeville, Maryland, is named, built Fair Hill before the war for independence. Legend has it that a slave baby burned to death in the fireplace beneath the kitchen, and that years later a potter from Ireland, allegedly depressed over being so far from home, hanged himself in the basement. Those two incidents are used to explain the horrible and painful screams of a baby and the sobbing of a man that are said to sometimes awaken residents and guests alike as they penetrate the darkness of the old home. *Courtesy Montgomery County Historical Society*

Bloomfield

Bloomfield, in Sandy Spring, is said to have one room haunted by the ghost of a small child. The house was built by Brookeville Post Master Caleb Bentley back in the 1700s. Ironically, another home that the Bentley's lived in also carries with it a legend about the ghost of a small child. *Courtesy Lee Shephard*

"We bought Bloomfield in 1950. Our son slept in this one room with a fireplace. When he started talking, at about three or four, he began to talk about a friend who would come visit him. His name was 'Aah.'"

For years the Washington attorney and his wife thought their son had an imaginary playmate. The lawyer had bought Bloomfield, the secluded old homestead in Sandy Spring because its country peacefulness provided a good escape from his hectic work in the District. It was a good place to raise a family.

He and his wife thought it quite creative of their son to dream up an imaginary friend, complete with "long blond hair and big nightshirt." The three-year old told his parents that Aah would sit on his bed. They talked and played.

A few years later, when the lawyer was preparing to take his family on vacation, he invited an associate in his law firm to bring his family out to the country and house-sit. That family had a four year old son.

When the lawyer and his family returned from their trip the house-sitters expressed their joy at having had the opportunity to live briefly in such a relaxed setting. They were particularly pleased at not having to coax their four-year old to bed every night. Instead of the usual struggle he went willingly. He told his parents he had a new friend, "Boo," who played with him at night. He had long hair and wore a big nightshirt!

There was a collective chill down the spines of the lawyer and his wife, but they said nothing—preferring to call it a co-incidence. They told themselves many small children, being raised without brothers or sisters, create imaginary friends to keep from being lonely. Afterall, when their son had turned six they had moved him into a larger room, and there had been nothing more said about "Aah" since then.

More than a decade passed, and then sometime in the 1970s a neighbor called the lawyer's home. She had a friend visiting her whose family once lived in Bloomfield many, many years earlier. Would it be possible, she asked, for her to bring this elderly friend over to see her old home? The lawyer and his wife greeted the neighbor and her guest warmly. The lawyer smiled broadly as he recalled how excited the woman seemed to be at being inside Bloomfield once again. After a few minutes of small talk, and an invitation to "see the rest of the house," the guest had a request of her own: Could they please start the tour with a visit to her former bedroom? She had so many pleasant memories of playing in it for hours on end. She smiled and her face lit up as she described how as a small child she used to have a little boy with long blond hair as a nighttime playmate. He was always dressed in a big nightshirt.

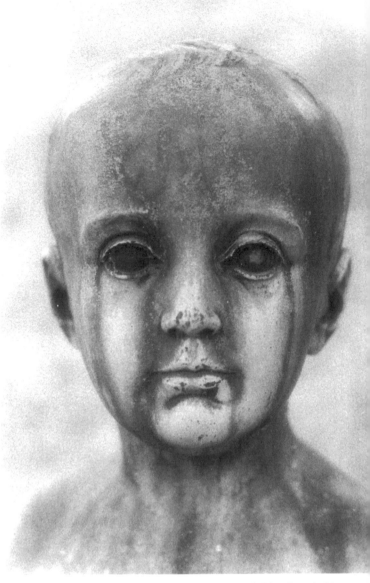

Just who the little child was that haunts Bloomfield will probably never be known. *Courtesy Lee Shephard.*

The President Slept Here

When President James Madison fled Washington as British troops advanced on the Capital in August of 1814, he and a very small contingent of American troops guarding him rode northward to Brookeville, Maryland. The President broke his journey to Montpelier, his Virginia estate, by spending the night in the home of Caleb Bentley, the Brookeville Postmaster.

Caleb Bentley and his wife lived here when President James Madison came through Brookeville in route to his Virginia home the night the British sacked and burned Washington. Although the Bentley's were Quaker and pacifists, they extended to the President their full hospitality. Whether Madison was visited by the ghost of a small child said to haunt the house is strictly conjecture. *Courtesy Montgomery County Historical Society*

Auburn

Bently was a well-liked man. His family had lived in the small Maryland community for quite some time. It is said that his wife was apprehensive about giving asylum to anyone connected with the war, but agreed to make an exception in the President's case. The Bentleys were devout Quakers.

At the house where Madison slept there was said to be a small unseen child who tugged at the dresses of women. Legend has it that many, many years ago a small child tumbled to its death from the staircase just off the kitchen. To this day, it is said, animals and small children are afraid to climb those stairs.

Whether that story was circulating at the time the Bentley's owned the small stone house is only conjecture. Several years after the President's visit, the Bentley family decided to move to Sandy Spring to be nearer the Quaker community. Their larger new home was Bloomfield. The first newspaper account of a reported encounter with "the little blonde boy of Bloomfield" places the incident around 1900—how much further back into the history of that old house it goes cannot be determined.

I read an account dated back to the 1930s or so of an apparition of a "pointy lady" who scolded a mischievous child whose family was visiting at Auburn. *Courtesy Montgomery County Historical Society*

Auburn is a charming brick house that was built behind the Friends Meeting House in Sandy Spring around 1818. William Henry Stabler built it for his bride. The Stabler's raised six children and spent many happy years in that house. It troubled them that three, Joseph, Ellen, and Lucy, never married. They never knew the kind of happiness experienced by their parents.

Joseph loved his livestock and treated them as though they were his children. Fences were not part of the Stabler farm, so old Joe could be seen frequently walking around the fields keeping his stock in the right pasture. It depends upon with whom you talk and which tavern they've been to, but some folks in the area still say they see old Joe every once in a while—looking for a stray calf, even though he's been dead more than a hundred years.

Aunt Lucy, as his sister was known to friends and neighbors, used to run a tight and tidy house with sister Ellen. Some said the persnickety habits of these spinster sisters were why you could usually find old Joe out tending the livestock. He would rather be in the fields with the cows than in the house with a couple of old hens.

When Joe Stabler died, Auburn was left to his nephew. It is from that era that I first saw a written account claiming Auburn to be haunted. Several times over the course of the summer of 1921 a "pointy little old lady wearing a cap and carrying a cane" visited the four year old son of the family's house guests. The little boy told his mother that the little old lady never said a word to him. She just stood at the foot of his bed and pointed her cane at him. The boy's description allegedly matched an old and much faded photograph of Aunt Lucy.

If the "pointy lady" ever appeared to anyone else in Auburn it has been a well kept secret, but then again perhaps none of the guests has brought along a mischievous child.

Montpelier

Near Laurel, Maryland, is the eighteenth century mansion Montpelier. It is said to be haunted by a woman who glides across the rooms about six inches off the floor. A maintenance worker described her to a *Washington Post* reporter. He said she wore a brownish dress of a quilt-like fabric and a white hood. The man watched the ghost glide across a hallway from one room to the next and decided to follow. "It was like being in the wake of a cold breeze," he said.

In that same article a jewelry maker, who works in a building adjacent to the old house, is quoted as saying she had an encounter while working late, *and alone,* one evening. There was a sound of books dropping outside her studio door, followed by a chill in the air. The large back door that was always kept locked from the inside, was ajar.

Some Ghosts in the Virginia Suburbs

Mount Vernon's Late-Night Rider

George Washington's plantation stretched south and east, from near the Federal District almost to Williamsburg, Virginia. Often he would make social calls on the Byrds of Westover, the Lees of Stratford, and the Carters of Shirley. He would ride up to Alexandria for fellowship too. Whether the General saw any of the ghosts that are said to frequent those old Virginia mansions is strictly conjecture, but there is some evidence that Washington, at least once, had an encounter with something that disturbed him tremendously.

It supposedly happened as he was working on a dispatch, alone in his tent, during the Revolutionary War. *The National Tribune* reported in a story in 1880 that Washington aide Anthony Sherman said that the General had confided in him that a wispy, "beautiful female figure" spread America's future before him. The spirit unfolded a vision that included not only the General's successes, but the nation's international destiny, too.

Some have theorized that the thought of that vision was with the President when he wrote his farewell address. In that speech he warned against permanent alliance with foreign powers, big public debt, a large military establishment, and the devices of "small, artful, enterprising minorities" to control or change the government.

The first President of the United States went back to Mount Vernon and his life as a gentleman planter at the end of his second term in 1797. Everything that he had done in office set a precedent, including his decision to retire after a second term. Washington not only established the model for the office, he shaped how future presidents would relate to Congress. He maintained a unity among the states that was so necessary if the young nation was to grow, and until it grew stronger, he insisted that it remain neutral in its foreign relations. Washington's personal and financial sacrifices during the war for independence, and while he served as President, had taken a severe toll. Mount Vernon showed his long absences and was in need of repairs. His other land holdings had dwindled. The "Father of Our Country" died at the age of sixty-seven, just two years after leaving office.

Some who have worked at Mount Vernon swear that Washington revisits his beloved estate from time to time. There have been various accounts down through the years of the General riding on horseback across his estate to the stables, much in the way he did on his last ride, on a cold and rainy December night so long ago.

Some say that on certain moonlit nights the ghost of George Washington can be seen riding his favorite horse across his estate toward Mount Vernon (sketch), just as he did on his last ride before he died. *Courtesy Mount Vernon Ladies' Association*

Woodlawn

Woodlawn, another stately old Virginia plantation, was a gift of George Washington to his niece. There is a presence that hovers over land and house, according to some staff members. Most theorize that a later owner, John Mason, may never have left his beloved home. They seem to base their speculation on the fact that Mason had a peg leg and the sounds that emanate from the stair well on occasion resemble the clumping of a man with one wooden leg trying to negotiate stairs.

Belle Grove

This handsome eighteenth century farm house near Middleburg, Virginia, was built for James Madison's sister and her husband, Eleanor Madison Hite and Isaac Hite. In the early days of the Republic many gala balls were staged here. Thomas Jefferson, it is said, was a frequent visitor along with other notables of that time.

The splendid home, with its huge, luxurious rooms and great fireplaces, was ideal for entertaining. The tables were dressed in multiple cloths of fine linen and ladened with imported china. Artificial flowers, more treasured than fresh ones, adorned the place settings. The food was always arranged in the most elegant and appetizing fashion.

It is said that a hunt at Belle Grove was something to behold. During the season the hunt table would be placed outdoors. Those returning from an invigorating chase could partake of a wide range of offerings. Casseroles and oyster stews were especially good. There was an abundance of cider—naturally fermented.

Isaac and Eleanor Hite never wanted for invitations, either. Indeed! It is said that many invitations were extended with the hope that the Hite's might be gracious enough to reciprocate. Life at Belle Grove was robust. It was a good life. Isaac Hite lived it to the fullest!

Even in death some say his ghost continues to travel the social circles of yesteryear. They claim to have seen the apparition of the jovial Hite sitting atop his ornate coach and pushing his gleaming ghostly steeds up the drive, much as he used to do during the late night hours after a neighbor's lavish party and a lot of drink. The crack of the whip, the thundering hooves, the churning of wheels, do not drown out the lusty yells and laughter as Hite haunts his beloved home—still intent on catching a few hours sleep before the sun comes up.

Cloverland

Cloverland, a clapboard house in Prince William County, Virginia, is believed to have been built shortly after the War for Independence by Charles Carter. It sports two ghosts.

Witnesses describe one ghost as an exuberant female, wearing slippers and crinoline petticoats that make a rustling sound, scurrying between upstairs bedrooms. An article in the *Washington Star* in the mid-1970s quoted a recent owner's wife as saying "I always had a pleasant feeling after seeing the ghost. I have no idea who she may have been." The woman said she had caught glimpses of the ghost at least a half-dozen times during the time she lived at Cloverland. "This wasn't anything you would dread," she added.

That remark doesn't hold true for the other ghost. It is a more frightening apparition, generally seen about dusk. This ghost is that of a man roaming the grounds, his head tucked underneath his arm. Some claim to have seen it at first light just as the fog is lifting off the fields.

Legend has it John Hill Carter was the first to see the apparition as he and his father were engaged in a discussion at the edge of the driveway. Most link the ghastly ghost to a nearby Revolutionary War battle. Apparently the shimmering image isn't clear enough for those who see it to provide a description of dress. However, I think if I encountered a man with no head approaching me at dusk I really wouldn't care what he was wearing. My only concern would be how fast my feet moved.

Gunston Hall

Near Lorton, Virginia, stands the elegant Georgian residence of George Mason who authored Virginia's Declaration of Rights and helped to frame our country's Constitution. The formal eighteenth century style gardens contain an English boxwood alley originally planted by Mason. It is said that he never aspired to a life of politics, preferring the quieter life of gentleman planter surrounded by family.

Mason loved his plantation which overlooks the Potomac. He was especially pleased with his serene gardens, in which he often strolled, and in which he often received inspiration.

Legend has it that if one ventures into these gardens on certain nights, when the moon is right, one may even get a glimpse of Mason himself. He is said to revisit his beloved home just to check on the health of his boxwoods; a pastime he found so relaxing in life and so pleasing to his spirit that the spirit seems to have continued the exercise for more than two-hundred years.

Mood Music

Across the Potomac there is a story of how music seems to summon a ghost that haunts the estate known as Seminary Hill. Once upon a time a young man visited the girl of his dreams but she shattered them by rejecting his love. She was not ready for marriage yet, and asked that they remain "good friends."

Disappointed and filled with remorse he decided to return to Washington. Darkness had descended and clouds obscured the moon. The young lady offered him a servant with a lantern to guide his way through the dark streets from Seminary Hill to the wharf where he would catch the ferry. The upset youth declined both, saying he needed no help in finding the wharf.

Unfamiliar with the region by the waterfront the young man stumbled into the Potomac and drowned. On that same summer eve, a year later, the young woman sat at her piano at twilight. She was playing a melody that had been a favorite of her departed friend. She was startled to see the door open and the apparition of her dead suitor pass silently through the room and out onto the verandah.

Old timers say that even today if someone plays a certain melody on the piano in that particular room at Seminary Hill, at twilight, on the anniversary of the youth's death, his apparition will stroll through.

Wall of Death

There is a house sometimes known as Belle Air that was built in the countryside outside of Alexandria in the late 1780s by Jonathan Swift for his lovely new bride Anne Foster. In later years, long after the Swifts departed this earth, the house is alleged to have come into the possession of a gambler who won it in a high stakes card game. Legend has it that sometime just before the Civil War he had a high brick wall erected around the property. It is from that era, and that wall, that the stories are spun. An infamous deserter was allegedly shot there after his capture in Alexandria by his own troops. It is also said that two other deserters were also shot against that wall.

A few years after the Civil War's end neighbors began to whisper of soldier ghosts haunting the wall. Shouts of life-taking commands and reverberating gunfire sometimes echo off the wall and through the garden.

Olde Towne

In the heart of the historic Olde Towne is another of Alexandria's haunted houses. The ghost that is said to frequent what is now the Alexandria Visitor's Center is that of William Ramsay. Ramsay, who built the house and lived there for years, founded the town and was the city's first Mayor. In addition to various noises and disconcerting goings on inside the house, Ramsay's ghost has been seen by passersby staring out of the upper windows of his old home.

Sometime around 1750 Lawrence Washington, the half-brother of George, built a home on what was then Waters Street (now Lee Street) in Alexandria. The house has survived down through the years in spite of the vast number of owners, none of whom can outlast the salty old ghost who remains determined to make a nuisance of himself. No one really knows who he is. He's been called salty, crusty, profane, and noisy. Those are some of the milder descriptions offered by witnesses down through the years. The ghost is described a "swarthy, with a beard." Most of the time when he appears he is wearing a sea captain's hat. No one seems to know when the old captain may have lived and died there, or why he still loves to try and intimidate during his revisits.

A few blocks away stands the home of another of the city's earliest inhabitants: Revolutionary War hero Light Horse Harry Lee. He was the father of Confederate General Robert E. Lee. There has been much conjecture and speculation over the years, but just who the little tyke is that is said to haunt that ancient house remains a mystery.

The Marshall House

During the early morning hours of May 24, 1861—the day after Virginia moved in favor of secession—Union troops moved quietly across the Potomac and into Alexandria in order to establish a defense of the Federal City. A small Confederate detachment in Alexandria had left quickly when they spotted Union regiments crossing Long Bridge and steamers landing still more troops at the wharf.

Among the first Union troops off the first steamer to dock was a 24-year old Colonel, Elmer Ellsworth—a dear family friend of President and Mrs. Lincoln. He landed with his First Fire Zouaves.

Ellsworth had gone to work for Lincoln's Springfield law firm in 1860. Law had always been his second career choice, but he lacked the preparation to get into the U.S. Military Academy at West Point. He satisfied his love of the pageantry and spectacle of marching and drilling troops by taking a rag-tag bunch of Chicago youth, and as a hobby, turning them into the National Champions. With exotic uniforms patterned after the original Algerian Zouaves—fierce Moslem fighters of the French Army in the Crimean War—Ellsworth toured them throughout the country. He was impulsive, energetic, and handsome. Young women swooned wherever the unit performed. Lincoln considered it an honor to have such a high profile celebrity working for his election.

By the time Lincoln won the election Ellsworth had become a confidant and accompanied the President-elect to Washington as one of his bodyguards. He worked within the administration and became such a close family friend that

Colonel Elmer Ellsworth, a close friend of President Lincoln and his family, had pulled strings to make sure his men would be among the first to invade Virginia when the Civil War started. His ghost is said to haunt the Marshall House in Alexandria where he was killed after pulling a Confederate flag from the roof. *Courtesy Library of Congress*

when the Lincoln sons caught measles Ellsworth came down with them, too.

Recognizing that war was inevitable, Ellsworth left for New York to form and equip a fighting regiment of zouaves. He was quoted in the *New York Tribune*, April 17, 1861 as saying, "They are sleeping on a volcano in Washington. I want men who can go into a fight now." In less than two weeks his Eleventh New York Regiment was in Washington, and Ellsworth was pulling strings—using his friendship with Lincoln—to insure that his unit would be among the first going into Virginia on this morning.

As the sun rose on May 24th Ellsworth took a small detachment, accompanied by Edward H. House, a correspondent for the *New York Tribune*, to take the telegraph office. He sent another detachment to capture the railroad station. As Ellsworth's contingent made their way down King Street the young Colonel spotted a large Confederate flag flying atop the Marshall House. Some say it was large enough to be seen from the White House across the Potomac. Ellsworth set out to haul down the enemy flag. His men followed.

The unit made their way to the roof. Ellsworth pulled down the flag and started back down the stairs. However, as the Union unit descended to the landing on the next floor, hotel keeper James Jackson was waiting with a shotgun. He fired. Ellsworth slammed against the wall and slumped to the floor, the bloody confederate flag he had just torn down clutched to his chest. Jackson was immediately killed by Private Francis E. Brownell, who is alleged to have bayoneted the body and pushed it down the stairs.

Both sides now had their martyrs.

"Jackson was killed in defense of his home and private rights," declared a southern newspaper. A northern paper mourned Ellsworth's death as "a beautiful and noble life ended."

Over the years there have been those who have reported scuffling sounds on the Marshall House stairs. Some have heard a loud thud against the wall. Sometimes these sounds are accompanied by muffled shouts and moans. More than a few swear that they have seen a shadowy silhouette on the stairs, and some have heard what sounded like a body tumbling down the stairs. Do the spirits of Jackson and Ellsworth replay their ill-fated encounter?

Others claim that from certain spots in Alexandria, on certain mornings at sunrise, if you look carefully to the roof of the Marshall House you can see the colorful uniform of a young Zouave near the flagpole.

Ghosts of Manassas

The juncture of two railroads in the 1850s created the town of Manassas, Virginia—and because it was a transportation hub the town was fought over and burned during the Civil War. The pain and suffering experienced during that bloody conflict is much in evidence, even today. Manassas was the scene of two major battles. It also contained fortifications, supply terminals, and hospitals for both sides.

It was on July 21, 1861 that picnickers, sightseers, and politicians—who had come to see the Union Army make quick work of the rebels—wound up scurrying for their lives when ill-trained Union soldiers were routed during ten hours of bloody fighting.

Up on Henry Hill, where a statue of General Thomas J. Jackson marks the place where he was given the nickname "Stonewall," it is said that more than once has the wispy silhouette of the old soldier been seen galloping across in front of where Confederate General Barnard Bee rallied his men by exclaiming loudly above the roar of the battle, "There is Jackson standing like a stone wall. Let us determine to die here, and we will conquer."

The second battle occurred in the heat of August, 1862—barely a year after the first engagement. Union General John Pope had a much larger army, but General Robert E. Lee demonstrated his military genius as he defeated Pope's forces in three days of fierce fighting.

The Marshall House was a hotel when the Civil War erupted. Hotel keeper, James Jackson, outraged that a company of Union soldiers had invaded his building, grabbed a shotgun and fired on them after their Colonel pulled down the Confederate flag flying over the hotel. Jackson was killed by return fire. Some say his ghost also haunts the Marshall House stairs on which he died. *Courtesy Library of Congress*

Down through the years there have been stories of specters of the horribly maimed wandering the plains of Manassas near the Bull Run stream. So much death and emotion flowed onto these fields that there is little doubt when someone hears a cry or a sob or catches a glimpse of a shadow in the moonlight that it is locked in time and space from another era.

Arlington House

The beautiful home that sits atop the hill overlooking the peaceful Potomac and Washington, D.C. in what is now the Arlington National Cemetery was once the abode where a young Robert E. Lee courted and married Mary Anna Randolph Custis.

Mary Anna's father George Custis, who was the grandson of Martha Washington. His father had given him the land just after the turn of the nineteenth century, and in 1802 he began building the home that stands there today. He passed it along to Mary Anna when he died.

General Robert E. Lee shared much happiness in this home from 1831 until the start of the Civil War. It was in this house that Lee agonized before deciding to resign his commission in the U.S. Army to defend his beloved Virginia.

When the Lees family vacated Arlington House, it was soon occupied by Union troops who recognized its strategic location atop high ground that commanded an excellent view of the river and the Union capital. When the Civil War ended,

General Lee and his family never returned to Arlington House. He lived in Richmond briefly and at Washington University in Lexington, Virginia, where he served as President until his death in 1870. After his death, the name was changed to Washington and Lee University.

Lee was a quiet, retrospective person. There is little doubt that some evenings, as he gently rocked in the drawing room of the University President's house, Lee would recall with warmness of heart those wonderfully quiet evenings he shared with his wife on the grand portico of Arlington House. Together, on serene summer nights, they would sit. Sometimes they talked. Sometimes they appreciated each others' silence as they watched the distant and shimmering lights of Washington, D.C.—spread before them across the Potomac like stars in the night sky.

Although Arlington House survived the war, it was in a state of disrepair for many years. Fortunately, it has been restored to its 1860 grandeur. Some of the original Custis and Lee furnishings have been returned. That may not be all that has returned.

Is that the General's likeness reported to have been seen on the grand portico on still summer nights? Or is it the ghost of old John Custis who believes his land still offers the best view of the nation's capital and cannot resist revisiting every now and then to gaze on what the capital of the young republic has become?

Final Words and Ghostly Sites

There is fact and there is fiction. One of the eternal quests of humanity seems to be the struggle to separate one from the other. Pleasant Dreams.

GHOSTLY SITES OF GEORGETOWN

1. Foxall is a private residence on Dumbarton Street allegedly haunted for more than a century by the "nocturnal nanny."

2. Oak Hill Cemetery, established in 1849, overlooks beautiful Rock Creek Park. The Van Ness mausoleum has been the scene of ghostly stallions sans heads. They are said to be the shimmering white stallions who pulled the coffin of one time Mayor John Peter Van Ness to his final resting place.

3. The Woodrow Wilson home is located at 2340 S Street NW. On more than one occasion the former President's ghost has been reported revisiting his old home.

4. Evalyn Walsh McLean spent her happiest days in Washington when she lived at 2020 Massachusetts Avenue, NW. That was before she acquired the Hope Diamond. The Indonesian Embassy now occupies her former home where legend has it a ghostly nude glides down the exquisite stairway from time to time.

5. The ghost of Susan Decatur, wife of Commodore Stephen Decatur, allegedly haunts a house in the 2800 block of N Street NW, where she moved after her husband was killed in a duel.

6. Halcyon House, Prospect and 34th Streets NW, has been restored more to the original plans approved by Benjamin Stoddert, the country's first Secretary of the Navy. Whether he still haunts his old home is something only the new owners know.

7. The river front home of Francis Scott Key was located on the south side of M Street, NW where the ramps to the Whitehurst Freeway and Key Bridge are now located. Before it was torn down there were many stories of his ghostly presence haunting the house.

8. The area around 37th and O NW is where old Georgetown legends place a mephesto spirit. It was known as the "Gaston Ghost" to Georgetown University students of another era. Even today, there are still old timers who blame it for any new campus havoc.

9. From the Key Bridge, spanning the Potomac River, one can get a good view of the Three Sisters Rocks in mid-channel. They are mute reminders of the curse placed on this section of the river by three Indian maidens more than five hundred years ago.

10. The old K Street NW Bridge used to cross Rock Creek from Georgetown into the District of Columbia, but now there is little to remind one of this area's ghostly past. Nevertheless, the legend of the "headless man of K Street Bridge," is still told.

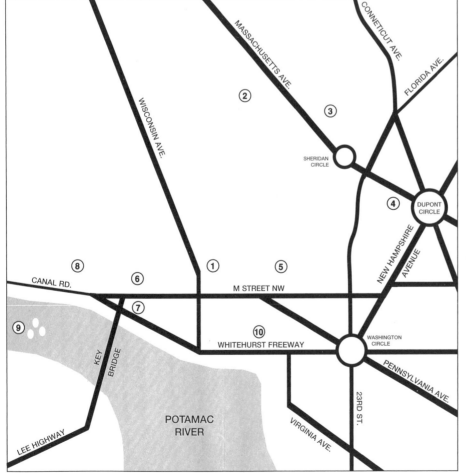

Map by Barry Lester

GHOSTLY SITES OF THE WHITE HOUSE AREA

(see next page for key)

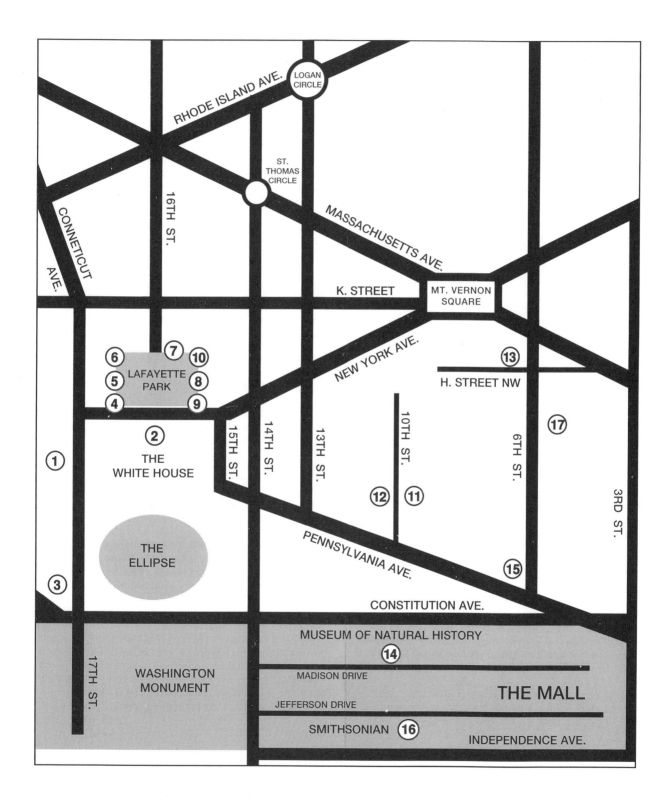

Map by Barry Lester

1. The Octagon House, at New York Avenue NW and 18th Street NW, is one of Washington's most haunted houses. Dolley Madison, who lived there briefly with her husband, President James Madison, revisits from time to time. Screams that allegedly reverberate from the ornate oval stairwell are chilling testimony to other ghosts haunting this stately town house.

2. The White House, 16th Street NW at Pennsylvania Avenue NW, is most noted for the ghostly presence of Abraham Lincoln. However, at least a half dozen other ghosts are said to haunt the house from time to time.

3. The estate of former Washington Mayor John Peter Van Ness used to stand at 17th Street NW and Constitution Avenue NW. The Pan American Union Building has replaced it, but stories of the ghostly goings on at the old Van Ness estate have survived.

4. Lafayette Square, across Pennsylvania Avenue NW from the White House, is haunted by more than a half-dozen ghosts. During the late 1800s passersby avoided walking past the former home of Major Henry Rathbone on Jackson Place because of the perceived evil they imagined lurked there.

5. Congressman Dan Sickles and his wife Theresa used to live on Jackson Place, too. When he was alerted that his wife's lover used to signal her from the park, Sickles watched from his home. Outraged when he saw Philip Barton Key's signal, Sickles set out to kill him. Key's ghost is said to still haunt the park and the sidewalk outside the old Washington Club where he died.

6. The home of Commodore Stephen Decatur was the first home built on the square. The handsome hero of the Battle of Tripoli reportedly still revisits his lovely home from time to time.

7. Many American Presidents have worshipped at St. John's Church. Legend has it that some of the spirits of those founding fathers materialize to pay their respects whenever one of the country's leaders dies.

8. Dolley Madison's peripatetic phantom has been seen on the porch of this house at Madison and H Streets NW where she spent her final years. Apparently, it wasn't uncommon for gentlemen leaving the old Washington Club (located just down the street) to tip their hat to the ghost of the elderly Mrs. Madison when they encountered her shimmering apparition at the bewitching hour.

9. The old Washington Club was one of the Federal City's most exclusive men's clubs for more than half a century. Afterwards, it was converted into living quarters and became home to Henry Clay, and later to President Lincoln's Secretary of State, William Seward. It's said Seward, who suffered so much tragedy there, haunted the place until it was eventually torn down.

10. Historian Henry Adams and his wife Marian "Clover" Adams used to live in a house that once stood here. After the mysterious death of the "poor unfortunate Mrs. Adams" visitors spoke in whispers of being overpowered by feeling of despair and deep loneliness, and of hearing muffled sobs.

11. Ford's Theater, on 10th Street NW, is where some claim to have seen Lincoln's ghost sitting in the President's Box where John Wilkes Booth shot him. A cold spot, experienced by some actors on the stage, is said to be a manifestation of Booth's ghost.

12. Across the street from Ford's Theater is the Petersen House where President Lincoln died. It too is said to be haunted. Not too many years ago a workman ran screaming into the streets and vowed never to return.

13. The old building at 604 H Street NW is where Mary Surratt maintained a boarding house. Ghostly cries and sobs are among the sounds said to still emanate from that structure.

14. The Museum of Natural History is home to the infamous Hope Diamond. A curse that allegedly enshrouds it is responsible for more than a dozen deaths.

15. The legendary gambler Colonel Beau Hickman is supposed to haunt the 6th Street NW and Pennsylvania Avenue NW area. Folks say they know the apparition is Colonel Beau because it's dressed in evening attire and sports the Colonel's beaver hat, diamond stickpin, and carries his fashionable cane.

16. The Smithsonian Castle, home to the bones of James Smithson who left money in his will to found the scientific institution, has been known to visit as a ghost a place and a country he never visited when alive.

17. The huge red brick building between F Street NW, G Street NW and 4th Street NW and 5th Street NW was originally labeled "Meigs Old Red Barn," after U.S. Quartermaster General Montgomery Meigs who is blamed or credited with its design. It served as The Pension Building, a home for some of the District of Columbia Courts, and most recently as The National Building Museum. It also is said to be home of a ghostly ill-tempered rider on horseback and at least one other ghost.

GHOSTLY SITES OF CAPITOL HILL

(see next page for key)

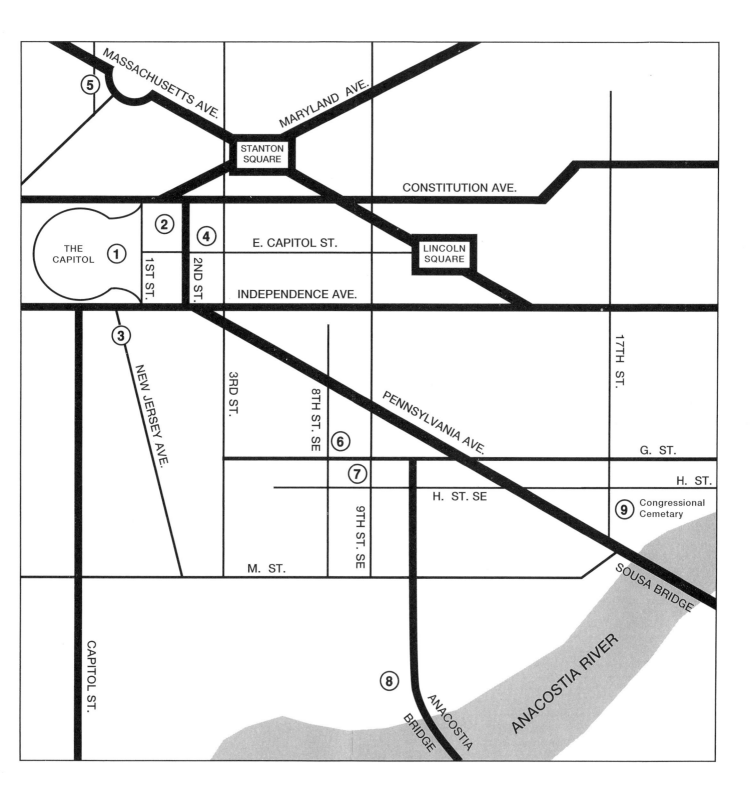

Map by Barry Lester

1. The U.S. Capitol building may be the most haunted site in all of Washington, D.C. It's most famous apparition is not that of a human, but of a dreaded Demon Cat that is said to make its home in the darkest, dankest corner of the Capitol cellar.

2. Across the street from the U.S. Capitol is the U.S. Supreme Court building. On certain nights it is said a full moon reflecting off the gleaming marble projects a shimmering apparition of The Old Brick Capitol which occupied this spot for a hundred years. It was built to house Congress while the Capitol was rebuilt after the British burned it in 1814. Later, it became a boarding house; served as a Union Prison during the Civil War; and was the home of the National Woman's Party. Airy figures and ethereal sounds also manifest themselves on this spot.

3. Judge Advocate General Joseph Holt, who presided over the military trial of the Lincoln Assassination Conspirators, insisted on the death penalty for Mary Surratt. It is said his ghost is doomed to search eternally until it finds evidence of Mary Surratt's guilt. For years it haunted his home in the 200 block of New Jersey Avenue SE until it was torn down. Then it was spotted along the sidewalk leading to the Old Brick Capitol where Mrs. Surratt was briefly imprisoned.

4. Maine Representative Jonathan Cilley, a reluctant participant in a fatal duel, lived in the 200 block of 3rd Street NW, where the Folger Shakespeare Library now stands. There have been some reports of workers having seen a shadowy figure resembling the bespectacled Cilley pacing the hallways of the Folger that are said to have been built on the spot where his home was. However, most of the tales of Cilley's ghostly appearance come from the Bladensburg Dueling Grounds.

5. The address of 224 North Capitol Street NW was quite a prestigious address for more than a century. It was on this site (now occupied by Union Station) that George Washington commissioned a row of townhouses to be built. Many well-to-do

and famous Washingtonians called these quarters home. However, it was an infamous incident that started the homes on the road to ruin and abandonment. Although a woman confessed to a murder in one of the homes in 1899, it didn't put to rest the ghost of the victim who allegedly haunted the homes for years. Even today there are those old timers who blame the malicious ghost for baggage lost and train delays.

6. The Marine Corps Barracks and Parade Grounds have been on 8th Street SE, between G Street SE and I Street SE, for nearly 200 years. It is said to have been haunted nearly that long by its' first commander Captain Samuel Nicholas.

7. An 1871 newspaper account began its story of another nearby ghost like this: "The neighborhood of 9th Street, between G and H Streets, SE has been the scene of great excitement this week, in consequence of stories in circulation that a two-story frame house in the rear of the garrison, occupied by a family named Bonehart, is haunted by the ghost of its former occupant, a marine by the name of Howard. He was the owner of the house, and died there some eight or nine months since. He is represented to have been a fearfully wicked man…"

8. The Navy's original commandant is said to occasionally survey his old home grounds, too. Thomas Tingey, serving under the first Secretary of the Navy, Benjamin Stoddert, supervised the building of the Washington Navy Yard from his home, Quarters A.

9. Congressional Cemetery is located seventeen blocks east of the U.S. Capitol, on the banks of the Anacostia River. It's an almost forgotten place because many of the notables buried there were, long ago dug up and re-interred back in their "home" states. However, famed march composer John Philip Sousa, Civil War photographer Mathew Brady, and former FBI Director J. Edgar Hoover are among those still there. Sousa and Brady, apparently are still rather active—if we are to believe some of the old stories.